The
Canadian Rockies
Trail Guide

A Hiker's Manual to the National Parks

Revised Edition

by Brian Patton and Bart Robinson

A Summerthought Publication

Box 1420, Banff, Alberta

ISBN 0-9690806-0-3

Revised edition, first printing, 1978

Published by
Summerthought Ltd.
P.O. Box 1420
Banff, Alberta T0L 0C0

Printed and bound in Canada

Preface to the Revised Edition

The publication of the first edition of *The Canadian Rockies Trail Guide* in 1971 inadvertently caught the leading edge of the wilderness boom, and the book has been popular in the intervening years. However, since that first printing, when backpackers were a rare breed and over ninety percent of mountain park hikers strayed no further than six or seven kilometres from the public thoroughfares, many things have changed. The upgrading of horse trails to hiker standards, the bridging of difficult river crossings, changes in trail heads, the closure and restoration of old fire roads, new park regulations, and a staggering increase in trail use have all worked to erode the contemporaneity of the guide.

Even as we worked on the manuscript for the first edition, we realized a revised edition of the guide would be necessary at some future point. In fact, not totally satisfied with the original production, we began work on a new edition soon after the first was released. By the time it was ready for press, just six years later, we found we had rewritten the guide from cover to cover.

Major alterations in the revised edition include a stronger emphasis on backpacking trips, with a section on extended trips of a week or more and a complete update on the proposed Great Divide Trail; a switch to metric measurement (English equivalents are still provided in the distance lines and trail summaries, however, and there is a conversion chart printed on the last page of the book); a narrowing of the territory covered in the guide—Glacier and Mount Revelstoke National Parks have been dropped in a purist's bid to provide additional space for the parks of the Rockies proper; and an increase in the number of sketch maps and an improvement in their quality. Physically the guide is thicker by some 48 pages, over a centimetre shorter and narrower (to help it fit into packs), and the cover is mylar-coated (to make it less water-soluble).

It is not without some hesitation that we present the second edition of *The Canadian Rockies Trail Guide*. It was not out of loneliness that we produced the first edition, and now, with the dramatic increase in backcountry use, we fear that those who were meant to help in the preservation of the national park wilderness may be speeding its destruction. More than ever, hikers need to exhibit a sensitivity toward the mountain environment and their fellow hikers if the nature of the wilderness experience is to be of a high quality. Increased trail use has necessitated a serious reappraisal of the fine line between wilderness use and abuse, and park officials are increasingly turning to permit and quota systems to control environmental wear and tear. If every person who uses this book could make the small effort necessary to leave the wilderness exactly as he or she found it, we might feel that providing this key to the backcountry has not been a detriment to our national parks.

Brian Patton
Bart Robinson
Canmore, 1978

Acknowledgements

In addition to those who helped us with the first edition of this book, we would like to express our gratitude to the following for their assistance in compiling this revision:

the many wardens, naturalists and other Parks Canada staff members who have selflessly added to our knowledge of the trails;

the hikers and backpackers who have corresponded with us or stopped to chat along the trail recounting tales of glory and woe and thereby providing much of the material that has gone into this revision;

marathon backpacker Mike McReynolds who, in completing two epic journeys through the Rockies, has added immensely to our storehouse of information and inspired our chapter on extended trips;

Ed Cavell, mountain photographer and photo archivist *extraordinaire*, who managed to salvage most of the authors' field snapshots in his darkroom;

Karine Bagley, who helped with manuscript editing and summer transportation and provided foreground variety for some of our photographic efforts;

and, of course, Dr. Jim Thorsell, whose advice and encouragement have been a constant source of inspiration (not to mention his gourmet trail lunches).

Photo credits: the cover was taken by Jim Thorsell. All other photographs in this book were taken by the authors.

Contents

Introduction

In 1885, the Dominion of Canada created a special ten square mile reserve near Banff, Northwest Territories, to protect the Sulphur Mountain Cave and Basin hot springs from commercial despoilation. The reserve, after name and boundary changes, became Banff National Park, the first such park in Canada. Today the park is one of five mountain national parks which together occupy over 20,000 square kilometres, or nearly 8,000 square miles, of prime mountain wilderness in the Canadian Rockies.

Though several million people visit the parks each year, a great many of them fail to experience the mountains on any other than a superficial level—the Canadian Rockies as seen from a rapidly moving automobile. Although the scenery is indeed magnificent, it represents only a small portion of what the Rockies offer. Just as it is necessary to leave the front seat of an automobile to fully appreciate a great museum or cathedral, so is it necessary to get out of a car and walk a bit (and preferably a great deal) to gain a true sense of these 'living museums of nature'. Hiking is a fitting, proper and effective way to appreciate the national heritage of the parks, and those who have walked the mountain trails are best prepared to understand the importance of preserving the park lands, leaving them 'unimpaired for the enjoyment of future generations.'

This book, then, is an invitation to the byways of the Canadian Rockies: to the more than 3,000 kilometres of trail that thread through the valleys and passes, by the lakes and glaciers of Banff, Jasper, Kootenay, Yoho and Waterton Lakes National Parks, as well as the adjacent Mount Assiniboine and Mount Robson Provincial Parks. It is an invitation to experienced hikers to examine a whole new realm—an area so large it would take a lifetime of summers to thoroughly explore. And it is an invitation to the novice to discover the three-dimensional 'living museum' which lies beyond the automobile window.

Weather, Climate and the Hiking Season

Despite their northerly latitudes, the Canadian Rockies have climate and weather patterns which compare quite closely with similar mountain areas hundreds of kilometres to the south. Because the elevation of the range increases progressively from north to south, mean temperature and annual precipitation in Banff relate almost to the degree and millimetre with those of West Yellowstone, Montana and Leadville, Colorado.

The following chart shows average daily maximum and minimum temperatures, precipitation averages for the months of May through October, and the average number of days per month with significant precipitation for Banff townsite. It should be remembered, though, that precipitation tends to increase and temperature to decrease as one gains elevation or approaches the continental divide. It should also be noted that in the five year period prior to this edition the month of August has been much wetter than the average and June drier, perhaps an indication of changing patterns.

1

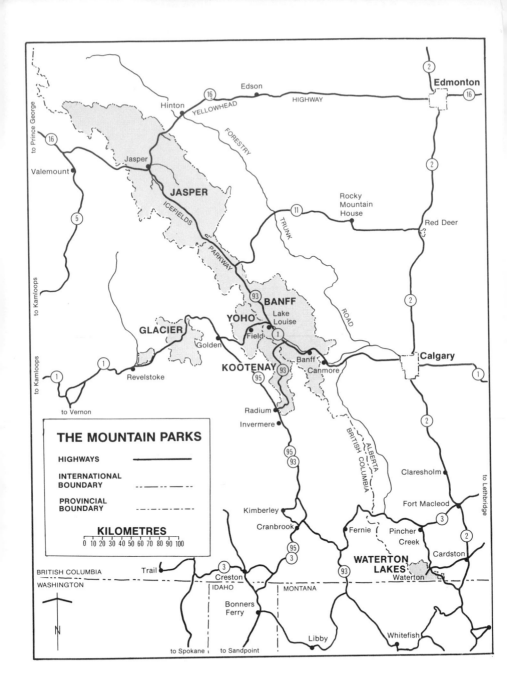

THE MOUNTAIN PARKS

HIGHWAYS ——————

INTERNATIONAL
BOUNDARY — ·· — ·· — ··

PROVINCIAL
BOUNDARY — · — · — · —

KILOMETRES

0 10 20 30 40 50 60 70 80 90 100

2

BANFF TOWNSITE CLIMATE:*	May	June	July	Aug.	Sept.	Oct.
Average max. temp./C.	14	18	22	21	16	9
Average min. temp./C.	1	4	7	6	2	-1
Mean rainfall/mm.	51	65	48	48	38	36
Average no. days rain	9	11	9	9	9	8

*Because of its location and lower elevation, Jasper townsite averages one degree warmer on all temperatures and is slightly drier.

Generally, as temperatures moderate in April the snowpack in the high country begins to disappear. By mid-May hiking is possible on a handful of low-lying trails situated in the major valleys and on south-facing slopes in the Front Ranges. By the first of July most trails below timberline are open, but many are still wet and muddy. In the alpine zone, trails open gradually from early July to early August depending on slope exposure and snowpack.

The hiking season often lingers into late October in the Rockies. High country temperatures start to drop in mid-August, and early September usually sees the first snow drifting down over the peaks. A fall of 15 centimetres or more is not unusual in the high country after late August. These initial storms are usually short-lived, however, and the latter weeks of September and early October often are characterized by beautiful Indian Summer weather. However, a wary eye must always be kept on changing weather at this time of year, and autumn backpackers should be prepared for cold, snowy hiking if a storm should move in overnight.

One final cautionary note: don't rush the season in the spring. Not only does hiking too high too early mean muddy boots and slippery trails, but it can be damaging to both the trails and the adjacent terrain. Check with the park information service for recent trail condition reports before starting any hike in the high country.

Equipment

Although the authors presuppose a certain amount of experience and common sense on the part of the reader, they also recognize that hiking conditions vary from one part of the continent to the other and thus suggest a few prerequisites for any day trip in the Rockies. Absolute essentials are good, sturdy leather hiking boots worn with wool socks, a raincoat or poncho, and an extra wool sweater or shirt. In other words, no matter how warm and promising the day may appear, always be prepared for weather which may include a combination of high wind, rain or snow, and freezing temperatures.

Other options for the day hiker include: sunglasses (particularly when the trail runs above timberline), wool toque, insect repellent, and extra pair of wool socks (wet feet are common in the Rockies), sun tan lotion, first aid kit, small flashlight (for longer trips which might end in darkness), map and compass.

There are dozens of publications dealing with the techniques of backcountry travel and camping, ranging from free government pamphlets to hiking bibles such as Colin Fletcher's *The Complete Walker* and Harvey Manning's *Backpacking: One Step at a Time*. Such manuals will help with the theoretical end of hiking, but, as with most things, experience is the true teacher. Novice hikers in the Rockies should start with short overnight trips and then move on to some of the longer treks outlined in this guide: don't tackle a hundred-kilometre epic as your first ever backpack if you want to keep hiking as a hobby.

Hiking and climbing specialty shops in both Banff and Jasper townsites carry a complete line of outdoor equipment. Freeze-dried food is also available.

Topographic maps

Most of the hikes in this book do not require a map. For the more remote wilderness trips, however, a topographic map is a prerequisite. Whatever the case, many hikers prefer to carry topo maps with them wherever they go, finding them invaluable for identifying natural landforms.

All areas in the mountain parks have been mapped on a 1:50,000 scale (approximately two centimetres equal one kilometre). These sheets provide a high degree of detail and are extremely useful both as tools of navigation and in landform identification. Unfortunately, it takes approximately 60 of the maps to cover the mountain parks. Furthermore, many of the cultural features (i.e., roads and trails) are often out-of-date or not accurately marked.

For casual hikers who can't read maps or for those who desire only a general overview of the parks and their trail systems, the national park topographic sheets are helpful. These are scaled from 1:50,000 (Waterton Lakes) to 1:250,000 (Jasper Park) and cover each of the mountain parks on a single sheet. Trails are marked with reasonable accuracy on most of the park maps (the Waterton Lakes sheet is excellent) and each provides a good overall picture of park features.

Produced by the Department of Energy, Mines and Resourcees, the park maps and the 1:50,000 sheets are available at park information bureaus and official map dealers in the major townsites. Maps may also be mail ordered from the Canada Map Office, Department of Energy, Mines and Resources, Ottawa, Ontario (write for a price list and ordering information).

Backcountry Information and Regulations

Although some slight differences exist between individual parks concerning the regulation of backcountry use, most operate on the same general principle.

In the four contiguous parks of Banff, Jasper, Yoho and Kootenay backpackers must obtain a backcountry use permit. These are issued at all main park information bureaus (locations are listed in the introduction to each park) and are mandatory for any trip involving an overnight stay in the backcountry.

The four parks also offer a voluntary registration option for hikers who feel there is a high risk involved in their backcountry activities. A registration form lists the hikers' route, destination and estimated time of return. If the hikers fail to register back in on schedule, the warden service will begin search operations. Needless to say, registered hikers must make every effort to return on time and register back immediately upon their return. Such registration is required of persons attempting any off-trail travel such as overland exploration or mountain climbing. While registration forms must be returned, backcountry use permits need not.

Waterton Lakes differs from its northerly counterparts in requiring registration for **any** overnight trip in the backcountry.

Day hiking on established trails requires no permit or registration in any of the parks.

While it doesn't affect the procedure which backpackers must follow, Jasper and Yoho Parks have, respectively, backcountry trail and campsite quotas. Such quotas could upset hiking plans, particularly when the objective is a popular backcountry area, and hikers should arrive at either park with several hiking alternatives in mind.

Campfires are still permitted in most designated backcountry campsites, but should be built only in existing fire circles or fireplaces. Several high country campsites are designated as 'camp stoves only' areas, usually because of a scarcity of wood. It is illegal to cut a living tree for firewood.

Hikers wishing to fish the backcountry lakes and rivers must purchase a national park license, available from any park information bureau.

4

It is recommended that all hikers stop by one of the information bureaus before beginning any serious hiking. The bureaus serve as centres for all hiking activity in the parks. In addition to issuing backcountry permits and registration forms, they dispense maps and up-to-date information on trail conditions, as well as a series of free publications covering everything from grizzly bears to hypothermia. And, they can update hikers on any policy changes which may have occurred since the last printing of this guide.

Using This Book

The Canadian Rockies Trail Guide was written with two objectives in mind: to catalogue most of the trails in the mountain parks of the Canadian Rockies, and to describe fully those which offer prime hiking opportunities. The trails have been loosely divided into two general categories:

Primary trails, or those routes commonly recognized as the most exceptional and scenically rewarding. These trails are given full description over two or more pages and all have been hiked at least once by the authors.

Secondary trails, a mixed bag of trips, ranging from short forest-enclosed nature hikes to long wilderness access routes. Because of their limited length or scenic reward, these trails are usually given briefer descriptions of a half to a full page. While the authors have hiked many of the secondary trails, there are many which they haven't personally surveyed. In such cases, as much detail as possible has been collected from reliable sources (usually the warden service and experienced hikers), and approximate distances have been calculated from 1:50,000 maps.

The primary trail displays are divided into four distinct elements: trail summary, outline, descriptive text and photo. These elements are largely self-explanatory, but a few notes may clarify their intended use.

Beneath the name of each trail is its one way distance and, in some instances, supplementary information if the hike is a loop trail or requires special transportation arrangements. All distances are listed in both kilometres and miles. The trails have been measured with an odometer attached to a bicycle wheel, pushed over the trails by the authors during their field work. Since the distances of most of the trails were previously only estimated by wardens on horseback, hikers will frequently find discrepancies between distances listed on trail signs and those found in the guide. Although Parks Canada has initiated its own program of trail measurement in recent years and is currently updating many of its signs, where major discrepancies exist, hikers would do well to use the figures recorded herein.

The general round trip duration of hikes is categorized as 'half-day,' 'day,' and 'backpack,' to assist hikers in finding outings tailored to their desires.

Hiking time is the number of hours, usually one way, the hiker can expect to spend on the trail. The times are usually calculated for the trip to the hiking objective, which, in most cases, takes a bit longer than the trip back because the route generally runs uphill. These times are a general estimate provided for those unaccustomed to estimating their own hiking speed. Strong hikers will find it easy to beat the times listed; less seasoned hikers, or those who take extensive breaks for nature study or photography, will probably find it takes longer to reach their destination.

The elevation gain is the total ascent, listed in both metres and feet, over the one way course of the trail. In cases where the trail both rises and falls significantly (e.g., a trail that carries the hiker over two high passes and through a deep connecting valley), a total elevation loss is recorded as well.

The maximum elevation is the highest point above sea level reached on the hike, usually at the trail's destination. This elevation is also expressed in both metres and feet.

The topographic map references given are for the 1:50,000 sheets covering the hiking area. In cases where the trail is not shown, or has been badly misplaced, such information is noted.

The trail outlines have been included to provide the reader with a brief, graphic profile of the route. All basic directions are given in the outline, thereby freeing the text for more interpretive material. The exact kilometre breakdown can be used either as an odometer for judging distance covered or to help locate natural features along the route. The outlines also contain important highway directions for reaching the trail heads.

The text has been written to describe the scenic rewards of the trail and to interpret some of the human and natural history of the area. Because most national park trails are fairly self-evident, a minimum number of words have been devoted to long, tedious directions. Where applicable, optional routes have been described at the end of the text.

All photographs were taken by the authors and selected because they represent a typical scene or the destination of the hike.

The maps included in the book were drawn by the authors using information from the Department of Energy, Mines and Resources maps in conjunction with corrections noted in the field. The maps are somewhat abbreviated and are provided to give the hiker a general impression of a given area rather than specific directions. In many cases the maps are included only to describe highway access to various trail heads.

The only complete listing of trails is provided in the index at the end of the guide.

Some Final Words

*Always pack out all garbage. Leave nothing behind. Bring plastic bags or pick some up from Parks Canada when obtaining a backcountry use permit.

*Never leave smelly garbage or food around your camp. Seal up all food and garbage and hang it in a tree a good 50 metres from your tent.

*Never disturb living trees or shrubs in setting up camp or building a fire. If dead wood is not available on the ground, use a stove.

*Care should be taken with all fires: make certain they are cold before being abandoned. Flood the fire circle and stir the ashes with a stick.

*Even where open fires are permitted, small stoves using gas, propane or other hydrocarbon fuels are often preferable. Natural fuels are dwindling rapidly around all backcountry campsites.

*While they are permitted on a leash, dogs in the backcountry are ill-advised. They can disturb wildlife and other hikers and may incite a grizzly bear to attack.

*Where facilities are not provided, one's toilet should be tended to well away from campsites and trails. Dig a small pit, burn toilet paper, and restore the ground as close as possible to its original state.

*Never pick wildflowers or edible plants in a national park.

*Be considerate of fellow hikers when sharing a campsite or backcountry shelter.

*Be considerate of horseback riders on the trail. Move well off the trail, remain still and be prepared to comply with the riding guide's requests.

In other words, hike the wilderness areas of the national parks as an experienced mountain traveller would, displaying at all times a keen awareness of the diverse and delicate mountain world.

6

Banff National Park

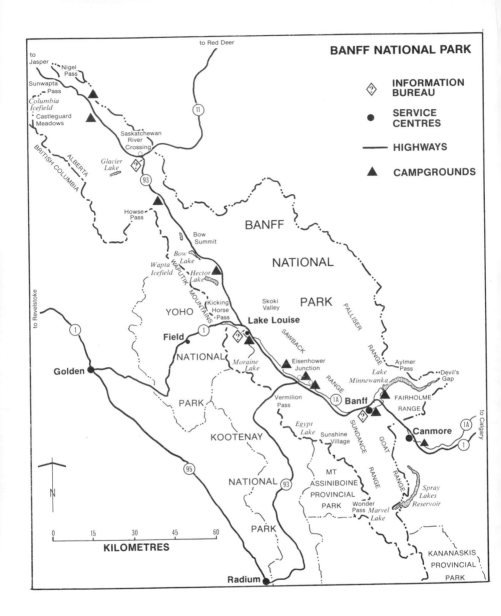

BANFF NATIONAL PARK

◈ INFORMATION BUREAU

● SERVICE CENTRES

— HIGHWAYS

▲ CAMPGROUNDS

KILOMETRES

Banff National Park

Situated on the eastern slope of the Rockies 120 kilometres west of Calgary, Banff National Park, with an area of 6,594 square kilometres, is the second largest mountain park. The Great Divide is its western boundary for more than 240 kilometres, with Yoho and Kootenay parks occupying the land immediately west of the divide. Jasper National Park shares a common boundary to the north.

There are hundreds of kilometres of trail stretching to all corners of the park, and it would be possible to spend an entire summer hiking and not come close to seeing all that the park offers. The hiking variety is extensive: short afternoon strolls, self-guided nature hikes, day trips of four to fourteen hours duration, and backpacking trips of any number of days are readily available. Terrains and life zones vary from the dense coniferous forests of the valley bottoms to the delicate lichens and wildflowers of high mountain passes set between sheer glaciated peaks.

Although it would be impossible to mention all the available hikes in Banff, several areas deserve special note. Lake Louise is perhaps the most famous of all hiking regions in the park, and the three major valleys of the area—Louise, Paradise and Moraine—offer extremely beautiful scenery but heavily used trails. Both the Skoki Valley and the Egypt Lake region provide interesting day hike or backpacking options, while Banff townsite is the centre of an extensive network of trails branching out in all directions and to all elevations. The northern section of the park, reached via the Icefields Parkway, features some interesting day trips, such as Dolomite Pass, Glacier Lake and Sunset Lookout, as well as access routes to the remote northeast section of the park where the travel is nearly as rugged and wild as it was 100 years ago.

All hikers planning an overnight trip in the backcountry must obtain a backcountry use permit from the warden service. Such permits, along with information on trails and open campfire regulations, are available in Banff from the information bureau on Banff Avenue and the wardens' office, located in the Banff industrial compound. The Lake Louise information bureau and wardens' office also issue permits as does the Saskatchewan River information centre. It is also possible to formally register hiking intentions with the warden service as a protective measure: if the party fails to register back in by a specified time the wardens will mount a search party. It should be emphasized that such registration is *voluntary* while the use of a backcountry permit is *mandatory*. Hikers should plan to pick up permits during regular office hours.

In both Banff townsite and Lake Louise the park visitor can find the usual tourist facilities of gas, food and accommodation (motels are booked solid throughout the summer). Banff townsite, a seasonally-active community of about 4,000 persons, is the site of the Park Administration Building and houses a number of hiking and climbing specialty shops.

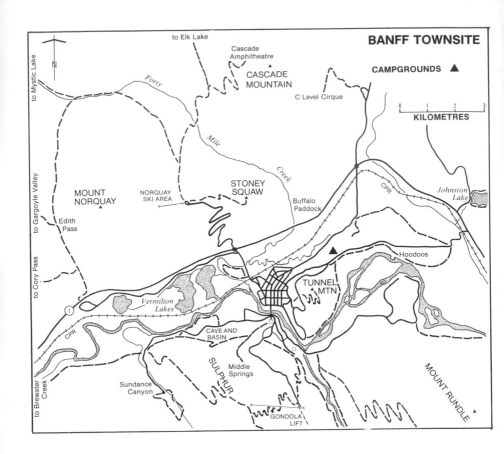

BANFF TOWNSITE

CAMPGROUNDS ▲

KILOMETRES
0 1 2 3

to Elk Lake

Cascade
Amphitheatre

CASCADE
MOUNTAIN

C Level Cirque

to Mystic Lake

N

Forty

Mile

Creek

CPR

Johnston
Lake

MOUNT
NORQUAY

NORQUAY
SKI AREA

STONEY
SQUAW

Buffalo
Paddock

Hoodoos

to Gargoyle Valley

Edith
Pass

to Cory Pass

Vermilion
Lakes

TUNNEL
MTN

CPR

CAVE AND
BASIN

to Brewster
Creek

Sundance
Canyon

SULPHUR

Middle
Springs

MOUNT RUNDLE

GONDOLA
LIFT

10

Banff Townsite Nature Trails

For the visitors who find themselves in Banff townsite for the day or staying at one of the nearby campgrounds, there are a number of short, interesting hikes of the nature walk variety that lead to natural features and viewpoints near the village. While most of these trails are limited to forested terrain on or just above the valley bottom, they seem all the more inviting after the summer crush and bustle of Banff. *Topo maps: Banff, 82 0/4 East.*

The Fenland Trail

2.1 kilometres (1.3 miles)

This short loop trail can be reached quite easily on foot from downtown Banff, and it offers a pleasant walk through an environment which most visitors would not associate with the mountains.

By walking or driving out of Banff on the Mount Norquay Road, one crosses the railroad tracks just south of the CPR station and immediately encounters the Fenland trail sign on the left hand side of the road. Approximately 100 metres into the forest the trail splits, making an elongated loop through the forest via a level pathway and returning to the junction in just under two kilometres. The main feature of this walk is the way in which a pond-marsh environment is slowly transforming into a mature valley bottom spruce forest. At various points along the trail hikers will encounter open swamps, streams where beaver have been at work, willow and shrub communities which have been 'pruned' by browsing deer and moose, and stands of towering spruce trees—the last stage of fenland succession. Along with the nearby Vermilion Lakes, the Fenland is one of the prime birding areas of Banff Park.

Sundance Canyon Loop

2.1 kilometres (1.3 miles)

The Sundance Canyon trail makes an interesting and easy one hour loop hike. From the trail head at the end of the Cave and Basin road, the hiker starts up the left hand branch of the trail, working up the canyon bottom alongside Sundance Creek for 800 metres. The canyon is hardly awe-inspiring, but it is pleasant and features an interesting variety of wildflowers in midsummer. At the 0.8 kilometre mark the trail arcs to the right, cutting across a spruce and pine-covered ridge. A viewpoint at Kilometre 1.4 overlooks the Bow Valley and the pinnacle of Mount Edith, directly across the valley to the northwest.

To reach the Sundance Canyon trail head, turn right on Cave Avenue after crossing the Banff Avenue bridge. Drive 5.6 kilometres (3.5 miles) to the termination of the road. The trail begins at the far end of the picnic area located there.

Tunnel Mountain

2.3 kilometres (1.4 miles)

The Tunnel Mountain trail provides a short, easy and readily accessible hike for Banff visitors. The trail is one of the oldest in the park and has probably been hiked more than any other in the Banff vicinity. Beginning at either St. Julien Road, just north of the Banff Centre, or at the trail sign on Tunnel Mountain Drive (the latter starting point reduces the hiking distance to 1.8 kilometres), the trail gradually ascends the western flank of Tunnel Mountain through a thick forest of pine and Douglas fir to reach the summit of the mountain and the Tunnel Mountain Fire Lookout.

The mountaintop, just 300 metres above the town, offers excellent viewing of the Banff environs, and, in particular, an impressive vista of the north ridge of Mount Rundle and the eastern Bow Valley. The mountain received its peculiar name in the 1880's when the CPR decided it would be necessary to run the railroad through it, a decision that the company soon rescinded.

The Hoodoos

4.7 kilometres (2.9 miles)

The trail to the Bow River Hoodoos is a short one, but it can be so pleasurably distracting that one can easily spend an entire afternoon hiking it.

The trip begins at the Hoodoos trail sign on Buffalo Street, just north of the Spray River Valley (and Banff Springs Hotel) viewpoint on the north bank of the river. From the sign the trail descends quickly to the backwaters of the Bow and proceeds along the riverbank beneath the sheer limestone cliffs of Tunnel Mountain to the Tunnel Mountain Meadows. It is this part of the hike that will waylay the casual traveller; a quiet river, a carpet of wildflowers, high rock walls and a blue sky create a most relaxing environment, and a short lunch often turns into a long nap. The trail also features some very old and beautiful Douglas fir trees which have managed to survive the forest fires of the past century.

Beyond the meadows the trail climbs to a ridge near the Tunnel Mountain Campground and then veers to the east, running parallel to the Tunnel Mountain Road as far as the Hoodoos, a little over three kilometres distant. The Hoodoos are tall, weather-sculpted forms of glacier sediment (or 'till') that have proved more resistant to erosion processes than the surrounding land mass and have thus stood solid while the earth around them has been carried away. The return to Banff is usually along the Tunnel Mountain Road.

Middle Hot Springs

1.3 kilometres (0.8 miles)

The trail to the Middle Hot Springs is short, gently-graded and cinder-finished, making a pleasant 1½ hour (return) stroll for Banff visitors with a bit of time to spare. Starting at the Upper Pergola in the Cascade Gardens behind the park administration building the trail climbs gradually through a rich pine and Douglas fir forest to three small, sulphurous springs. The Middle Hot Springs are only three of several originating in Sulphur Mountain and companion springs, at the site of the old Cave and Basin Pool, first attracted people to the Banff area.

The springs are formed by surface water seeping through fissures in the mountain, eventually reaching depths where the rock is extremely hot. From such depths the water reverses course, percolating up through another set of fractures to the earth's surface. The water, carrying dissolved lime and hydrogen sulfide from the rocks below, issues from the mountainside as the hot mineral springs. The hydrogen sulfide gas gives the water its rotten egg smell while the lime forms the interesting mantle of 'tufa' around the springs. The meadow at the springs provides a good view of the Banff area, featuring, across the valley, Mount Cory, Mount Norquay, Cascade Mountain and Mount Aylmer.

Stoney Squaw

2.1 kilometres (1.3 miles)

One of the highest viewpoints in the Banff townsite vicinity, the summit of Stoney Squaw offers an excellent survey of the many interesting features in the Bow Valley. The trail from Mount Norquay is enclosed in a dense forest of pine and spruce for much of its length, but within 200 metres of the trail's end the hiker begins to catch glimpses of the Banff environs to the south and east. Spread out below are Banff townsite, Tunnel Mountain and the Bow Valley. Mount Rundle, the Spray Valley, Sulphur Mountain and the Sundance Valley are all visible, while the towering south face of Cascade Mountain (2998 m) looms above.

The trail starts at the trail sign in Winter Parking Lot #3 at the Mount Norquay ski area. The area is 6.5 kilometres (4 miles) north of Banff on the Mount Norquay access road.

Mount Rundle

5.3 kilometres (3.3 miles)

The trail which climbs the southwest slope of Mount Rundle is one of the most arduous in the Banff townsite vicinity, and its primary function is as an access route for summit-bound climbers.

To pick up the trail, travel to the Banff Springs Golf Course, cross the bridge to the east side of the Spray, and look for the Spray Fire Road just beyond the first green. Follow the road for 800 metres and watch for the Rundle trail cutting up into the forest to the left. From this junction the trail climbs through closed forest for 2.4 kilometres before switchbacking out onto open slopes where there are good views of the Spray Valley and the Banff townsite vicinity.

At the 4.5 kilometre mark, the route to the first peak of Mount Rundle cuts uphill to the left; just 800 metres farther along the slope the main trail ends at a large gully. The climber's route to the second peak of Mount Rundle continues up the forested ridge on the opposite side of the gully. Any ascent of Mount Rundle beyond the established trail requires previous climbing experience and a registration slip from the warden service. And remember, a number of inexperienced hikers have lost the route and their lives on this 'easy' climb.

Be sure to carry water on the hike or the climb, as this slope of Mount Rundle is usually bone dry.

Spray River Loop

11.1 kilometres (6.9 miles)

The Spray River Fire Circle loop is one of several hiking options centring on the lower Spray Valley and provides an interesting three hour excursion for those limiting their hiking to the immediate Banff vicinity.

The initial portion of the walk coincides with the first 5.8 kilometres of the Spray River Fire Road, tracing the west bank of the Spray River. The fire road starts to the south of the Banff Springs Hotel just past the bus garage; a metal gate restricts access to motorized vehicles. The road rises gradually above the river, winding through the predominant Banff forest of lodgepole pine and white spruce. A bridle path cuts off to the left at Kilometre 0.6, as does a foot path at Kilometre 0.8 (a quick route to the golf course for those with little time or energy).

Bypassing a Canadian Youth Hostel (Kilometre 3.7), the road intersects another trail at the 4.7 kilometre mark. This trail leads to the right and constitutes a four kilometre hike to the Upper Hot Springs, emerging from the forest at the Sulphur Mountain Gondola right-of-way.

At Kilometre 5.8 the road passes the Spray River Fire Circle. Hikers should veer to the left at this point, cross the bridge over the Spray and pick up the trail heading back toward town, now following the east bank of the river. The trail ends at the golf course near the first green, a few hundred metres below the Bow Falls. From there it is a short walk either back to the Banff Springs Hotel or on into downtown Banff.

Cory Pass-Edith Pass

Trans-Canada Highway to Cory Pass—5.3 kilometres (3.3 miles)

Cory Pass—Edith Pass Loop—12.6 kilometres (7.8 miles)

Day trip

Allow 3 hours to Cory Pass

Elevation gain: 945 metres (3,100 feet)

Maximum elevation: 2350 metres (7,700 feet)

Topo maps: Banff, 82 0/4 East
(trail not shown)

Point of Departure: Drive to the Banff townsite west exit overpass. Take the Vermilion Lakes Road which branches west 100 metres south of the overpass and follow it five kilometres to its termination beneath the Trans-Canada Highway. Cross the highway to the Edith Pass trail sign.

0.0—Trail head (1405 m).

0.5—Cory Pass trail branches left from Edith Pass trail.

—Extreme uphill climb.

1.9—Crest of narrow forested ridge.

—Trail rolls along ridge, then climbs steeply across valley headwall to pass.

5.3—Cory Pass (2350 m).

Cory Pass. A rugged defile that stands over 2300 metres above sea level and looks out upon the monolithic south face of Mount Louis, Cory Pass is the objective of the most spectacular hike in the immediate Banff vicinity. But after gaining a vertical kilometre of elevation in just over five kilometres of hiking, the traveller will have paid dearly for the view.

The hike to Cory Pass starts at the trail head for Edith Pass, most easily reached by driving to the small parking area at the end of the Vermilion Lakes Road 5 kilometres west of Banff townsite. The trail starts on the opposite side of the busy Trans-Canada Highway.

The Cory route branches from the Edith Pass trail 500 metres from the trail head, and after emerging from the trees onto an open south-facing slope, the heart-pounding climb begins. After what may seem like an eternity, a forested ridge is crested and the grade relents somewhat. From this viewpoint, the sharp summit of Mount Edith is visible ahead with the notch of Cory Pass just below and to the left. The trail follows along the uneven ridge for the next kilometre or so before ascending across a broad open slope to the pass (take care if steep snow gullies are lingering across the trail).

Despite the usual warm, dry climb on the southerly exposed trail, Cory Pass itself is often a very cold and windy place. Sandwiched between the rocky summits of Mount Edith (2555 m) on the east and Mount Cory (2800 m) on the west, this high, rockbound gap might more appropriately be called a col.

However, the views are worth any discomforts of trail or pass, the highlight being the towering slabs of grey limestone which form the 500 metre face of Mount Louis. Known as a 'dogtooth' mountain, Louis' extraordinary shape was eroded from layers of sedimentary rock which

14

Gargoyle Valley

were tilted almost vertical during the uplift of the Rockies some 60 million years ago. Because of its spectacular and unapproachable aspect, the peak is a popular ascent for experienced rock climbers.

Gargoyle Valley Option. Instead of returning via the approach trail, the hiker may wish to continue on into the Gargoyle Valley. Barring late season snow, a vague trail can be followed down the steep talus slope north of the pass. After a quick initial loss of elevation, the track traverses high and just beneath the cliffs of Mount Edith to a narrow opening between that mountain and Mount Louis. The valley has an appropriate name as rugged cliffs and rock pinnacles loom on all sides, the stark landscape relieved only by a small, green meadow nestled at the foot of Louis' south face.

Stay high and to the right once out of the Gargoyle Valley (the trail is faint here) and watch ahead for a well-defined route

which traverses the lower slopes of Mount Edith and finally descends onto the forested crest of Edith Pass.

The Gargoyle option makes a fine day-long excursion for the strong hiker, the complete circuit of Mount Edith totalling nearly 15 kilometres.

Edith Pass. Many people hike to this pass as a point of destination. It has little to recommend it, however, as the trail is forest-enclosed all the way to the top; the only view of any note is a glimpse of Mount Louis obtained about a kilometre north of the summit. It is a short but steep trip of four kilometres.

Any hiker not up to the strenuous circuit of Mount Edith but who has a couple of vehicles at his disposal, can drop one car at the Edith Pass trail head, then drive to the Mount Norquay ski area and hike back via Forty Mile Creek—a somewhat more pleasant outing covering 12.2 kilometres. (See *Mystic Lake* trail.)

Cascade Amphitheatre

Mount Norquay to Cascade Amphitheatre—6.6 kilometres (4.1 miles)

Day trip
Allow 2½ - 3 hours one way
Elevation gain: 610 metres (2,000 feet)
Maximum elevation: 2195 metres (7,200 feet)
Topo maps: Banff, 82 0/4 East
(last 3.5 kms not shown)

Point of Departure: Follow the Mount Norquay
Road north from Banff townsite across the
Trans-Canada Highway and up 5.8 kilometres
(3.6 miles) of twisting switchbacks to the ski
area complex. Enter Parking Lot #3 and drive
to the far end.

0.0—Trail sign.

—Follow the valley bottom path leading
through the ski area development.

0.8—Trail enters woods on old fire road.

1.1—Junction. Trail to Edith Pass and Mystic
Lake cuts left. Keep straight ahead for
Cascade Amphitheatre.

3.1—Forty Mile Creek bridge.

—Steady uphill.

4.3—Junction. Cut uphill to right for Cascade
Amphitheatre.

6.6—Trail levels out into Amphitheatre.

7.7—Head of Amphitheatre.

One of the more popular hikes in the
Banff environs is a 6.6 kilometre trek up
the western flank of Cascade Mountain
to a large natural amphitheatre lying
some 2200 metres above sea level.
Featuring the beauties of subalpine
meadows, glacial-carved rock and an
excellent survey of Elk Valley, the trip is
certainly worth a day's outing.

From the trail sign at the third
Norquay parking lot, the trail ambles
north past the ski development. The first
section might be a bit confusing as the
development of the area has left the valley
floor covered with bits and pieces of road
and trail which intersect frequently.
However, with a small amount of
perseverance and a generally northerly
orientation, the hiker will soon find the
bits and pieces consolidating into one
trail running above Forty Mile Creek on
the west side of the valley.

At the 3.1 kilometre mark the trail
descends into the valley and crosses Forty
Mile Creek before angling up the western
slope of Cascade. For late season hikers
the bridge is a good place to fill a canteen
as the trail beyond is fairly dry and quite
steep.

Shortly beyond the crossing the trail
offers a good view of the sheer 390 metre
face to Mount Louis (2682 m) which lies
directly west across the valley. The
precipitous Palliser limestone "pope's
hat" of Louis is one of the better-known
rock climbs in the Banff region. The
summit of Mount Edith (2554 m),
another popular climb, can be seen to the
south of Mount Louis, behind Mount
Norquay (2523 m).

The last trail fork of the hike is the Elk
Lake junction, 1.2 kilometres beyond
Forty Mile Creek. The right hand fork to
the amphitheatre climbs steeply through
a forest of white spruce and lodgepole
pine for 2.3 kilometres to reach the hike's
maximum elevation. From this point it is
possible to view five major peaks to the

Cascade Amphitheatre

west. Running from the south, they are Mount Norquay, Mount Edith, Mount Cory (although the main summit is not visible from the trail), Mount Louis and Mount Brewster.

Beyond the viewpoint the path begins a gradual descent, and a few minutes bring the hiker to the centre of a delicate subalpine meadow sheltered on three sides by the rugged limestone of Cascade's crest. This natural amphitheatre is a fine example of a glacier-carved cirque—a great bowl-shaped depression ground out by an accumulation of ice over an extended period of time. Today the pika and alpine fir have replaced the ice, but its incredible power is still evidenced by the high carved rock of the amphitheatre's walls.

For the hardier hiker the ridge forming the southern wall of the amphitheatre represents the popular route to the summit of Cascade Mountain (2998 m). Although this is considered a climb and thus requires registration, the route (at least as far as a false summit some 300 metres short of the true summit) is little more than a rough scree scramble and the view is quite spectacular. A crude but discernible trail runs up the ridge as far as the false summit.

Elk Lake

Mount Norquay to Elk Lake—13.5 kilometres (8.4 miles)

Day trip or backpack
Allow 4½ hours one way
Elevation gain: 610 metres (2,000 feet)
Maximum elevation: 2165 metres (7,100 feet)
Topo maps: Banff, 82 0/4 East
　　　　　Mount Eisenhower, 82 0/5 East
　　　　　(trail not marked)

Point of Departure: Follow the Mount Norquay access road to the third (#3) winter parking lot. A directional sign at the far end of the lot indicates the trail head.

0.0—Trail sign.

—The first 4.3 kilometres of trail are as described for the Cascade Amphitheatre hike.

4.3—Elk Lake junction. Follow the left hand branch.

6.8—Trail enters high subalpine meadows.

12.6—Maximum elevation (2165 m) and viewpoint.

13.5—Elk Lake.

Miles of subalpine meadow and the sight of distant mountain peaks characterize the 13.5 kilometre Elk Lake hike. Although a bit long for an "easy" day trip, the hike is most pleasant and offers fine overnight possibilities.

The first 4.0 kilometres of trail are the same as for the Cascade Amphitheatre hike, cutting across the flank of Mount Norquay, down to and across Forty Mile Creek and then proceeding up the western flank of Cascade Mountain. At the Elk Lake junction the traveller should stay to the left. The path here is wide and well-defined, running through a typical Banff Park coniferous forest of lodgepole pine, western white spruce and alpine fir.

A little over two hours of walking will bring the hiker to an extensive subalpine meadow, characterized by few trees, low willows and a profusion of delicate wildflowers. The scenery is dominated by Mount Brewster (2859 m) to the west, named for one of the early residents in the Banff area. The trail wanders through such terrain for some five kilometres—a beautiful piece of hiking where an occasional over-the-shoulder glance reveals a long and clear view down the Elk Valley to Mount Norquay (2522 m), Sulphur Mountain (2451 m) and, beyond Sulphur, portions of the Sundance Range.

The trail eventually crosses the valley and gradually ascends the side of Mount Brewster a short distance before dropping into the amphitheatre that houses Elk Lake. The high point on Brewster offers an excellent unobstructed view of the length of Elk Valley.

Not far from timberline, backed by a sheer limestone face of 720 metres, the lake's aspect differs markedly from the gentle meadows leading up the valley from Mount Norquay. The forest cover at the lake, predominantly alpine larch, offers a distinct contrast to the earlier

18

Elk Lake and Mount Brewster

canopy—a good indication of a transitional life zone.

A feeling of silent and solemn grandeur pervades the environs of the lake, a feeling which is best realized by spending a night or two in the area. For those following such a course of action and who are armed with map and compass, the rugged upper portion of Elk Valley and the northern slopes of Cascade Mountain ought to provide many interesting hours of exploration.

Mystic Lake

Mount Norquay to Mystic Lake—19.6 kilometres (12.2 miles)
Mount Norquay to Johnston's Canyon—36.8 kilometres (22.9 miles)

Backpack
Allow 6 hours to Mystic Lake
Elevation gain: 150 metres (500 feet)
        loss: 120 metres (400 feet)
Maximum elevation: 1980 metres (6,500 feet)
Topo maps: Banff, 82 0/4 East
        Mount Eisenhower, 82 0/5 East
        Mount Eisenhower, 82 0/5 West

Point of Departure: Follow the Mount Norquay access road to the third (#3) winter parking lot. A directional sign at the far end of the lot indicates the trail head.

0.0—Trail sign.

1.1—Mystic Lake trail junction and sign. Take the left fork.

4.0—Bridge over Forty Mile Creek. Trail follows close to the creek's east bank.

6.0—Edith Pass trail junction. Follow the right fork.

9.3—Campsite.

15.6—Trail crosses a short boggy area and swerves abruptly to the left, angling down toward Forty Mile Creek.

15.9—Major unmarked trail junction. Take the left fork.

16.0—Small stream and old log cabin. Trail proceeds through the camp and ascends a low ridge.

19.1—Mystic Pass trail junction and campsite. To the left, Mystic Lake (0.5 kilometre); to the right, Mystic Pass.

21.9—First larches. Trail approaches treeline.

22.7—Crest of Mystic Pass (2285 m).

23.3—Narrow rocky defile signifies end of pass. Steep descent.

29.3—Campsite (primitive) and Luellen Lake junction. Proceed straight ahead, crossing stream.

31.2—Hillsdale Meadow junction. Keep right and cross bridge over Johnston Creek.

31.5—The Ink Pots.

36.8—Johnston's Canyon Lodge.

The Mystic Lake and Mystic Pass trail combination offers a classic two day backpack through the heart of the Rocky Mountain Front Ranges. Fast-running streams, forest-ringed lakes and a high alpine pass are all to be enjoyed during the course of the 36.8 kilometre hike.

The hike divides itself nicely into two parts, the first day spent on a quiet and essentially level 19.6 kilometre walk to Mystic Lake, while the second day is spent on a shorter but considerably more challenging traverse of Mystic Pass and a long descent to Johnston's Canyon. Both are full hiking days, but the scenery justifies the effort involved for the complete trip. Because of the altitude difference between Mount Norquay and Johnston's Canyon, it is strongly recommended that the hike begin at Mount Norquay. The trail throughout is in good shape and, although secondary trails branch off the main route from time to time, the trail is adequately obvious.

The first portion of the hike involves a gently graded traverse of the northern flank of Mount Norquay, the trail rising and falling through a forest of lodgepole pine and spruce. At the 4.0 kilometre mark Forty Mile Creek is crossed, and the trail proceeds along its eastern bank, with Mount Brewster to the east and, across the valley to the west, some of the more striking peaks in the Sawback Range: Mount Louis, Mount Fifi and Mount Cockscomb. Although much of this section of trail is forested, avalanche paths and willow flats give the hiker frequent chances to examine the valley.

An unmarked trail junction at Kilometre 15.9 and a second crossing of Forty Mile Creek move the hiker into the side valley which leads to Mystic Lake. Passing a weathered log cabin, the trail begins to alternate between steep, short climbing sections and fairly level (though rocky and rooty) patches. At the 19.1

kilometre mark the trail reaches the Mystic Lake campsite (primitive and very small) and the junction to Mystic Pass. A scant 500 metres beyond lie the shores of Mystic Lake, a quiet body of water settled in the bottom of a great rock cirque.

For people wishing to go beyond Mystic Lake, the next day's hike is a full one. From the Mystic Pass junction the trail climbs 300 metres into Mystic Pass and then descends a long and often steep 14 kilometres to meet the old 1-A Highway at Johnston's Canyon. The total descent is 840 metres. The pass itself is a kilometre-and-a-half in length, running through beautiful alpine meadows flanked by the gnarled and twisted Devonian limestone strata of the Front Ranges of the Rockies. Beyond the pass the trail drops through some spectacular rockslide and avalanche paths, bypassing delicate waterfalls, to meet Johnston Creek at Kilometre 29.6. The Ink Pots (see *Johnston's Canyon*) and the option of the Johnston Canyon falls provide the possibility of continuing points of interest all the way to the highway and the trail's end.

Aylmer Lookout

Minnewanka Parking Area to Aylmer Lookout—11.8 kilometres (7.3 miles)
Minnewanka Parking Area to Aylmer Pass—13.5 kilometres (8.4 miles)

Day trip or backpack

Allow 4-5 hours one way

Elevation gain: 760 metres (2,500 feet)

Maximum elevation: 2255 metres (7,400 feet)

Topo maps: Lake Minnewanka, 82 0/6 West

Point of Departure: Drive 9 kilometres (5.6 miles) north from Banff townsite to Lake Minnewanka via the Minnewanka Road. Park in the large parking lot adjacent to the boat concession.

0.0—Trail head at boat concession access gate.

—Route follows paved trail through picnic area.

0.6—Pavement ends, official trail begins (trail sign).

1.4—Stewart Canyon and bridge.

—Trail climbs, then emerges above lakeshore.

7.8—Junction: Take left fork to Aylmer Lookout and Pass. Campground and lakeshore to right.

—Trail rises steeply.

10.1—Junction: Right fork for lookout. Straight ahead 3.4 kilometres for Aylmer Pass.

11.8—Aylmer Lookout.

In August, 1841, Sir George Simpson, Governor of the Hudson's Bay Company, travelling with twenty-two men and over forty horses, entered the Canadian Rockies and passed along the shores of Lake Minnewanka. Sir George commented in his *Narrative*: "This valley is from two to three miles in width, contracted in several places, forming basins, in which there lie four beautiful lakes, connected to each other by small streams . . . the fourth is upwards of fifteen miles in length and three in width . . . The surrounding Mountains were very grand, of every varied form . . . their craggy summits resembling battlements among which dizzy heights the goat and sheep delight to bound."

Today, owing to the damming of the Cascade River, Minnewanka is much larger than it was when Sir George made his marathon journey through the Rockies, the water level having been elevated by some 25 metres. Likewise, where the Hudson's Bay Company explorers bushwhacked, a well-defined trail skirts the north shore of the lake. Most hikers, however, prefer to follow the shore for less than half that distance, then climb the steep spur trail to the outstanding views of Aylmer Lookout and the extensive alplands of Aylmer Pass.

Though the first 7.8 kilometres of trail are gentle, non-demanding walking, hikers should beware of the ordeal beyond. Forking uphill, away from the beauties of the lake, the trail to the lookout and pass is strenuous climbing indeed. Canteens should be filled at the stream near the junction in preparation for gaining 600 vertical metres in the next two kilometres. The next water is at least an hour beyond this stream, and on warm sunny days this slope is one of the hot spots in the Canadian Rockies.

Most day hikers opt for the shorter trip to the fire lookout, situated on the crest of

Lake Minnewanka from Aylmer Lookout

an open ridge which descends from the summit of Mount Aylmer. From this lofty viewpoint nearly all of Lake Minnewanka may be seen. The water, over 500 metres below, is of the deepest blue, while boats look much like tiny water insects skimming to and fro.

Across the lake stand the twin peaks of Mount Inglismaldie (2965 m) and Mount Girouard (2995 m), displaying massive cliffs of limestone which date back to the Mississippian and Devonian ages. Directly behind the lookout, a short distance to the north, is Mount Aylmer (3162 m), the highest mountain in this section of the park. To the southwest lie the Mount Rundle massif and the Bow Valley near Banff townsite, with range upon range beyond, disappearing into the distance.

This open ridge abounds with mountain sheep, and in early summer large flocks are often seen in the vicinity of the lookout. Another form of wildlife which proliferates on the ridge in early summer, partially due to the presence of the sheep, is the wood tick (check your bodies carefully upon returning from this trip).

Though strong hikers can visit the lookout and return in one long day, the hike lends itself well to overnight camping. An excellent campsite exists on the shore of Lake Minnewanka near the 7.8 kilometre junction.

Aylmer Pass Option. From the junction at Kilometre 10.1, the left fork continues on to the park boundary and the alpine tundra of Aylmer Pass. The pass is a prime alpine area above the last forest cover. Views open into the highly folded and faulted mountains of the Palliser Range, and directly above to the summit of Mount Aylmer. Like the Aylmer Lookout ridge, the slopes above the pass are frequented by flocks of mountain sheep.

The pass side trip should be considered a must for those backpacking in the area, and if hikers have a few days to spare they may wish to continue over the pass to explore the Ghost River Wilderness Area.

Lake Minnewanka—Carrot Creek

Minnewanka Parking Area to Ghost Lake #2—25.5 kilometres (16.0 miles)
Lake Minnewanka—Carrot Creek Circuit—48.5 kilometres (30.2 miles)

Backpack

Allow 8 hours to Ghost Lakes

Elevation gain: 460 metres (1,500 feet)

Maximum elevation: 1920 metres (6,300 feet)

Topo maps: Lake Minnewanka, 82 0/6 West
Lake Minnewanka, 82 0/6 East
Canmore, 82 0/3 West

Point of Departure: Drive 9 kilometres (5.6 miles) east from Banff townsite to Lake Minnewanka via the Minnewanka Road. Park in the large parking lot adjacent to the boat concession.

0.0—Boat concession access gate. Follow paved route through picnic area.

1.4—Stewart Canyon and bridge.

—Trail rolls up and down along the north shore of the lake for the next 21 kilometres.

7.8—Junction and campsite: Aylmer Pass and Lookout to left. Lakeshore trail straight ahead.

22.7—East end of Lake Minnewanka.

23.7—First Ghost Lake.

25.4—Trail crosses channel between 1st and 2nd Ghost Lakes turning eastward toward Lake Minnewanka.

27.8—Trail reaches east end of Lake Minnewanka then skirts above south shore.

34.4—Trail cuts away from lake and begins steep climb.

37.9—Carrot Creek Summit (1920 m).

40.8—First of approximately 25 crossings on Carrot Creek.

—Trail enters canyon.

45.9—Last crossing on Carrot Creek.

—Trail emerges from canyon and crosses pine and aspen flats.

48.5—Trans-Canada Highway, 1.9 kilometres west of Banff Park East Gate.

This loop trip around Banff's largest lake is definitely a departure from the usual alpine meadow—cirque lake routine, and it is especially attractive to early and late season backpackers since its lower elevations and easterly situation in the range often result in dry, snow-free hiking from May until autumn.

Departing from the boat dock complex and picnic area at Lake Minnewanka's western tip, the trail bends back into Stewart Canyon, crosses that chasm and follows along the north shore of the lake for the next 20 kilometres. In some respects this part of the journey is uneventful, but the scenery is far from dull as views are continually opening to the sheer cliffs of Mounts Inglismaldie and Girouard across the lake. There are also many well-appointed campsites along this shore, and pleasant driftwood-covered beaches provide numerous rest-stops (though not as pleasant on week-ends when motor boat traffic is heavy on the lake).

Approaching the eastern end of Lake Minnewanka, the countryside becomes noticeably drier. Limber pines are scattered among the ubiquitous lodgepole stands, while western wood lilies bloom on the open forest floor in midsummer; this is one of the few areas in Banff Park where this showy prairie flower grows in profusion.

Lake Minnewanka's first recorded visit came in 1841 when a party led by George Simpson, Governor of the Hudson's Bay Company, passed along its northern shore on a route-finding journey through the Rockies. (Damming near its west end during this century has created a lake which is 25 metres higher and eight or so kilometres longer than that seen by Sir George.)

Nearing the Ghost Lakes and Devil's Gap, new summits come into view—

Lake Minnewanka from the lakeshore trail

peaks which are even more stark and rugged than those already encountered. Typical of the eastern edge of the Front Ranges, these mountains are composed primarily of Cambrian and Devonian limestone—layers of sedimentary rock which have been tightly folded and severely fractured by the forces of mountain building.

After passing beyond the eastern end of the lake, the trail skirts the first of the three Ghost Lakes, crosses through an arm of forest and emerges on the short channel connecting the first and second lakes. An easy ford can be made here and the journey continued by turning west to follow the trail back toward Lake Minnewanka (another trail continues east, skirting the south shoreline of both the second and third Ghost Lakes to reach the park boundary in the Devil's Gap in less than five kilometres).

The rather haunting names found in this part of the park relate to local Indian legends concerning a ghost which was observed picking over the bones of Stony warriors killed in a battle on the nearby Ghost River—just a bit of local colour to ponder as you slip into your sleeping bag for the night.

After reaching the eastern end of Lake Minnewanka once more, the trail rolls along the south shore for nearly seven kilometres, then turns south to begin a short but steep climb to the Carrot Creek Summit. Totally enclosed within a mature spruce forest, the route crosses back and forth over a sparkling moss-fringed stream. Other pleasures are few.

The Carrot Creek Summit is just under 2000 metres above sea level, so it is still below the timberline. But a short walk uphill and to the west of the pass will soon bring you out into the beautiful meadows which skirt the lower ramparts of Mount Peechee. It is fine country for wandering with views to the south of Princess Margaret Mountain, Mount Charles Stewart and an even more extensive alpine region which leads over a divide and into the Grotto Creek watershed.

The trip is completed by descending the Carrot Creek Canyon. Many have cursed this narrow gorge for its numerous stream crossings (the trail is forced back and forth across the creek by the canyon walls), but the descent of this cool canyon can be quite pleasant if you are willing to relax and take your time. Waders will find none of the fords more than knee-deep while acrobatic log walkers and rock hoppers may even escape with dry feet.

25

C Level Cirque

Half-day trip

Allow 1½ hours one way

Elevation gain: 455 metres (1,500 feet)

Maximum elevation: 1920 metres (6,300 feet)

Topo maps: Banff, 82 0/4 East
(trail not shown)

Point of Departure: Drive 3.4 kilometres (2.1 miles) north from the Trans-Canada Highway on the Lake Minnewanka Road to the Bankhead Historical Site. Turn left onto a dirt access road a half kilometre past the Bankhead interpretive exhibit. Follow the road 300 metres to the parking area for the trail. The trail starts at an old access road gate across a meadow 100 metres to the north.

0.0—Wood and cable gate.

—Steady uphill through closed forest.

1.1—Old mine buildings.

1.3—Lake Minnewanka viewpoint.

1.8—Old mine vent shaft.

—Steady climb through forest.

3.9—C Level Cirque.

Despite its short length, the C Level Cirque trail is one of the more attractive hikes in the Banff townsite vicinity. In less than four kilometres it climbs past the remains of a long defunct coal mine, a spectacular viewpoint for the broad Minnewanka Valley, and finally emerges in a high, rockbound pocket beneath the looming east face of Cascade Mountain.

The hike begins its ascent through a pleasantly varied forest of lodgepole pine, spruce and aspen where calypso orchids, blue clematis and many colourful violets bloom in early summer.

Within a half-hour two skeletal buildings are reached, remnants of an anthracite coal operation which flourished from 1904 to 1923. From a tailings pile 100 metres beyond the old buildings there is an excellent view out to Lake Minnewanka. Above the viewpoint several fenced holes in the ground indicate the location of old mine vent shafts.

For the remainder of the hike travel is through closed forest. At Kilometre 3.9 the trail opens out into a cirque on the eastern flank of Cascade Mountain. Snow often lingers in this small basin into midsummer, and as it retreats, a carpet of yellow glacier lilies spreads across the damp, subalpine soil. A small pond at the cirque mouth provides water in all but the driest years.

Views from near the mouth of the cirque are to Mount Inglismaldie, the western tip of Lake Minnewanka and the Two Jack Lake area. The trail continues up to the right of a large talus slope to an even higher vantage point on a knoll above the basin. The hiker may also wish to take a seat on any convenient rock in the midst of the great debris slope and watch the antics of the cirque inhabitants—the hoary marmots, pikas and golden-mantled ground squirrels.

Brewster Creek

Sundance Canyon to Bryant Creek Warden Cabin—40 kilometres (25 miles)*

Wilderness access
Allow 2 days one way
Elevation gain: 1035 metres (3,400 feet)
Maximum elevation: 2410 metres (7,900 feet)
Topo maps: Banff, 82 0/4 East
          Mount Assiniboine, 82 J/13

Point of Departure: The trail begins from the Sundance Canyon Road, 5 kilometres (3 miles) west of Banff townsite. Watch for the fire road cutting right just before the picnic area at Sundance Canyon.

*distance approximate

The Brewster Creek trail is a broad, well-travelled fire road and horse route running from Sundance Canyon up Brewster Creek. The trail travels beneath the western slope of the Sundance Range and then climbs steeply up and over Allenby Pass and descends toward Bryant Creek and the Mount Assiniboine vicinity. Though the trail offers no hazards and is well-defined, its use as a major horse route to Assiniboine creates obvious problems for the hiker.

An alternate trail head at the Healy Creek Warden Station (on the Sunshine Road east of Banff) cuts some 5 kilometres off the total distance but necessitates a ford of Healy Creek which could be troublesome during the early season.

Spray River Fire Road

Banff Springs Hotel to Bryant Creek trail head—44.4 kilometres (27.6 miles)

Wilderness access
Allow 2 days one way
Elevation gain: 365 metres (1,200 feet)
Maximum elevation: 1735 metres (5,700 feet)
Topo maps: Banff, 82 0/4 East
          Canmore, 83 0/3 West
          Spray Lakes Reservoir, 82 J/14

Point of Departure: The fire road begins a short distance beyond the Banff Springs Hotel, just past the parking lot. Traffic control gate indicates the trail head.

Starting near the Banff Springs Hotel in Banff townsite, the Spray River Fire Road approximates the course of the Spray River to its source at the western end of the Spray Lakes Reservoir, working first up the Sulphur Mountain-Mount Rundle valley and then up the valley between the Goat and Sundance Ranges. It is a closed access road but well-maintained and is the major warden access route to the southern portion of Banff Park. Although not recommended as a hiking route because of a variety of shorter and more 'authentic' hiking trails (see *Assiniboine* and *Burstall Pass*), it does have several fine campsites and passes through some beautiful country. It should be considered a two day hike. From the warden camp at the 44.4 kilometre mark the hiker will find trails both to the Palliser Pass area and Mount Assiniboine Provincial Park.

Mount Assiniboine

Mount Assiniboine, rising 3618 metres above sea level, is the seventh highest peak in the Canadian Rockies and the highest peak between the International Boundary and the CPR mainline. Lying 37 aerial kilometres southwest of Banff, the mountain soars spectacularly above its neighbors and is visible for many kilometres in all directions. Mount Assiniboine and its environs constitute one of the splendid scenic areas in the Canadian Rockies, an area popular with hikers and climbers alike. It is not, needless to say, an area sought out by those seeking extended wilderness solitude.

The peak, reminiscent of the Matterhorn (and thus labelled 'the Matterhorn of the Rockies'), was named in 1885 by Dr. G.M. Dawson of the Dominion Geological Survey. The name is derived from the Assiniboine Indian tribe, and means 'stone-boiler,' coming from the Indians' practice of cooking their food by dropping heated rocks into animal paunches or holes filled with water.

The first white men to explore the immediate Assiniboine vicinity were R.L. Barrett and Tom Wilson, who made an expedition to the foot of the mountain in 1893. Unsuccessful attempts to climb the peak were launched in 1899, 1900 and the early summer of 1901, and it wasn't until September of 1901 that a party comprised of James Outram, a British alpinist, and Christian Hasler and Christian Bohren, two Swiss guides, succeeded in reaching the summit via the southwest face. Outram later eloquently described the mountain when he wrote, "it rises, like a monster tooth, from an entourage of dark cliff and gleaming glacier, 5,000 feet above the valley of approach; the magnificent triangular face, barred with horizontal belts of perpendicular cliffs and glistening expanses of the purest snow and ice, which constitutes the chief glory of the mountain, soaring more than 3,000 feet directly from the glacier that sweeps its base." Since Outram's day the mountain has been climbed many times from many directions and remains a very popular ascent.

Although extensive horse use in the area in the recent past has created trail damage distracting to people on foot, there are many kilometres of trail in the region which provide good hiking. Three continental passes, Og, Assiniboine and Wonder, are within easy hiking distance of Magog Lake; the circuit of Sunburst, Cerulean and Elizabeth Lakes in the Sunburst Valley offers a good half day trip; and the somewhat longer journey to Wedgewood Lake provides a view of Assiniboine not seen by many. Most of the area lies within the upper reaches of the subalpine life zone, from 1950 to 2100 metres, and true alpine terrain is never more than a few minutes scramble away. The fragility of the area is readily apparent and hikers in this high use region should react accordingly.

Backpackers have two camping options in the immediate Assiniboine area. One is the tenting site about halfway down Magog Lake above its eastern shore, and the other is the provincially owned Naiset Cabins, 300 metres south of Mount Assiniboine Lodge. A small nightly fee is charged for people wishing to use the cabins and, owing to high use, hikers should not be surprised to find them full anytime from mid-June to Labour Day.

Three days should be the absolute minimum allotted to an Assiniboine trek: one day travel each way plus a day in the area. Additional days of travel should be tacked on for the longer access routes: Ferro Pass, Brewster Creek or the Spray Fire Road.

Mount Assiniboine

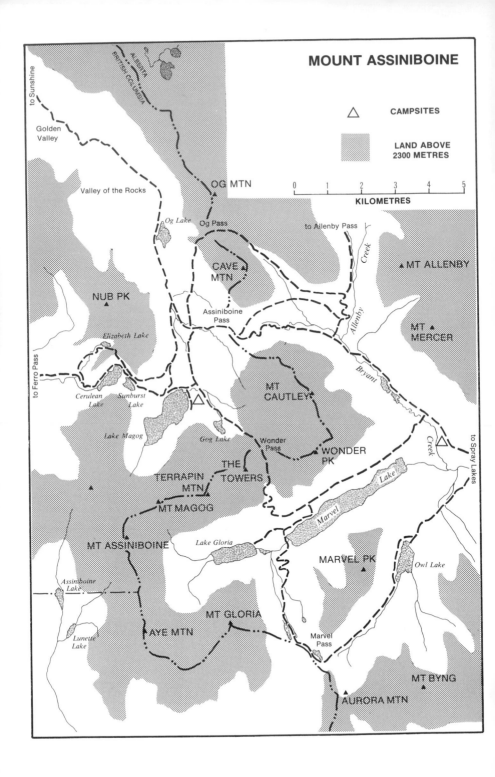

MOUNT ASSINIBOINE

△ CAMPSITES

LAND ABOVE 2300 METRES

KILOMETRES
0 1 2 3 4 5

to Sunshine

Golden Valley

ALBERTA
BRITISH COLUMBIA

Valley of the Rocks

Og Lake

OG MTN

Og Pass

to Allenby Pass

Allenby Creek

▲ MT ALLENBY

CAVE MTN

NUB PK ▲

Assiniboine Pass

MT MERCER ▲

Elizabeth Lake

to Ferro Pass

Cerulean Lake

Sunburst Lake

MT CAUTLEY

Bryant Creek

Lake Magog

Gog Lake

Wonder Pass

WONDER PK

Creek

to Spray Lakes

THE TOWERS

TERRAPIN MTN

▲

MT MAGOG

Marvel Lake

MT ASSINIBOINE

Lake Gloria

Marvel Creek

MARVEL PK ▲

Owl Lake

Assiniboine Lake

MT GLORIA

Luneue Lake

AYE MTN

Marvel Pass

MT BYNG ▲

AURORA MTN

Assiniboine via Sunshine Village

Sunshine Village to Lake Magog—27.2 kilometres (16.9 miles)

Backpack
Allow 2 or more days
Elevation gain: 335 metres (1,100 feet)
loss: 490 metres (1,600 feet)
Maximum elevation: 2360 metres (7,750 feet)
Topo maps: Banff, 82 0/4 East
Banff, 82 0/4 West
Mount Assiniboine, 82 J/13

Point of Departure: Drive to the Bourgeau parking lot, following the Sunshine Village turn-off 9.0 kilometres (5.6 miles) west of Banff. From the Bourgeau lot either hike or take the bus (call Brewster's in Banff for summer schedules) up the six kilometres of access road. The trail begins at Sunshine Village, running south up the Dell.

0.0—Sunshine Village.

—Trail climbs up and over the Dell to extensive alpine meadows beyond.

1.4—Junction. Assiniboine to the left (south)

5.2—Summit of Quartz Ridge spur.

5.8—Howard Douglas Lake.

9.3—Summit of Citadel Pass (2360 m). Assiniboine straight ahead.

—Steep 390 metre descent to the Simpson River and Golden Valley. (Near the valley bottom, watch for the elevation-saving high route striking off across the open slopes to the left.)

—Trail forks occasionally; main route proceeds up valley, runs through a large natural bowl and enters Valley of the Rocks.

??.?—Og Lake.

24.1—Old corral fence.

25.6—Sunburst Lake junction. High trail to Sunburst to the right. Main route to Assiniboine Lodge and the Naiset Cabins, straight ahead.

27.2—Assiniboine Lodge.

The 27 kilometres from Sunshine Village to Lake Magog in Mount Assiniboine Provincial Park constitute a full day's hiking and can be quite tiring on a hot summer's day. It is recommended that hikers do not choose this as the first backpack of the season. However, the route is one of much beauty, the trail winding through a variety of terrains and always running close beneath the peaks of the continental divide.

From Sunshine Village to Citadel Pass the trail ambles across open, fragile subalpine meadows, angling south-east between Lookout Mountain and Quartz Hill, bypassing the diminutive Howard Douglas Lake and gradually climbing to the summit of Citadel Pass (2360 metres). A steep 390 metre descent on the far side of Citadel puts the hiker at the bottom of Golden Valley and near the headwaters of the Simpson River, the last spot to fill water bottles for nearly 13 kilometres. From the valley bottom the trail runs southeast along the foot of the continental divide, passing through a forest of pine and spruce, into and out of a large natural amphitheatre and into the Valley of the Rocks, a long and dry valley featuring a wild array of peculiarly shaped boulders. Og Lake marks the end of the valley and the trail veers south, rounding the eastern flank of Nub Peak to reach Lake Magog.

A highline trail cuts off to the left from the main trail on the south side of Citadel Pass, a good distance above the Golden Valley floor. The trail contours off at some elevation above the valley bottom and provides an interesting option to the lower valley route, saving both distance and elevation for the hiker.

Assiniboine via Assiniboine Pass

Spray Reservoir to Lake Magog via low route—17.7 kilometres (11.0 miles)
Spray Reservoir to Lake Magog via high route—19.4 kilometres (12.1 miles)

Backpack
Allow 6 hours one way
Elevation gain: 455 metres (1,500 feet)
Maximum elevation: 2165 metres (7,100 feet)
Topo maps: Spray Lakes Reservoir, 82 J/14
            Mount Assiniboine, 82 J/13

Point of Departure: Drive or hike the 40 kilometre (25 mile) Spray Lakes access road from the town of Canmore. Cross the dam at Kilometre 16 to the west side of the reservoir and proceed as far as Canyon Dam. The 1.5 kilometres of road beyond the dam is usually in wretched shape, and some hikers will prefer to start the hike at this point. The trail head is approximately six kilometres beyond the dam at a Warden Service access gate.

0.0—Warden Service access gate.

8.0—Bryant Creek trail junction and sign. Stay straight ahead.

10.6—Small creek crossing. Trace trails to left and right.

11.4—Trail sign for Assiniboine. Keep right.

11.5—Stream crossing and trail junction. To the left, across the stream, the low route to Assiniboine Pass; to the right, the trail to Allenby and Og Passes and the high route to Assiniboine Pass.

12.0—Trail junction and sign. Turn left.

16.4—Trail merges with low route and switchbacks up through rock bands.

17.0—Assiniboine Pass and entrance to Assiniboine Provincial Park.

17.3—Trail map in O'Brien Meadows.

18.9—Trail fork. To the left, the Naiset Cabins; to the right, Assiniboine Lodge.

19.4—Assiniboine Lodge.

The hiker attempting to reach Mount Assiniboine via Assiniboine Pass has two options. He can follow either a low, fairly direct route close to the base of Gibralter and Cascade Rocks; or a higher, more scenic and slightly longer route which contours across the southern flank of Cave Mountain. Both trails begin at the same point and reach the pass at the same point, so the decision boils down to one of time and distance versus scenery.

Both trails begin at the Bryant Creek Warden Cabin and work northwest along the east bank of Bryant Creek as one trail for 3.5 kilometres. The first portion of the hike is very easy, the trail travelling across extensive willow flats. There are minor trail branches both to the left and right, but there should be no trouble following the main route.

At Kilometre 11.4 (from the Spray Reservoir) the hiker will find a sign for Assiniboine and shortly thereafter will reach a trail junction at the edge of Bryant Creek, marking the splitting of the low and high routes. To the left, across the stream, the low route proceeds in a direct fashion around the base of Gibralter Rock and on to the pass, some 3.5 kilometres distant. The high route keeps to the east of Bryant Creek, following the Allenby Pass trail for 500 metres before branching off to the left at a clearly marked trail junction. From the junction the trail contours up and across the southern flank of Cave Mountain, climbing toward the pass.

Descending the pass, the hiker reaches O'Brien Meadows within 300 metres of the top where he will find a large photographic map of the Assiniboine area directing him to the various camping areas in the park. From this point it is 2.1 kilometres to Assiniboine Lodge, 2.3 kilometres to the Naiset Cabins and 3.0 kilometres to the tenting sites east of Lake Magog.

Assiniboine via Wonder Pass

Spray Reservoir to Lake Magog—20.3 kilometres (12.6 miles)

Backpack
Allow 7½ hours one way
Elevation gain: 685 metres (2,250 feet)
Maximum elevation: 2395 metres (7,850 feet)
Topo maps: Spray Lakes Reservoir, 82 J/14
Mount Assiniboine, 82 J/13

Point of Departure: Drive or hike the 40 kilometre (25 mile) Spray Lakes access road from the town of Canmore. Cross the dam at Kilometre 16 to the west side of the reservoir and proceed as far as Canyon Dam. The 1.5 kilometres of road beyond the dam is usually in wretched shape, and some hikers will prefer to start the hike at this point. The trail head is approximately six kilometres beyond the dam at a Warden Service access gate.

0.0—Trail head.

0.8—Palliser Pass junction. Stay right.

3.7—Major stream (bridged).

6.1— Junction. Stay right.

7.2—Bryant Creek Shelter and campsite.

8.0—Bryant Creek Warden Cabin and junction. Turn left for Wonder Pass.

9.1—Trail fork. Stay ahead on main trail.

14.0—Marvel Lake junction. Stay right.

—Trail makes steep ascent.

17.4—Wonder Pass (2395 m).

20.0—Naiset Cabins.

20.3—Assiniboine Lodge.

Wonder Pass is more often used as an exit rather than an approach route to Assiniboine owing to the arduous 390 metre climb from Marvel Lake to the pass summit. However, for hikers planning to start their trip at the Spray Lakes Reservoir and continue on through Assiniboine, exiting via Sunshine Valley or Ferro Pass, Wonder Pass deserves serious consideration as an approach.

From its start at the Spray Lakes Reservoir, the trail (a rough access road) runs along the reservoir shoreline for 800 metres before veering off to the right at a clearly marked trail junction. From the junction the trail cuts through dense lodgepole pine forest, working northwest up the Bryant Creek drainage between Cone Mountain and Mount Turner. At Kilometre 7.2 the hiker reaches the Bryant Creek Shelter and campsite. The shelter is open to the public but is usually well-populated from June through Labour Day.

A little less than a kilometre from the shelter is the Bryant Creek Warden Cabin and the Wonder Pass junction. Cutting left, to the southwest, the hiker crosses Bryant Creek (a wooden bridge is slightly downstream from the horse crossing), and spends the next six kilometres on a gradually ascending traverse of the southeast flank of Wonder Peak, paralleling the shore of Marvel Lake. At the 14.0 kilometre mark the trail bypasses a cutoff to Marvel Lake and begins the steep ascent to the pass, a tough climb on a hot day. However, the scenery encountered near the pass summit more than compensates for the work involved in getting there, and the view back to Marvel Peak, Mount Gloria and Eon Mountain is truly spectacular.

From the summit of the pass the trail gradually descends through subalpine meadows toward tree line, Gog Lake and Assiniboine Lodge.

Assiniboine via Ferro Pass

Vermilion River to Lake Magog—32.2 kilometres (20 miles)

Backpack
Allow 2 days one way
Elevation gain: 1005 metres (3,300 feet)
loss: 275 metres (900 feet)
Maximum elevation: 2165 metres (7,100 feet)
Topo maps: Mount Assiniboine, 82 J/13

Point of Departure: Drive the Banff-Radium Highway to the Simpson River trail head, 37.0 kilometres (23 miles) south of the Alberta-B.C. boundary. Cross the Vermilion River bridge and take the first turn to the right. A parking area lies 30 metres ahead.

0.0—Access road.

—Trail passes corrals on right.

—Trail reaches Simpson River and swings east.

8.5—Kootenay Park boundary.

10.6—Junction. Stay right and cross bridge for Ferro Pass.

10.7—Surprise Creek Cabin.

—Steep climb 2.5 kilometres.

18.1—Rock Lake junction. Stay left.

22.6—Ferro Pass (2165 m).

—Moderate to steep descent.

27.0—Trail reaches valley bottom. Begins ascent.

28.6—Elizabeth Lake junction. Stay right.

29.4—Wedgewood Lake junction at Cerulean Lake. Stay straight ahead.

31.3—Provincial Park Headquarters at Sunburst Lake.

32.2—Lake Magog campsite.

The Ferro Pass trail represents an arduous two day aproach to Assiniboine, involving 32 kilometres of trail and well over 1000 metres total elevation gain. It should probably be considered an exit rather than an approach route, but of all the routes to Assiniboine it has the most direct access to a public thoroughfare and will thus be a serious consideration to those hikers without the transportation necessary for two car shuttle arrangements.

Beginning at the Vermilion River, the trail works its way a short distance to the Vermilion-Simpson confluence and swings east up the north bank of the Simpson, reaching Surprise Creek at the 10.6 kilometre mark. There the Simpson is crossed via a cable suspension bridge, and the trail begins a long and steep climb up the Surprise Creek drainage, passing Rock Lake at Kilometre 18.1 and reaching the Ferro Pass summit 4.5 kilometres beyond.

From Ferro Pass the trail drops 300 metres to the headwaters of the Mitchell River, descending gradually across the southern flank of Nestor Peak and then climbing again to the Sunburst Valley and the Assiniboine area.

The first portion of the hike, to Rock Lake, is scenically unimpressive as the trail confines itself to dense, closed forest of pine, fir and spruce, but above Rock Lake the scenery becomes increasingly impressive, featuring the massive rock wall of Surprise Peak and Indian Mountain. From Ferro Pass the hiker gains a wonderful view of Mount Assiniboine, The Marshall, Mount Watson and Wedgewood Lake. Beyond the pass the hike remains memorable, with Mount Assiniboine and The Marshall keeping the trekker company nearly all the way to Cerulean Lake in the Sunburst Valley.

The trail is in good shape throughout and is well marked the entire distance.

34

Clark's nutcracker—a campground companion

Owl Lake

Day hike or backpack
Allow 2½ hours one way
Elevation gain: 185 metres (600 feet)
Maximum elevation: 1890 metres (6,200 feet)
Topo maps: Spray Lakes Reservoir, 82 J/14
　　　　　Mount Assiniboine, 82 J/13

Point of Departure: Drive or hike the 40 kilometre (25 mile) Spray Lakes access road from the town of Canmore. Cross the dam at Kilometre 16 to the west side of the reservoir and proceed as far as Canyon Dam. The 1.5 kilometres of road beyond the dam is usually in wretched shape, and some hikers will prefer to start the hike at this point. The trail head is approximately six kilometres beyond the dam at a Warden Service access gate.

0.0—Spray Lakes Reservoir parking area (1705 m).

　—Trail begins as access road and runs through a packer's camp.

0.8—Palliser Pass trail junction and sign. Stay right.

1.1—Trail Centre Warden Cabin junction. Stay right.

3.7—Bridged stream crossing.

6.0—Owl Lake junction and sign. Take the left fork.

6.3—Trail crosses Bryant Creek. Footbridge upstream 200 metres.

8.0—Trail crosses top of rise and enters Owl Lake basin.

9.5—Trail junction. Left fork leads to lakeshore at north end (100 metres); right fork proceeds along west bank to south end of lake (1.5 kilometres).

9.6—Owl Lake (1890 m).

The Owl Lake trail represents a relatively easy hike which can be undertaken either as a full day's effort from the Spray Reservoir or a somewhat shorter trip from an overnight camp at the Bryant Creek Shelter.

The day's objective is a charming blue-green body of water, measuring approximately 1.5 by 0.5 kilometres and occupying the central portion of a valley formed by Marvel Peak to the west and Mounts Morrison and Byng to the east. Good fishing and a pleasant alpine setting make it worthy of a day's outing in itself, but it is usually considered a side trip for hikers occupied with the thought of the more grandiose objectives of the area: Assiniboine, Marvel Pass or Marvel Lake.

The trail begins as a warden access road at the southern tip of the Spray Lakes Reservoir and, as such trails often are, is fairly level and scenically uneventful for the first six kilometres as it works its way along the foot of the Sundance Range.

At the 6.0 kilometre mark the Owl Lake trail branches off to the left, gradually descending to the valley bottom and the swift-flowing Bryant Creek. By staying up on the creek's bank and working upstream for 200 metres the hiker will find a solid bridge and a good track leading back to rejoin the main (horse) trail.

Beyond the creek the trail climbs moderately for a little over 1.5 kilometres to enter the Owl Lake basin. Once the valley bottom elevation has been reached the hiker begins to traverse some intriguing meadows, characterized by low ridges of peculiarly jumbled rock, probably the remnants of a terminal moraine. This section of twisted and broken terrain also provides a good opportunity for the hiker to take his bearings on the surrounding country.

Mount Alcantara from Marvel Pass

At the 9.5 kilometre mark the hiker encounters a trail split and must decide either to descend to the shore of the lake (to the left) or continue on around its western shore (to the right), the trail running some 30 metres above the shoreline to the lake's south end.

Marvel Pass. Lying 4.3 kilometres beyond and 300 metres above the southern end of Owl Lake, Marvel Pass offers an interesting option for experienced hikers visiting the southern portion of Banff Park. Located at the apex of three high alpine valleys, the pass is a truly spectacular spot in an area celebrated for its scenic wonders.

From the end of Owl Lake a clear-cut trail exists as far as an old trail riders' camp in a broad meadow 400 metres distant. There the hiker is confronted with a variety of trails leading back into the woods and should look for the distinctive combination of a double-topped fir and a dead snag in the trees at the edge of the meadow. The main trail lies about 20 metres on the uphill side. At any junction from then on the hiker should take the fork that leads to the right (uphill) to avoid some stints of discouraging bushwhacking.

For adventuresome backpackers, the trek can be extended beyond Marvel Pass by descending into the Marvel Creek drainage, following it down to Marvel Lake and then steeply up the northern shore to the Wonder Pass trail. However, some rather sketchy pieces of trail across boggy meadows and a double ford of Marvel Creek just above Marvel Lake make a good nose for trail and some solid wilderness experience prerequisites for this option. The total distance of the Owl Lake, Marvel Pass and Marvel Creek combination, starting and ending at the Spray Lakes Reservoir, is 36.0 kilometres (22.4 miles).

37

Palliser Pass

Spray Lakes Reservoir to Palliser Pass—21.4 kilometres (13.3 miles)

Backpack
Allow 7-8 hours to pass
Elevation gain: 380 metres (1,250 feet)
Maximum elevation: 2085 metres (6,850 feet)
Topo maps: Spray Lakes Reservoir, 82 J/14
           Kananaskis Lakes, 82 J/11

Point of Departure: Drive or hike the 40 kilometre (25 mile) Spray Lakes access road from the town of Canmore. Cross the dam at Kilometre 16 to the west side of the reservoir and proceed as far as Canyon Dam. The 1.5 kilometres of road beyond the dam is usually in wretched shape, and some hikers will prefer to start the hike at this point. The trail head is approximately six kilometres beyond the dam at a Warden Service access gate.

0.0—Spray Lakes Reservoir parking area (1705 m).

0.8—Palliser Pass and Bryant Creek trail junction and mileage sign. Follow left hand fork.

4.5—White Man Pass junction and Spray River. For Palliser Pass, ford the Spray and proceed straight ahead.

7.9—White Man Pass south cutoff joins main trail.

10.5—Palliser Warden Cabin.

12.7—First of several unmarked trail junctions. To the right is the low (river edge) trail and Leman Lake cutoff 600 metres distant. To the left, the high (bench) trail to Palliser Pass.

13.5—Skyline Hikers' camp on bench trail.

15.4—Unmarked cutoff to Burstall Pass. Keep right for Palliser Pass.

19.3—Second of two small stream crossings and beginning of steep ascent toward Palliser Pass.

21.4—Palliser Pass and Banff Park boundary (2085 m).

The valley of the headwaters of the Spray River forms the extreme southern tip of Banff Park. It is a narrow valley just over 20 kilometres in length running from the southern end of the Spray Lakes Reservoir to Palliser Pass. Flanked by the craggy peaks of the Spray Mountains, the valley offers a variety of hiking options in an area receiving only moderate use during the hiking season.

Using Palliser Pass as a basic objective, a hiker may spend several days in the valley, taking side trips to White Man Pass and Leman Lake, and, having reached Palliser Pass, either continue beyond the pass for longer treks to Kananaskis Provincial Park or turn back down the Spray to exit via Burstall Pass.

Starting at the gate of the Bryant Creek access road, the trail first works south as part of the Bryant Creek route. At the 1.0 kilometre mark, the track up Bryant Creek turns west while the trail to the Upper Spray continues south, crossing Bryant Creek via a sturdy pony bridge.

The only major obstacle on the entire hike is encountered at Kilometre 4.5, where the hiker is faced with a ford of the Spray River. Even though the river at the ford is even-running and smooth-bottomed, the volume of water in the spring and early summer makes it a difficult thigh-deep crossing and the early season traveller is advised to check with the warden service concerning the feasibility of the ford. (If the river is high, Burstall Pass serves as an excellent alternate route into the valley.) The north side of the ford also marks the main White Man Pass trail junction.

At the 7.9 kilometre mark the trail passes the southern cutoff to White Man Pass and at the 10.5 mark the Palliser Warden Cabin is bypassed.

A short distance (2.2 kilometres) beyond the cabin the hiker, now travelling through the open meadows that characterize the upper portion of the

valley, encounters what will prove to be the first of many unmarked trail junctions. Poor management of horses has left the area criss-crossed with seemingly dozens of trails and the hiker must rely on his "trail nose" to choose the most serviceable. Theoretically, there are two main trails, one that runs along the river's edge and another that stays high along the benchland above the river. Both trails eventually reach Palliser Pass, but the bench trail, being higher and drier, is the preferred route.

At Kilometre 13.5 the hiker encounters a narrow fir-ringed meadow with a small stream running through it. A fire circle and a bundle of teepee poles identifies it as an old Skyline Hikers' camp, a good staging area for further exploration to Leman Lake, Palliser Pass and Burstall Pass. The trail runs through the camp and continues south, passing the unmarked Burstall Pass cutoff at the base of a large avalanche slope some two kilometres

beyond the camp. At the cutoff the hiker should veer to the right and continue his journey up the valley.

At Kilometre 19.3 the second of two small streams is crossed and the trail begins a steep ascent toward the pass, eventually leaving the forest for the open subalpine meadows surrounding Belgium Lake. The boundary marker of Banff Park at Kilometre 21.4 indicates the crest of Palliser Pass.

Leman Lake. Lying at 1935 metres between Mounts Leval and Leman, Leman Lake is often a primary objective for backpackers visiting the valley of the Upper Spray. The trail to the lake splits from the main Spray trail at a signed junction just beyond the 13 kilometre mark. The hiker fords the Spray (about knee depth but slow moving in midsummer) and follows the trail on the west bank for a short distance to the Leman Lake campsite. From the campsite the trail climbs a short but steep ridge and then descends to the Leman Lake shore, just under a kilometre from the Spray trail junction. The trail continues high along the western shore of the lake to the park boundary at Spray Pass, 2.2 kilometres from the Spray River.

White Man Pass. Although the White Man Pass trail is seldom hiked today, it is a pass of historical significance and offers an interesting day's diversion from the main Spray trail. It presents few obstacles to the backpacker, although unbridged crossings of both Currie and White Man Creeks can be troublesome in the early season. From the north side of the main Spray River ford (Kilometre 4.5 on the Spray trail), the route crosses the eastern flank of Mount Currie and travels west up the White Man Creek drainage to a small lake and the 2150 metre pass, 7.2 kilometres from the Spray ford junction. For those wishing to continue up the Spray River to Palliser Pass, a shortcut back to the valley bottom splits off from the main White Man Pass trail 3.8 kilometres below the pass and rejoins the Spray trail at Kilometre 7.9. The trip to White Man Pass and back to the Spray via the southern cutoff is 15.3 kilometres.

Burstall Pass. This is an excellent option for hikers desiring a quick and scenically different exit from the Upper Spray. It also provides an interesting route into the valley for those fearful of an early season crossing of the Spray. Taken from either side, the pass is a beautiful one and offers an excellent vantage point for viewing the Leman Lake environs.

From the Upper Spray side, the unmarked cutoff to Burstall Pass starts 1.9 kilometres south of the Skyline Hikers' camp on the high Spray trail, branching abruptly to the east up an avalanche slope. A short distance up the slope the trail swings to the north and begins a steep traverse toward the pass. Early season hikers may find snow patches in the pass and should be aware that the main route crosses high on the southern side of the large bowl just west of the pass proper. (Likewise, hikers coming from Burstall Lakes should know the trail does not follow the obvious low gap west of the pass, but stays on the shoulder above the gap and then swings away south from the pass.)

From the pass the trail descends to subalpine meadow and then steeply down through coniferous forest to the gravel flats above Burstall Lakes. Some faded red flagging and split log bridges carry the hiker across the braided stream running through the flats and to the Burstall Lakes parking area. It is 8.9 kilometres from the Spray trail cutoff to the parking area.

Access to the Burstall Lakes parking area: from Canmore follow the Spray Lakes Road along the east shore of the reservoir 45 kilometres (28 miles) to the small logging camp at Mud Lake. Turn right, crossing the small earth dam, then take the next two lefts in quick succession and follow the rugged main track for 3.2 kilometres (2 miles). A wide, slanted section of road indicates the place to park.

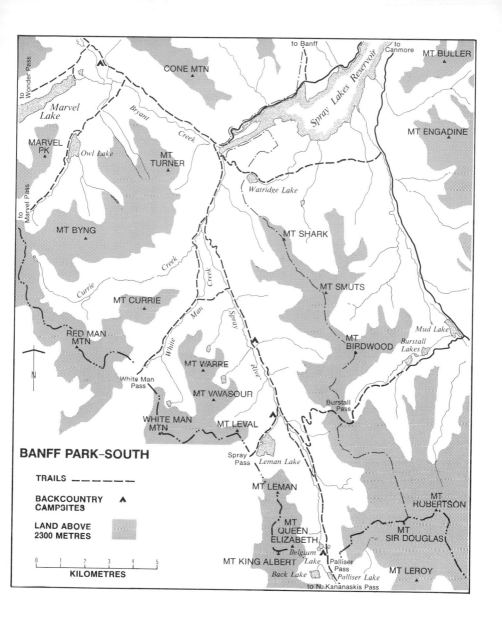

BANFF PARK–SOUTH

TRAILS — — — — —

BACKCOUNTRY ▲
CAMPSITES

LAND ABOVE
2300 METRES

0 1 2 3 4 5
KILOMETRES

MT BULLER

to Banff

to Canmore

CONE MTN

Spray Lakes Reservoir

MT ENGADINE

to Wonder Pass

Marvel Lake

Bryant Creek

MARVEL PK

Owl Lake

MT TURNER

Watridge Lake

to Marvel Pass

MT BYNG

MT SHARK

MT SMUTS

Currie Creek

White Man Creek

Spray River

Mud Lake

MT CURRIE

Burstall Lakes

RED MAN MTN

N

MT WARRE

MT BIRDWOOD

White Man Pass

MT VASASOUR

Burstall Pass

WHITE MAN MTN

MT LEVAL

Spray Pass

Leman Lake

MT ROBERTSON

MT LEMAN

MT SIR DOUGLAS

MT QUEEN ELIZABETH

Belgium Lake

MT KING ALBERT

Palliser Pass

MT LEROY

Back Lake

Palliser Lake

to N. Kananaskis Pass

41

Bourgeau Lake

Trans-Canada Highway to Bourgeau Lake—7.5 kilometres (4.6 miles)

Day trip

Allow 2½-4 hours one way

Elevation gain: 730 metres (2,400 feet)

Maximum elevation: 2160 metres (7,100 feet)

Topo maps: Banff, 82 0/4 West
(trail not shown)

Point of Departure: Drive west from Banff, 16.4 kilometres (10.1 miles) on the Trans-Canada Highway. Watch for a trail sign on a high bank along the southwest side of the roadway. Vehicles may be parked at the Wolverine Creek Picnic Area, 300 metres west of the sign.

0.0—Trail sign (1430 m).

　—Moderate but steady uphill.

1.6—Trail stops switchbacking, heading straight up the southeast side of the valley.

3.7—Trail crosses tributary.

5.5—Wolverine Creek crossing. Cascades.

　—Steep switchbacks.

6.8—Trail levels out into meadows.

7.5—Bourgeau Lake (2160 m).

Set within an amphitheatre carved from the limestone walls of the Massive Range, Bourgeau Lake exhibits a wide variety of alpine and subalpine life forms. Bordering its waters are fir-laced meadows and barren talus slopes where ptarmigan, marmots and pikas are often seen pursuing their daily chores. In spring, avalanches thunder down through the couloirs above, and mountain goats stroll placidly on the slopes of Mount Brett to the north. These attractions, coupled with the lake's solitude and easy access from Banff townsite, make the lake a popular spot with local hikers.

Rising from the Trans-Canada Highway, the trail quickly buries itself in a fire succession forest of lodgepole pine and spruce, then slowly gains altitude up the Wolverine Creek drainage. After 2.4 kilometres views open back to the Bow Valley and the sharp, serrated peaks of the Sawback Range beyond. The broad summit of Mount Brett (2984 m), the highest mountain in the Massive Range, dominates the scenery ahead.

At the 5.5 kilometre mark the trail crosses Wolverine Creek, passing beneath a long cascade of tumbling white water. The log bridge offers an excellent spot for rest and refreshment before tackling the steep switchbacks that climb into the cirque above.

The amphitheatre containing the lake is carved into the northwest side of Mount Bourgeau (2930 m). Like other peaks in the range, it is composed of Devonian and Mississippian limestones and shales—formations which bear fossils of brachiopods, corals, and other early species of ocean life. Dr. James Hector named the mountain for the French botanist Eugene Bourgeau, his comrade-in-exploration with the Palliser Expedition during the summer of 1858.

Snowbanks often linger in the meadows bordering the lake until mid-July,

Bourgeau Lake

their meltwaters feeding a wide variety of subalpine wildflowers. White-tailed ptarmigan nest in the talus above the lake, their mottled summer plumage making them all but invisible among the piles of broken rock. Pika, golden-mantled ground squirrels and chipmunks scurry back and forth through the boulders, watching any passing hikers closely for a possible handout.

Strong hikers may wish to explore beyond Bourgeau Lake into the alpine basin which lies above and to the west. A path follows above the forested north shore of Bourgeau Lake then climbs steeply toward a notch dividing the ramparts of Mounts Bourgeau and Brett. After some strenuous climbing, the track emerges into an open, alpine bowl complete with small tundra ponds.

While this lofty cirque is quite pleasant, hikers will want to continue upwards and to the south to yet another pass at the foot of the long ridge which descends from the main peak of Mount Bourgeau. In less than fifteen minutes of hiking the traveller will crest this col and be greeted with unparalleled views to the south—the matterhorn peak of Mount Assiniboine framed perfectly within the narrow pass. A small tarn set within this gap is known locally as Harvey Lake.

Citadel Pass

Sunshine Village to Citadel Pass—9.3 kilometres (5.8 miles)

Day trip

Allow 3 hours one way

Elevation gain: 150 metres (500 feet)

Maximum elevation: 2360 metres (7,800 feet)

Topo maps: Banff, 82 O/4 East
                 Banff, 82 O/4 West

Point of Departure: Drive the Trans-Canada Highway west from Banff townsite 9 kilometres (5.6 miles) and turn onto the Sunshine Village access road. Follow this road for nine kilometres to the Bourgeau Parking Lot. Hike or take the shuttle bus the last six kilometres to the Sunshine Village Lodge (check at the Banff bus depot concerning bus schedules and fares).

0.0—Sunshine Village Lodge.

—Cross beneath the Strawberry Chairlift and into the Dell beyond. Follow up the left-hand side of the Dell to the meadows above.

1.4—Junction: Citadel Pass trail continues across meadows to left. Short spur trail cuts right to Rock Isle Lake.

5.2—Trail climbs over crest of ridge below Quartz Hill.

5.8—Howard Douglas Lake.

9.3—Citadel Pass. (2360 m).

The hike to Citadel Pass is one of the longer and more popular day trips radiating out from Sunshine Village. Following up the Dell—a small draw just beyond the Strawberry Chairlift, the trail soon levels out into open alpine meadows and rolls its way through timberline stands of larch, spruce and fir to this rocky and barren pass situated between Citadel Peak and Fatigue Mountain. Throughout most of its distance, the trail is never more than a few hundred metres from the crest of the Great Divide and small passes along the way provide continual vistas of the rugged peaks of British Columbia to the west.

The trail remains fairly level throughout its course except for a short climb at Kilometre 5.2 when it traverses a short spur ridge beneath Quartz Hill. On the opposite side of this ridge the trail drops to the shore of Howard Douglas Lake, a beautiful little tarn named after Banff Park's first superintendent.

Another small lake lies off to the right of the trail less than two kilometres beyond Howard Douglas, its basin set beneath a gap in the Great Divide which serves as a window to the great 3618 metre horn, Mount Assiniboine. This is one of the best views of this famous mountain from the Sunshine Meadows trail system, and though its summit seems to loom near, it is over 15 aerial kilometres from this lookout point.

Citadel Pass offers several options to the day hiker with a little time to spare and a yen for exploration. Just an extra half-hour of climbing above the pass to the east will bring the hiker to an even loftier viewpoint on the 2400 metre crest of Fatigue Pass. Meanwhile, the main trail continues on across the summit of Citadel and drops sharply into British Columbia and the forested Golden Valley (see *Assiniboine via Sunshine Village*).

Howard Douglas Lake and the meadows leading to Citadel Pass

Simpson Pass

Sunshine Village to Simpson Pass—5.3 kilometres (3.3 miles)
Sunshine Village to Egypt Lake—13.4 kilometres (8.3 miles)

Day trip

Allow 2½-3 hours to Healy Creek trail

Elevation gain: 155 metres (500 feet)

Maximum elevation: 2350 metres (7,700 feet)

Topo maps: Banff, 82 0/4 West

Point of Departure: Drive the Trans-Canada Highway west from Banff townsite 9 kilometres (5.6 miles) and turn onto the Sunshine Village access road. Follow this road for nine kilometres to the Bourgeau Parking Lot. Hike or take the shuttle bus the last six kilometres to the Sunshine Village Lodge (check at the Banff bus depot concerning lodge buses and schedules).

0.0—Sunshine Village Lodge (2195 m).

—Walk around the day-lodge to the Wa Wa T-bar lift (on the north edge of the resort complex). Follow up the ski run on the extreme right.

1.9—Crest of Wa Wa Ridge (2350 m).

—Gradual descent into subalpine forest.

5.3—Simpson Pass (2107 m).

—Short climb into meadows.

7.6—Junction: Trail from Eohippus Lake merges from south.

7.9—Junction with Healy Creek trail: Healy Pass and Egypt Lake to left, Healy Creek and Bourgeau Parking Lot to right.

This is an interesting trip which can be used either by day-trippers looking for a scenically varied hike in the Sunshine Village vicinity or by backpackers as a highline route to Egypt Lake and beyond. One word of warning, however: more than any other trail in the area this can be a very sloppy hike early in the season or during wet weather.

Ascending the most northerly ski run on Wa-Wa Ridge, the trail soon climbs through the upper fringes of the subalpine forest and onto the treeless summit of the ridge at Kilometre 1.9. From this high crest, hikers can see most of the Sunshine Meadows country. Views include the Citadel Pass region and the sharp summit of Mount Assiniboine to the southeast, and the massive pyramid of The Monarch to the southwest. This is definitely the best viewpoint on the trail.

Beyond Wa-Wa Ridge the trail begins to drop back into the forest of Engelmann spruce, alpine fir and larch. Small ponds fringed with cotton grass dot the open meadows and, like all trails in the Sunshine vicinity, this walk is a flower paradise.

After following along a low but sheer rock escarpment for nearly two kilometres, the trail drops down to an open meadow on the summit of Simpson Pass. The pass was crossed by Sir George Simpson, Governor of the Hudson's Bay Company, in the summer of 1841, and while it was a disappointment as an improved route for the company's fur brigades, the governor did linger long enough to allow his guide to carve their initials and the date in a nearby tree—a monument which was discovered and salvaged by a local outfitter in the early part of this century.

On the west side of the Simpson Pass meadow, the trail rises quickly onto the open, lake-studded meadows which lie beneath the long ridge of the Monarch

The Healy Lakes area near Simpson Pass

Ramparts. At Kilometre 7.6 a less-defined trail enters from the south, coming from Eohippus Lake about 5 kilometres distant—a good option for strong hikers who have time and energy to spare.

Just five minutes or so beyond the Eohippus junction, the hiker will reach the Healy Creek trail, 1.4 kilometres below Healy Pass and 7.7 kilometres above the Bourgeau Parking Lot. From here, the hiker can either continue into the Egypt Lake country by veering left and ascending the pass (see Egypt Lake trail), make a loop back to the Bourgeau Parking Lot by descending Healy Creek or simply retrace the route back to Sunshine Village.

Egypt Lake

Egypt Lake Campsite via Healy Creek—12.4 kilometres (7.7 miles)
Egypt Lake Campsite via Simpson Pass—12.6 kilometres (7.8 miles)
Egypt Lake Campsite via Pharaoh Creek—19.6 kilometres (12.2 miles)

Backpack

Allow 4-6 hours via Healy Creek

Elevation gain: 640 metres (2,100 feet)
          loss: 335 metres (1,100 feet)

Maximum elevation: 2330 metres (7,650 feet)

Topo maps: Banff, 82 0/4 West

Point of Departure: Drive the Trans-Canada Highway west from Banff townsite 9 kilometres (5.6 miles) and turn onto the Sunshine Village access road. Follow this road for nine kilometres to the Bourgeau Parking Lot.

0.0—Follow the ski-out trail, which is to the right of the upper access road descending from Sunshine Village at the west end of the parking lot (1690 m).

0.8—Junction: Turn right as trail leaves ski-out.

3.1—Bridge over Healy Creek.

5.2—Old cabin foundation.

5.5—Campsite.

—Trail begins to climb.

7.7—Junction and campsite: Straight ahead for Healy Pass and Egypt Lake. Turn back to left for Simpson Pass and Sunshine Village.

—Open meadows with alpine larch.

9.2—Healy Pass (2330 m).

—Steady downhill grade.

12.2—Junction: Trail hub for Egypt Lake, Pharaoh Creek and Natalko Lake. Cross creek for Egypt Lake.

12.4—Egypt Lake Shelter Cabin and Campsite (1995 m).

Egypt Lake, a popular backpacking area, lies near the continental divide just 25 aerial kilometres west of Banff townsite. Though Egypt Lake itself is often the focal point of trips into the area there are many other beautiful lakes, bearing exotic names such as Scarab, Mummy, Haiduk and Sphinx, scattered about in the open subalpine environment. The options for the hiker are many, limited only by time.

Most people hike to Egypt Lake by way of the Healy Creek trail since that route is shortest and the trail head can be reached by car. Climbing from the Bourgeau Parking Lot below the Sunshine Village ski area, the route follows along a wide, bulldozed ski-out for 800 metres before cutting off into a forest of spruce and alpine fir. Gradually, but steadily, it ascends the Healy Creek drainage, rising into open subalpine meadowland. Sir George Simpson followed this route in 1841 during his epic round-the-world journey for the Hudson's Bay Company, branching up to the nearby pass which bears his name and then down the western slope into present day British Columbia.

The climb finally culminates among the last scattered alpine larch on Healy Pass. At an elevation of 2330 metres above sea level, the pass offers an excellent perspective on the surrounding landscape. The block of peaks beyond the ridge to the northeast is the Massive Range, dominated by Mount Brett (2984 m) on the left and Mount Bourgeau (2930 m) to the right. Standing as a landmark to the southeast—nearly 30 kilometres distant—is the 'horn' spike of Mount Assiniboine (3618 m), the highest mountain in Banff National Park. Less than four miles away to the south is the massive pyramid of The Monarch (2904 m), while the long, wall-like ridge which

The Monarch and Ramparts from Healy Pass

extends from its flanks to Healy Pass is known as the Monarch Ramparts.

Here, for the first time, the hiker catches sight of his objective—Egypt Lake at the base of the Pharaoh Peaks. The trail drops rapidly downhill from the pass, reaching the junction near the Egypt Lake shelter cabin in just over three kilometres. In addition to the shelter cabin, constructed in 1969 to house approximately 16 backpackers, the meadow below the cabin is designated as a backcountry campsite. (Don't mistake the warden's cabin downstream for the shelter; the shelter is directly across the creek from the junction and a short ways upstream.)

Egypt Lake lies only 800 metres beyond the cabin-campsite, but there are several other interesting options for those who have a day or more to spend in the area. A five kilometre trail runs south from the campsite, following the Pharaoh Creek tributary upstream to Redearth Pass and climbing steeply in the last two kilometres to Natalko Lake just west of the continental divide in Kootenay Park.

Another half-day option leads in the opposite direction, running 500 metres down the Pharoah Creek trail then 800 metres up a steep branch trail to Pharaoh and Black Rock lakes.

Whistling Valley Option. A short distance beyond Egypt Lake, the main trail jogs sharply to the left across a small stream and begins a steep series of switchbacks. With an occasional rewarding glance back to Egypt Lake, the trail grinds upward for more than a kilometre, finally emerging near Scarab and Mummy lakes. A short spur trail visits the two tarns, both of which have outstanding settings—Scarab at the upper edge of the subalpine forest, surrounded by larch and scree; Mummy in the alpine zone, rimmed by tundra and talus. To reach Mummy, you must ford the outlet from Scarab, above the waterfall, and scramble up a short but steep track.

From near Scarab Lake the main trail continues upward for another 500 metres into the Whistling Valley which is actually a high pass between Haiduk

Peak and the Pharaoh Peaks. Its larch-laced meadows and rockslides are the home of the hoary marmot, whose shrill whistle of warning gives the valley its name. Another inhabitant is the pika, an elusive bundle of fur that may be seen darting among the rocks. From the summit of the pass, views open on Haiduk Lake and the long escarpment of the Ball Mountain Group.

Concerning the exotic names which are scattered about the area, pioneer survey-or and mountaineer A.O. Wheeler once wrote: "How Pharaoh Peaks received the name is not recorded. Egypt, Scarab and Mummy Lakes were named by me as a sequence when mapping that area. Haiduk Lake was named from a Polish word meaning 'lively, vigorous,' and when first seen with the sun, like diamonds, sparkling on its wind-blown ripples the name seemed to apply. . . . Black Rock Lake is from the high rock amphitheatre enclosing it. . . ."

Shadow Lake Option. Those who can arrange transportation may want to continue on through the Whistling Valley, visiting Haiduk Lake and Shadow Lake and following Redearth Creek to the Trans-Canada Highway 11 kilometres east of Eisenhower Junction. Total one way distance from the Bourgeau Parking Lot for this popular trip is 39.9 kilometres, and campsites are conveniently placed below both Haiduk and Shadow lakes. (See *Shadow Lake* trail.)

Other Access Routes. Two other trails are sometimes used as access to the Egypt Lake vicinity, though not nearly so commonly as Healy Creek.

The high trail running from Sunshine Village via Simpson Pass is undoubtedly the most scenic route to the area, the distance is virtually the same as the Healy Creek trail, and there is a lot less climbing along the way. But, without bus access to Sunshine Village, an extra six kilometres of ski-out or access road must be hiked. This can also be a wet, muddy trail throughout much of the summer. (See *Simpson Pass* trail.)

The Pharaoh Creek route to Egypt Lake is much longer than the other two, but it runs at lower elevations. This makes it a good trail early in the season before Healy Pass is free of snow. It is also used as an optional exit by backpackers who have entered over Healy Pass. Despite the length, the trail is good (ignore the new hiker's trail on Pharaoh Creek), the grade gentle, and strong hikers can make nearly as good time on this route as either of the shorter options. (See *Shadow Lake* trail.)

One final word concerning the Egypt Lake area. This is one of the most heavily-used backcountry destinations in the mountain parks. Don't go there seeking solitude. The shelter cabin is inevitably crammed to the rafters during the summer months, and because the area seems to attract an inordinate number of inexperienced backpackers there are many horror stories concerning inconsiderate individuals clattering about the premises at all hours of the night. Because of this high impact and the delicate nature of the subalpine environment, it behooves all hikers to take special care when visiting the area.

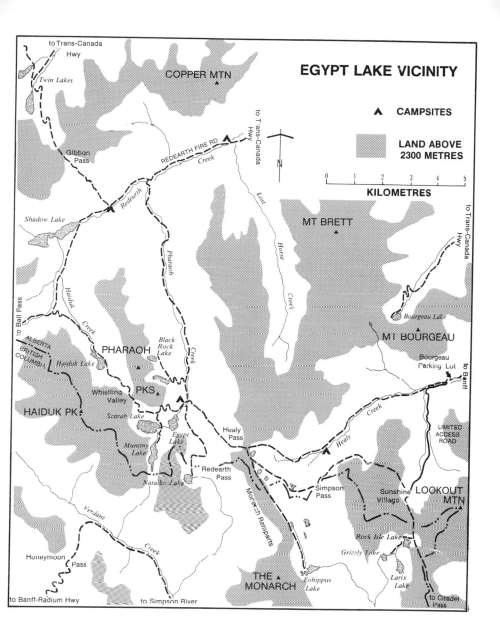

EGYPT LAKE VICINITY

▲ CAMPSITES

LAND ABOVE
2300 METRES

KILOMETRES
0 1 2 3 4 5

to Trans-Canada Hwy

Twin Lakes

COPPER MTN ▲

REDEARTH FIRE RD

Creek

to Trans-Canada Hwy

N

Gibbon Pass

Redearth

Shadow Lake

Pharaoh

MT BRETT ▲

Lost

Horse

Creek

to Trans-Canada Hwy

to Ball Pass

Haiduk

Creek

ALBERTA
BRITISH COLUMBIA

PHARAOH

Black Rock Lake

Creek

Bourgeau Lake

MT BOURGEAU ▲

Bourgeau Parking Lot

to Banff

Haiduk Lake

PKS ▲

Whistling Valley

▲

Healy

Pass

Creek

Healy

LIMITED ACCESS ROAD

HAIDUK PK

Scarab Lake

Egypt Lake

Mummy Lake

Redearth Pass

▲

Simpson Pass

Sunshine Village

LOOKOUT MTN

Natalko Lake

Verdant

Morraine Ramparts

Rock Isle Lake

Grizzly Lake

Honeymoon Pass

Creek

THE MONARCH ▲

Eohippus Lake

Larix Lake

to Banff-Radium Hwy

to Simpson River

to Citadel Pass

Shadow Lake

Trans-Canada Highway to Shadow Lake—14.3 kilometres (8.9 miles)

Day trip or backpack

Allow 4-5 hours one way

Elevation gain: 460 metres (1,500 feet)

Maximum elevation: 1860 metres (6,100 feet)

Topo maps: Banff, 82 0/4 West

Point of Departure: Drive to the Redearth Creek parking area, situated on the south side of the Trans-Canada Highway 10.8 kilometres (6.7 miles) east of Eisenhower Junction and 19.6 kilometres (12.2 miles) west of the Banff townsite overpass.

0.0—Trail starts at the east end of the parking lot (1400 m).

—Foot trail climbs up through forest and merges with the Redearth Fire Road within 300 metres. Gradual to moderate uphill on fire road.

7.2—Redearth Creek and bridge. Campsite.

10.8—Junction: Shadow Lake trail cuts away from road to right. Pharoah Creek approach to Egypt Lake (8.8 km) follows road to left.

—Moderate uphill grades.

13.4—Meadow and campsite. Junction: Gibbon Pass trail cuts uphill to north from campsite. Shadow Lake route continues up the valley.

14.3—Shadow Lake (1860 m).

Situated beneath the massive cliffs of Mount Ball, Shadow Lake is one of the more impressive subalpine lakes along the Great Divide. In addition to its own charms, the lake has gained popularity as a centre for a number of excellent side trips: Egypt Lake, the Whistling Valley, Ball Pass and Gibbon Pass are all within one day's travel of its shores.

The first 10.8 kilometres up the Redearth Fire Road are somewhat tedious, but the grade is gradual and it is easy to make good time. At Kilometre 10.8 the Shadow Lake trail cuts away from the fire road and climbs into a forest of lodgepole pine, spruce and alpine fir. From this junction with the fire road it is only 2.6 kilometres to the Shadow Lake campsite located on the edge of a large meadow within sight of the rugged peaks of the Ball Mountain Group.

By climbing into the forest a few metres above the campsite, the main trail to Shadow Lake can be found leading on up-valley (the trail to Gibbon Pass and Twin Lakes strikes off from this point as well, climbing northward from the campsite). From the camp it is less than a kilometre to the lake and the long footbridge which spans its outlet stream.

Shadow is large compared with most subalpine lakes, stretching for over two kilometres to the base of Mount Ball (3312 m). Carved from Cambrian strata and laced with glaciers, the Ball Mountain Group provides a particularly photogenic backdrop for the lake (though the east-facing cliffs are often in shadow). The mountain was named in 1858 by Dr. James Hector for John Ball, the British Under-Secretary of State for the Colonies—a man who assisted in the organization of the Palliser Expedition of which Dr. Hector was a member.

From the outlet bridge a good trail continues around the south shore of the lake for a kilometre before breaking away towards Haiduk Lake and Ball Pass.

Shadow Lake and Mount Ball

Gibbon Pass Option. This is a fine option for strong day hikers and backpackers. The trail starts off from the Shadow Lake campsite and climbs north through subalpine forest and larch-fringed meadowland to the treeless summit of the pass. Total distance to the pass from the campground is only 3.1 kilometres and views from the 2285 metre summit stretch from Mount Assiniboine on the south to Mount Hector on the north. Beyond the pass the trail continues its northerly journey, descending to Lower Twin Lake in another 2.9 kilometres. From Twin Lakes it is only seven kilometres out to the Trans-Canada Highway at Eisenhower Junction or the Banff-Radium Highway at Storm Mountain Lodge. (See *Twin Lakes* trail.)

Egypt Lake Option. Shadow Lake also serves as an entrance to the beautiful Egypt Lake area. The most scenic approach is by way of the trail leading around the south shore of Shadow Lake.

In four kilometres the trail splits left to Haiduk Lake, Whistling Pass and Egypt Lake. Total distance from the Shadow Lake outlet bridge to the campsite-shelter near Egypt Lake is 12.7 kilometres.

A somewhat quicker approach to the Egypt Lake region can be made via Pharaoh Creek. This trail cuts away from the Shadow Lake route at Kilometre 10.8 and reaches the Egypt Lake shelter cabin 8.8 kilometres beyond. (See *Egypt Lake* trail.)

Ball Pass Option. Situated on the Great Divide between Alberta and British Columbia, the 2200 metre summit of Ball Pass can easily be visited as a day hike from Shadow Lake or traversed as a through-route into Kootenay Park. The pass is reached by following the trail which continues around the south shore of Shadow Lake. Keep right at the Haiduk Lake-Ball Pass junction 4.0 kilometres beyond the outlet bridge and climb to the pass in another 2.5 kilometres.

Twin Lakes

Storm Mountain Lodge to Upper Twin Lake—7.6 kilometres (4.7 miles)

Altrude Picnic Area to Lower Twin Lake—8.1 kilometres (5.0 miles)

Day trip or backpack

Allow 2½-4 hours one way

Elevation gain: 745 metres (2,445 feet)
 loss: 360 metres (1,180 feet)

Maximum elevation: 2270 metres (7,450 feet)

Topo maps: Banff, 82 0/4 West
 Mount Eisenhower, 82 0/5 West

Point of Departure: Drive the Banff-Radium Highway west from Eisenhower Junction for 5.2 kilometres (3.2 miles) to Storm Mountain Lodge. Park at the Vermilion Pass Burn viewpoint across the highway from the lodge.

0.0—Trail sign at viewpoint (1705 m).

 —Steep descent.

0.8—Trail enters burn.

1.3—Valley bottom (1525 m). Trail crosses Altrude Creek.

 —Steady climb.

5.3—Arnica Lake.

6.1—Trail summit (2270 m).

 —Steep descent.

7.6—Upper Twin Lake (2090 m).

8.5—Junction: Keep right for Lower Twin Lake.

8.7—Lower Twin Lake (2055 m).

"The Twin Lakes lie at the base of the scarped and nearly vertical front of the watershed range, which rises above them in stupendous cliffs, in the rifts and hollows of which, snow remains throughout the year."

So wrote government geologist George M. Dawson following a visit to the lakes on August 5, 1884, with a Silver City prospector named Joe Healy. His description should serve today's hiker in good stead—an apt introduction to a very pretty subalpine area on the southwest slope of the Bow Valley.

Storm Mountain Route. Two trails of almost equal length lead to the Twin Lakes region, and though it must be considered the more arduous of the pair, the hike from Storm Mountain Lodge on the Banff-Radium Highway is far more scenic and varied than the grim forest climb from the Eisenhower Junction vicinity.

Starting from the Vermilion Pass Burn viewpoint opposite the lodge the trail immediately drops 150 vertical metres in altitude, crosses Altrude Creek, then proceeds to climb 700 metres in the next five kilometres. For much of the distance, the hiker passes through the charred aftermath of a fire that swept over the Great Divide from Marble Canyon in 1968. However, far from being a drab and depressing scene, the burn is filled with wildflowers throughout the summer and allows expansive views stretching from Storm Mountain to Mount Eisenhower.

At Kilometre 5.3, the tiny but beautiful Arnica Lake is found nestled against the rocky face of Storm Mountain, and just 800 metres further along the summit of the trail is reached in a small meadow surrounded by stands of alpine larch. This lush meadow is a typical snowbed plant community filled with arnica,

Lower Twin Lake

fleabane and other showy wildflowers through most of July and August. While views from the meadow are limited, a five minute climb above the trail allows excellent vistas both north and south.

A quick 1.5 kilometre descent brings the hiker to the shore of Upper Twin Lake, a relatively small, narrow body of water set directly below the main peak of Storm Mountain (3161 m). Just a little over a kilometre south of Upper Twin is Lower Twin Lake, its rocky, open shoreline an excellent viewpoint for the glowering cliffs of the Great Divide.

Eisenhower Junction Route. This trail to the Twin Lakes might be considered a quicker and more direct approach than the stenuous hike from Storm Mountain Lodge, but since it boasts little scenery, an unrelenting uphill climb through closed forest, and nearly two kilometres of boggy, rough walking, it's probably best reserved as an optional exit from the area.

Gibbon Pass Option. From Lower Twin Lake, a trail extends southward over the alpine meadows of Gibbon Pass to Shadow Lake. The pass itself is only 2.9 kilometres distant and can be easily reached in a half-day from Lower Twin. It is six kilometres across to the Shadow Lake campground from which a multitude of options exists. (See *Shadow Lake* and *Egypt Lake* trails.)

55

Johnston's Canyon

Johnston's Canyon Lodge to Lower Falls—1.1 kilometres (0.7 miles)
Johnston's Canyon Lodge to Upper Falls—2.7 kilometres (1.7 miles)
Johnston's Canyon Lodge to Ink Pots—5.8 kilometres (3.6 miles)

Day trip
Allow 2 hours to Ink Pots
Elevation gain: 215 metres (700 feet)
Maximum elevation: 1645 metres (5,400 feet)
Topo maps: Banff, 82 0/4 West
             Mount Eisenhower, 82 0/5 West

Point of Departure: Drive to the Johnston's Canyon lodge complex located on Highway 1-A, 17.8 kilometres (11 miles) west of the 1-A cutoff. The trail begins at the northern end of the parking area beyond the lodge.

0.0—Trail sign (1430 m).

1.1—Lower Falls.

2.7—Upper Falls.

3.2—Trail joins fire access road. Keep to the right for the Ink Pots.

5.3—Road narrows to trail width, descends gradually to the Johnston Valley bottom.

5.8—Ink Pots (1645 m).

The Johnston's Canyon hike is one of the most popular day trips in Banff Park. The first 1.1 kilometres to the Lower Falls is not only very easy walking (street shoes are adequate) and highly photogenic, but is supplied with 'self-guiding' information pamphlets which serve to acquaint the hiker with some of the predominant geological and biological features of the area. The additional kilometres to the Upper Falls and Ink Pots are a bit more rugged and not self-guiding, but they are aesthetically well-worth the effort made to cover them.

The path to the Lower Falls stays close to Johnston's Creek, hanging to the canyon walls in several places on sturdy bridges. The sheer walls rising above the creek and trail are limestone dating to the Paleozoic and Mesozoic eras, and the first viewpoint (0.8 kilometre) clearly shows the evidence of a geologically young stream cutting itself a more mature bed in the ancient rock.

A bit beyond the first viewpoint the hiker reaches the Lower Falls, which can be viewed from either the bridge below the falls or through a tunnel in the rock slightly above and to the right of the bridge. The water cascades some ten to twelve metres into a deep 'pothole,' or cylindrical depression carved in the rock by the pressures of water over time.

Across the bridge the trail continues to the Upper Falls, winding through forest of pine, spruce and Douglas fir. Several smaller falls may be seen from the trail before the Upper Falls is reached. Here the water plummets well over 30 metres to the bed below. Until early June the falls wear a mantle of blue ice which greatly enhances their beauty, but the late season hiker will also take pleasure in the texture and colour of the rock directly opposite the falls' viewpoint, the work of recently precipitated lime.

Johnston's Canyon

Above the Upper Falls the trail cuts away from the creek and into the forest where it joins a fire access road leading to the Ink Pots. From this junction it is possible to see Copper Mountain across the Bow Valley, and, to the south, Pilot Mountain, used as a landmark by early travellers in the region. The trail runs for two kilometres with the road, hemmed in on the left by a 'dog hair' stand of lodgepole pine and on the right by white spruce.

After crossing the southeastern flank of Mount Eisenhower the road narrows to single file trail width once more and descends to the bottom of Johnston Valley. To the right are the Ink Pots, six clear green springs which issue forth water at a constant 1° Celsius. The valley and Ink Pots together constitute a beautiful setting for a noontime meal and rest before starting either the trek back or further exploration up the valley. Luellen Lake and Mystic Pass (described elsewhere) offer overnight extensions of the Ink Pots trip, while the Hillsdale Meadows trail provides an extended day hike of 8.4 kilometres behind Mount Ishbel (2,907 m) back to the 1-A Highway.

For those wishing a direct route back to the trail head, it is possible to follow the fire access road directly to the lodge, 5.3 kilometres from the Ink Pots.

Luellen Lake—Pulsatilla Pass

Johnston Canyon Lodge to Luellen Lake—18.0 kilometres (11.1 miles)
Johnston Canyon Lodge to Pulsatilla Pass—26.2 kilometres (16.2 miles)

Backpack

Allow 6 hours to Luellen Lake

Elevation gain: 915 metres (3,000 feet)

Maximum elevation: 2345 metres (7,700 feet)

Topo maps: Mount Eisenhower, 82 0/5 West

Point of Departure: Drive to Johnston's Canyon Lodge, located on Highway 1-A 23.5 kilometres (14.6 miles) west of Banff and 6.4 kilometres (4.0 miles) east of Eisenhower Junction. The trail begins at the nature trail sign behind the lodge.

0.0—Trail sign (1430 m).

5.8—Ink Pots.

7.9—Bridge, campsite, and trail junction: Mystic Lake and Forty Mile Valley to the right; Luellen Lake and Pulsatilla Pass straight ahead.

11.6—Johnston Creek Warden Cabin.

16.4—Junction: Luellen Lake to the left, 1.5 kilometres. Pulsatilla Pass straight ahead.

16.9—Main trail crosses to west bank of stream. Faint trail follows along east bank.

18.0—Main trail crosses to east bank, rejoining hiker's trace.

21.7—Creek crossing.

21.9—Junction: Badger Pass to right. Pulsatilla Pass straight ahead.

23.3—Creek crossing.

23.5—Trail begins climb to pass. Stay left.

25.8—Pulsatilla Pass (2345 m).

26.9—Pulsatilla Lake.

—Steep descent down Wildflower Creek Valley.

32.2—Campsite and junction with Baker Creek trail (1815 m). 1-A Highway left (14 kilometres); Baker Lake right (6 kilometres).

Luellen Lake has long been a popular destination for backcountry fishermen, but with each passing year more and more backpackers are finding their way not only to this pretty lake but to the headwaters of Johnston's Creek and the lofty summit of Pulsatilla Pass as well. Once into this high, open country, the options for side trips and exploration are numerous as seldom visited passes, glaciers and lakes beckon from every side. In addition, this trail can be used as a segment for even longer journeys both north and south along the sawtooth mountains of the Front Ranges.

The first 5.8 kilometre section of the Luellen Lake-Pulsatilla Pass route travels over one of the most popular day-hiking trails in Banff Park, ascending Johnston's Canyon to the Ink Pots—a beautiful if somewhat congested beginning to the trip. (See *Johnston's Canyon* trail.)

Above the Ink Pots, the trail is less travelled than below and very straightforward as it ascends the Johnston's Creek valley at a steady but moderate grade. The creek, bordered by open willow flats, is never far away and there are many pleasant forest glades in which to stop and rest.

At Kilometre 16.4 the spur trail to Luellen Lake cuts left from the valley trail and descends through the forest for 200 metres to a campsite on Johnston's Creek. The creek is usually bridged in one fashion or another just below the campsite, and a brief climb of five or ten minutes brings the hiker to the east end of Luellen Lake.

Luellen is a long, thin lake situated at just under 2000 metres above sea level and totally surrounded by a subalpine forest of spruce and fir with stands of alpine larch scattered on the ridges above. It is backdropped by rugged east-facing cliffs which extend northward from

Descending into the Wildflower Valley from Pulsatilla Pass

Helena Ridge, an escarpment which hides the well-known turrets of Mount Eisenhower just a few kilometres beyond.

Continuing up the main Johnston's Creek trail, the valley soon opens out into beautiful meadowland where there are fine views to the east of the steeply tilted limestone peaks of the Front Ranges. For much of the remainder of the journey to Pulsatilla Pass the trail follows along the strike of the Castle Mountain Thrust Fault, a great fracture in the strata which separates the Main Ranges of the Rockies from the Front Ranges and creates a 200 million year 'jump' in geological history.

After passing the Badger Pass junction and the final creek crossing of the valley, the trail begins its ascent to Pulsatilla Pass. Unless the hiker wants to explore the large alpine cirque just east of the pass (a worthwhile pursuit), stay left beneath the glacier-draped cliffs of Pulsatilla Mountain and pick up the trail which climbs to the obvious low notch above (a more obvious horse trail pulls many hikers across the slope to the east and adds a kilometre of strenuous climbing).

The view beyond the 2435 metre summit is one of the classic wilderness scenes in the Canadian Rockies—the sparkling waters of Pulsatilla Lake perfectly framed between two rugged mountain chains which march away to the north. Pulsatilla is an old *genus* name for the white flowered western anemone, just one of a myriad of wildflowers which spread over the alpine tundra in July and August.

As well as the many options for exploration in the Pulsatilla environs (a campsite at the Badger Pass junction makes an excellent base camp for such activity), the Wildflower Creek trail continues northward from the pass to intersect with the Baker Creek trail 6.4 kilometres below. From this junction you may either climb to the Baker Lake-Skoki Valley region or exit to the 1-A Highway. Though the latter trip is popular, the lower Baker Valley has little to recommend it and, as of this writing, the trail is vague as it nears the highway causing many to lose their way; the upper Baker Valley trail is rough, mucky and steep in sections, but the destination is worth the day of effort.

Rockbound Lake

Eisenhower Warden Station to Tower Lake—7.7 kilometres (4.8 miles)

Eisenhower Warden Station to Rockbound Lake—8.4 kilometres (5.2 miles)

Day trip

Allow 3 hours one way

Elevation gain: 760 metres (2,500 feet)

Maximum elevation: 2210 metres (7,250 feet)

Topo maps: Mount Eisenhower, 82 0/5 West

Point of Departure: Drive to the Eisenhower Warden Station on Highway 1-A, 0.8 kilometre (0.5 mile) east of Eisenhower Junction. The trail begins directly behind the station.

0.0—Trail sign (1450 m).

0.3—Trail fork. The right hand branch leads to Silverton Falls, the left to Tower and Rockbound Lakes.

5.0—Trail narrows from road width to single-file path.

5.3—Trail becomes indefinite—boggy in early season.

7.7—Tower Lake.

8.4—Rockbound Lake (2210 m).

The Tower and Rockbound Lakes trip is a rather rigorous 8.4 kilometre hike carrying the trekker high behind the ramparts of Mount Eisenhower to the snow-fed waters of Rockbound Lake. Much of the trail is a quite steep access road, and the early season traveller must be prepared to face short sections of boggy terrain in order to reach the lakes and enjoy the scenery found there—the lakes, Mount Eisenhower and an extensive view down the Sawback Range to the Bow Valley.

The trail begins as an old access road and is scenically modest for 2.4 kilometres as it gradually climbs up and across the southeastern flank of Mount Eisenhower. At the 0.3 kilometre mark a fork to the right leads to Silverton Falls, 800 metres distant.

However, a bit beyond Kilometre 2.4 the trail gains sufficient elevation to grant glimpses of the Bow Valley and the mountains to the west. Prominent are Copper Mountain, rising like a great pyramid above the valley floor, and, to the south a bit, Pilot Mountain, an early landmark in the area. The trail, still access road, continues its traverse around Eisenhower, eventually gaining entrance to the long narrow valley running northwest between the ramparts and Helena Ridge.

At the 5.3 kilometre mark the trail narrows to single file width and, just a bit farther on, opens up to the southeast tower of Mount Eisenhower, a 2752 metre mass of Cambrian limestone well-known to local rock climbers. The tower is actually the southernmost extension of the ramparts of Mount Eisenhower, one of the best examples of a 'castellate' mountain found in the park—indeed, until World War II, it was known as Castle Mountain.

The trail beyond this point is rather

erratic, particularly in the early season when the entire area is likely to be marshy. The trail branches frequently, disappears in places, yet is clearly marked and easy to follow in other spots. The hiker picks a way as best he can up the valley for the remaining 2.4 kilometres. The lakes are at the upper end of the valley, a quite obvious goal.

The first lake reached is Tower, a small body of water located in a semicircle of rock which would seemingly indicate the end of the trail. However, the trail does continue to the right of the lake and climbs steeply up the headwall of Tower Lake.

At the top of the wall one first sees Rockbound Lake and immediately appreciates the lake's name, for it is totally enclosed by rock. Limestone of the Middle Cambrian Cathedral Formation forms the immediate bed of the lake, while limestone of the Stephen and Eldon formations constitutes the high walls of the cirque. The geological position of the lake is also most interesting as it lies precisely in the centre of a great syncline, or downfold in the strata, which runs from Rockbound Lake to Mount Kerkeslin in Jasper Park, some 260 kilometres to the northwest. The syncline is evidenced by the easterly dip in the strata of Mount Eisenhower and the westerly dip in the strata of Helena Ridge.

From the top of the wall one may choose to stroll the short distance to the lakeshore or remain where he is to enjoy the scenery to the southeast, down the valley and past the Sawback Range to the Bow Valley beyond.

Eisenhower Lookout

1-A Highway to Eisenhower Lookout—3.7 kilometres (2.3 miles)

Half-day trip

Allow 1½-2 hours one way

Elevation gain: 520 metres (1,700 feet)

Maximum elevation: 1980 metres (6,500 feet)

Topo maps: Mount Eisenhower, 82 0/5 West
(trail not shown)

Point of Departure: Drive 5.0 kilometres (3.1 miles) west of Eisenhower Junction on the 1-A Highway and watch for a narrow dirt fire road emerging from the forest on the north side of the highway. Turn off and park in any of the many good parking spots alongside the fire road. The trail starts at the closed gate approximately 100 metres from the highway.

0.0—Fire road gate.

—Road ascends through closed forest.

1.4—Old cabin.

2.1—Fire road reverts to trail and begins switchback ascent of open slopes below lookout.

3.7—Eisenhower Lookout cabin.

This relatively short but steep hike leads to the Mount Eisenhower fire lookout cabin and an outstanding panorama of the Bow Valley stretching from the grey limestone peaks near Banff townsite to the glacier-capped summits surrounding Lake Louise. And because it climbs along an open slope with a southwesterly exposure the trail is one of the earliest to be free of snow in the spring and the latest to close in the autumn.

From the fire road gate beyond the parking area the route follows a steep, wide pathway upward through forest of lodgepole pine, spruce and Douglas fir. Only a few glimpses are afforded beyond the forest canopy during the first two kilometres, but an old cabin offers a stop of interest at Kilometre 1.4, its dilapidated remains possibly a relic of the short-lived mining boom which sprang to life in this part of the Bow Valley in 1884.

The fire road eventually reverts to foot trail not far beyond the cabin and traverses out onto the steep, open slopes below the lookout. From mid-June until August, these meadows rank among the finest of wildflower gardens in the Rockies, overflowing with yellow columbine, heart-leaved arnica, Indian paintbrush and many other colourful species.

With increasing altitude the views of the Bow Valley become increasingly impressive. Finally the trail twists up through a cliff, enters a stand of white-bark pine and contours above the precipice for 100 metres or so to the lookout.

At an elevation of 1980 metres above sea level, it is possible to scan from the lookout cabin southward to the prominent peaks of Copper Mountain (2795 m) and Pilot Mountain (2954 m). The most obvious summit to the northwest is snowcapped Mount Temple, at 3544 metres the highest mountain in the Lake Louise vicinity.

Baker Creek

Baker Creek Picnic Area to Wildflower Creek—14 kilometres (9 miles)*
Baker Creek Picnic Area to Baker Lake—20 kilometres (12 miles)*

Wilderness access

Allow 7 hours to Baker Lake

Elevation gain: 715 metres (2,350 feet)

Maximum elevation: 2210 metres (7,250 feet)

Topo maps: Lake Louise, 82 N/8 East

Point of Departure: Drive the 1-A Highway to the Baker Creek Picnic Area, located on the north side of the roadway 14.3 kilometres (8.9 miles) west of Eisenhower Junction. Enter the picnic area and watch for the trail sign on the western edge of the site.

*Distances approximate.

Scenically Baker Creek is rather mundane, and few people use it as a destination trip. More often the lower valley is hiked as an optional exit from Pulsatilla Pass or Baker Lake, while the upper one-third of the trail is being used more each season as a connecting link between the Pulsatilla Pass and Skoki Valley environs.

Ascending from the picnic area, the trail climbs over a low ridge covered by 'dog-hair' stands of lodgepole pine and eventually descends onto the broad Baker Valley plain.

A pleasant campsite is passed near the 10.5 kilometre mark, and a short distance above this camp the valley narrows as the trail begins a more noticeable ascent through a mature spruce forest. Just 2.7 kilometres above the campsite the trail crosses to the east bank of Baker Creek (rock-hop and wade), and another 800 metres brings the hiker to a forest-enclosed campsite at the Wildflower Creek junction.

Continuing up-valley, the trail crosses Wildflower Creek at the campsite and stays on the east side of Baker Creek. Two kilometres or less above the camp the trail crosses a boggy meadow (becoming indistinct at times) and, shortly thereafter, begins a steep, direct ascent through a closed forest. Emerging into open meadowland at the top of the grade, the hiker is not far from the Baker Lake cutoff and less than three kilometres from the lake itself.

For those descending lower Baker Creek to the 1-A Highway, beware of misleading blazes and false trails over the last three kilometres. If the trail is lost, as often happens, keep the prominent summit of Mount Temple on the right. Eventually the hiker will run into the trail again or emerge on the 1-A just west of Baker Creek.

Boom Lake

Half-day trip
Allow 1½-2 hours one way
Elevation gain: 185 metres (600 feet)
Maximum elevation: 1895 metres (6,220 feet)
Topo maps: Mount Goodsir, 82 N/1 East
　　　　　 Lake Louise, 82 N/8 East
　　　　　 (trail incorrectly marked)

Point of Departure: The trail begins at the Boom Creek Picnic Area, 7.1 kilometres (4.4 miles) southwest of Eisenhower Junction on the Banff-Radium Highway.

0.0—Trail sign.

　　—Trail crosses Boom Creek. Bridged.

4.3—Trail fork. Stay left below the rock slide.

4.5—Trail fork. The faint trail cutting left leads to the foot of the lake. Main route is straight ahead.

5.0—Trail narrows from cat-cleared track to a single-file foot path.

5.1—Boom Lake (1895 m).

The Boom Lake trail is an easy five kilometre trek to a beautifully formed and exceptionally clear body of water lying 1895 metres above sea level. Named for a natural log boom at its outlet, the lake is backed to the south by a massive 600 metre limestone wall and to the west by a glacier-mantled mountain—features which contribute to the dramatic aesthetic appeal of the area. The hike is particularly pleasant early in the season when the snowpack on Boom Mountain's heights is breaking up: on a sunny spring day a lucky hiker will see numerous avalanches cascade down the north face of the mountain to the lake below.

For most of its length the trail is a wide, bulldozed track which, after crossing Boom Creek at the Boom Creek Picnic Area, climbs moderately above the creek through a coniferous forest of spruce, lodgepole pine and fir. In the spring many small streams make the trail a bit boggy in spots, but the runoff redeems itself by offering an opportunity for many fine drinking stops—something the late season hiker will miss.

Just before the trail reaches the lake it narrows from its wide cat-cleared track to the more traditional single file foot path. This actually signifies the end of the hike, for 100 metres farther on the path ends abruptly on a rockslide just above the lake. A bit of rock hopping takes the hiker to the water's edge.

Across the lake soars the north face of Boom Mountain and the glaciated spires of Mount Quadra (3173 m) and Bident Mountain (3084 m), the latter named for its tooth-like appearance. A better view of Quadra and Bident is obtained from the lake's outlet (the eastern end), although this entails the bushwhacking and wet feet mentioned above for the spring hiker.

Boom Lake

Taylor Lake

Taylor Creek Picnic Area to Taylor Lake—6.3 kilometres (3.9 miles)

Day trip

Allow 2-3 hours one way

Elevation gain: 580 metres (1,900 feet)

Maximum elevation: 2070 metres (6,800 feet)

Topo maps: Lake Louise, 82 N/8 East

Point of Departure: Drive west of Eisenhower Junction on the Trans-Canada Highway 8 kilometres (5 miles) to the Taylor Creek Picnic Area.

0.0—Trail sign (1490 m). Cross bridge at rear of picnic area.

—Gradual to moderate uphill grade.

1.0—Bridge across Taylor Creek.

—Steady uphill.

5.8—Bridge across Taylor Creek.

6.3—Taylor Lake (2070 m).

Taylor Lake is typical of several cirque lakes set high on the west side of the Bow Valley: situated just below the timberline, carved into a wall of rugged, heavily-glaciated peaks, and surrounded by subalpine forest and meadow.

The trail to Taylor Lake is straightforward and not overly inspiring, consisting of little more than an old fire road track which switchbacks steadily upwards. Views beyond the forest canopy of lodgepole pine and spruce are nonexistent.

The goal is well-worth the drudgery of the climb, however, as the trail suddenly emerges into the open meadowland near the lake's outlet—an area carpeted with western anemone, marsh marigold, buttercups and mountain laurel throughout much of the summer. Fringing the meadow and much of the lakeshore is a typical forest of the upper subalpine zone —a dense, cool cover of alpine fir and Engelmann spruce dotted with the pale green foliage of alpine larch.

The north face of Mount Bell rises abruptly in a wall of over 750 metres from the south shore of the lake. The low notch of Taylor Pass to the west separates Mount Bell from Panorama Ridge and serves as a rock scrambler's route to the Consolation Valley and Moraine Lake. Beneath the pass, at the far end of the lake, a lacy waterfall flows over ancient rocks formed during the Precambrian Era.

O'Brien Lake Option. Located in a smaller cirque 2.1 kilometres to the south, O'Brien Lake is a worthwhile side trip for those with time and good footwear. Ford Taylor Creek at the trail signs just below the lake and follow the faint track which drops below the Mount Bell cliffs and then rises back up into the O'Brien cirque. The trail is all but nonexistent through the last 500 metres of boggy morass to the lake and it is best to stick as close to the outlet stream as possible.

Taylor Lake

Panorama Ridge Option. Leaving from the north edge of the Taylor Lake meadow this trail climbs high onto the eastern slope of Panorama Ridge, contours along for several kilometres at near the 2300 metre level, then turns the north end of the ridge to drop into the mouth of the Consolation Valley. Total distance from Taylor Lake to the junction with the Consolation Lakes trail is just over 11 kilometres, and the trail is an excellent highline route to Moraine Lake and beyond.

Thor's Folly Option. This unofficial Bow Valley highline trail also runs south from Taylor Lake emerging on the Boom Lake trail. The trail is reported in very rough shape, however, and few have completed the journey without a good deal of bushwhacking.

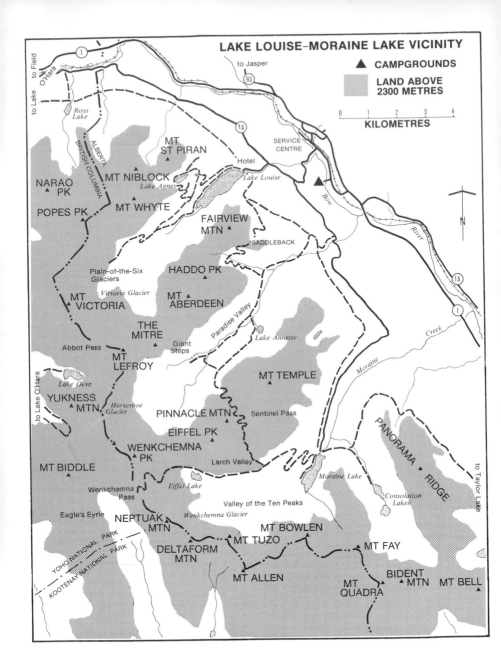

LAKE LOUISE–MORAINE LAKE VICINITY

▲ CAMPGROUNDS

LAND ABOVE
2300 METRES

0 1 2 3 4
KILOMETRES

to Field

to Lake O'Hara

Ross
Lake

to Jasper

93

SERVICE
CENTRE

Hotel

Lake Louise

MT
ST PIRAN

MT NIBLOCK

Lake Agnes

NARAO
PK

BRITISH COLUMBIA
ALBERTA

POPES PK

MT WHYTE

FAIRVIEW
MTN

SADDLEBACK

Bow

River

1A

1

N

Plain-of-the-Six
Glaciers

HADDO PK

MT
VICTORIA

Victoria Glacier

MT
ABERDEEN

Paradise Valley

Lake Annette

Creek

THE
MITRE

Giant
Steps

Moraine

Abbot Pass

MT
LEFROY

MT TEMPLE

Lake Oesa

YUKNESS
MTN

Horseshoe
Glacier

PINNACLE MTN

Sentinel Pass

PANORAMA

RIDGE

to Lake O'Hara

EIFFEL PK

WENKCHEMNA
PK

Larch Valley

Moraine Lake

to Taylor Lake

MT BIDDLE

Wenkchemna
Pass

Eiffel Lake

Consolation
Lakes

Eagle's Eyrie

NEPTUAK
MTN

Valley of the Ten Peaks

Wenkchemna Glacier

DELTAFORM
MTN

MT TUZO

MT BOWLEN

MT FAY

YOHO NATIONAL PARK

KOOTENAY NATIONAL PARK

MT ALLEN

MT
QUADRA

BIDENT
MTN

MT BELL

68

Lake Louise and the Valley of the Ten Peaks

There are few day-hiking areas in the Canadian Rockies or, in fact, in all of North America, comparable to the Lake Louise-Moraine Lake region. Compressed within 100 square kilometres are seven major hikes with their spur trips and options—a total of over 70 kilometres of trail which climb and wind through some of the most rugged alpine scenery on the continent.

Indeed the Lake Louise-Moraine Lake environs can be said to be the birthplace of recreational hiking in the Canadian Rockies. Shortly after the completion of the Canadian Pacific Railroad, tourists began making their way into the area. One of the first high trails cut in Banff Park was to Lake Agnes—named in honor of one of its earliest visitors Susan Agnes, wife of Prime Minister John A. Macdonald, who travelled through the Rockies with her husband in 1886. A small chalet was constructed on the shore of Lake Louise in 1890 by the CPR, and its manager, W.J. Astley, directed the clearing of many of the early trails in the immediate vicinity of the lake.

In 1894, a party of young collegians from the United States, who called themselves the Yale-Lake Louise Club, began a systematic exploration of the region. Over the next five years members of the club discovered and explored Paradise Valley, the Valley of the Ten Peaks and Consolation Valley and completed first ascents of many of the surrounding peaks. As the adjoining valleys and scenic wonders were discovered, CPR employees constructed trails from the chalet at Lake Louise providing access for less-adventuresome travellers. As the trails became more heavily used, tealhouses and shelters were also built along the way, and indeed much of the trail system was maintained by hotel staff through the middle of the 20th Century.

Today these trails are the most heavily travelled in the Canadian Rockies. On a warm sunny day you will be in continual contact with other hikers—just a few of the 50,000 plus who use the trails in this area every summer. Yet these trips are still some of the most spectacular to be found anywhere and, in the autumn when the crowds have thinned out somewhat, there is probably no finer place to be in the Rockies.

Lake Agnes

Lake Louise to Lake Agnes—3.4 kilometres (2.1 miles)

Day trip

Allow 1-2 hours to Lake Agnes

Elevation gain: 367 metres (1,205 feet)

Maximum elevation: 2099 metres (6,885 feet)

Topo maps: Lake Louise, 82 N/8 East

Point of Departure: Drive to Lake Louise, following the 6 kilometre (3.7 mile) access road from its junction with the Trans-Canada Highway. A large parking area is available adjacent to the hotel. Follow along the lakeshore to the trail sign just west of the hotel.

0.0—Trail sign (1731 m).

  —Lake Agnes trail branches uphill to the right. Steady uphill climb.

1.6—Switchback and viewpoint.

2.4—Junction with horse trail.

2.6—Mirror Lake (2031 m). Junction: branch trail to left contours beneath the Big Beehive to the Plain-of-the-Six Glaciers; keep right for Lake Agnes.

  —Trail continues to switchback upward.

3.1—Junction: Shortcut to Little Beehive and Mount St. Piran cuts uphill to right. Lake Agnes straight ahead.

3.4—Lake Agnes and teahouse (2099 m). Branch trail to Little Beehive summit (1 km) begins climb directly behind teahouse. Trail to Big Beehive continues on around lake, reaching the summit in 1.6 kilometres.

Hidden in a small cirque above Lake Louise, Lake Agnes has long been the most hiked-to area in the mountain parks. In addition to its own charms, the lake and its adjacent "Beehives" provide breathtaking views of Lake Louise and the Bow Valley.

The first half hour of ascent from the hotel is through a dense subalpine forest of Engelmann spruce and alpine fir, and not until the 1.6 kilometre mark does a break in the trees allow a clear view down to the pale, glacier-fed waters of Lake Louise.

At Kilometre 2.6 the hiker emerges at Mirror Lake—a small body of water that receives its name from its round looking-glass appearance. Above loom the dark cliffs of the Big Beehive, and in the gap to the right, the red roof of the Lake Agnes Teahouse is visible—still a steep 800 metres away.

Arriving at the narrow opening where Lake Agnes tumbles from its basin, the entire length of the lake can be seen stretching westward to the foot of Mounts Whyte (2983 m) and Niblock (2976 m). The lake, contained on the south by the long flank of the Big Beehive, is often ice-covered into mid-June.

Looking back to Mirror Lake, views are open to Lake Louise and the Bow Valley far below. From this viewpoint it is easy to see how Lake Agnes sits within what is called a 'hanging valley.'

The lake was named for one of its earliest visitors, Lady Agnes Macdonald, wife of Canada's first Prime Minister. Lady Agnes is also known as the first woman to ride the cowcatcher of a locomotive over the Rockies. Travelling the transcontinental railway with her husband in 1886, she boarded her precarious perch at the Lake Louise station and announced with great aplomb: "This is lovely! I shall travel on this cowcatcher

from summit to sea." And so she did, though Sir John A. thought the whole idea "rather ridiculous."

The area surrounding Lake Agnes abounds in the wildlife and flora of the upper subalpine forest zone. Garbage-debauched chipmunks, ground squirrels, nutcrackers and 'whiskey jacks' beg crumbs from hikers on the teahouse porch, while hoary marmots and pikas whistle and cheep from the rocky slopes above.

Pioneer mountaineer and photographer Walter Wilcox writes of an early visitor to the lake who cut short his stay and hurried back to Lake Louise upon hearing the shrill whistle of a marmot "which he thought must be the signal of robbers or Indians about to commence an attack."

The Beehives. Anyone with energy to spare once they reach the lake should continue on to the summit of either the Big Beehive or Little Beehive. Both of these lofty viewpoints offer excellent vistas of the Bow Valley and are well worth the extra energy to get there. The trail to the Little Beehive leaves from behind the teahouse and climbs to the northeast along a partially forested ridge for approximately one kilometre to a fire lookout, while the route to the Big Beehive continues around the far end of Lake Agnes, climbs a short steep incline, then traverses eastward along the summit ridge to the overlook—a total distance of 1.6 kilometres from the teahouse. Both Beehives are crowned with stands of alpine larch—particularly beautiful in late September when their needles have turned to gold.

Plain-of-Six Glaciers Option. Strong hikers who wish a full day of activity may continue over the Big Beehive, dropping down to the highline trail from Mirror Lake, then traversing up-valley to the Plain-of-Six Glaciers overlook and teahouse. Total distance for this loop trip return to Lake Louise is 18 kilometres. (See *Plain-of-the-Six Glaciers* trail.)

71

Plain-of-the-Six Glaciers

Lake Louise to Plain-of-Six Teahouse—5.3 kilometres (3.3 miles)
Lake Louise to Plain-of-Six Viewpoint—6.6 kilometres (4.1 miles)

Day trip

Allow 2 hours to teahouse

Elevation gain: 670 metres (2,200 feet)

Maximum elevation: 2410 metres (7,900 feet)

Topo maps: Lake Louise, 82 N/8 East
Lake Louise, 82 N/8 West

Point of Departure: Drive to Lake Louise, following the 6 kilometre (3.7 mile) access road from its junction with the Trans-Canada Highway. A large parking area is available adjacent to the hotel. Walk along the lakeshore to the trail sign just west of the hotel.

0.0—Trail sign (1731 m).

—Trail follows the shore of Lake Louise.

1.9—West end (inlet) of Lake Louise.

2.4—Trail begins uphill grade.

3.2—Junction: Straight ahead for Plain-of-Six. Descent route from Big Beehive enters from right.

—Trail becomes steep, entering an area of morainal deposits.

5.3—Plain-of-the-Six Glaciers Teahouse.

6.3—Narrow crest of lateral moraine.

6.6—Viewpoint. Trail disappears on a high talus slope.

The Plain-of-the-Six Glaciers trail, rising from Lake Louise to a spectacular viewpoint at the base of Mount Victoria, passes through some of the most interesting glaciated scenery in Banff Park. Unfortunately for those seeking solitude, it is also one of the park's busiest trails.

Starting from the trail sign just west of the Chateau Lake Louise, the hiker spends the first 30 minutes walking along the shore of Lake Louise. Away from the crowds and confusion surrounding the hotel, he might better appreciate the description given the lake by the British mountaineer Sir James Outram shortly after the turn of the century: "At every season, every hour, it is wonderful. . . . As a gem of composition and of colouring it is perhaps unrivalled anywhere."

At the lakehead, a trail side cliff exposes the Lower Cambrian quartzites which comprise the lower reaches of the surrounding mountains. A short distance beyond, the trail begins to climb, entering a forest arm of spruce and alpine fir.

At Kilometre 3.9 the trail enters into the wasteland produced by the advance and retreat of the Victoria Glacier. All round, beyond and below, ridges of rock and gravel bear mute testimony to the forces that have passed this way. Farther on the trail passes along the top of a morainal ridge, where views improve toward Mount Victoria, Mount Lefroy, the Lefroy Glacier and The Mitre.

The Plain-of-the-Six Glaciers Teahouse, surrounded by a stunted forest typical of the altitude, is an ideal resting spot where lunch and refreshments can be purchased during the summer months. In a boulder field just beyond the teahouse the hiker should watch for the whistling marmots and pikas that make their home in these rough surroundings.

From the teahouse the trail soon leaves the last trees behind, emerging onto the narrow ridge of a lateral moraine. This

The Mitre from Plain-of-the-Six Glaciers trail

steep ridge of debris was formed over many centuries as the Victoria Glacier retreated into the valley. (Travellers along the last 300 metres of trail should take care on this precarious path.)

Mount Victoria (3464 m) and Mount Lefroy (3441 m) dominate the scene from the viewpoint. The gap between Victoria and Lefroy is Abott's Pass (2922 m), named for Philip Stanley Abbot who died climbing Mount Lefroy in 1896—the first alpinist to perish in the Rockies. Looking closely at the skyline of the pass it is possible to see the alpine hut—a rather substantial stone structure constructed by Swiss guides in the early 1920's.

Beehive-Lake Agnes Option. Strong hikers desiring a full day outing can take the highline route back to Lake Louise, cutting up to the Big Beehive and down past Lake Agnes and Mirror Lake on the other side. This option adds approximately 5 kilometres to the normal 13 kilometre round trip and includes a very strenuous climb to the 2268 metre elevation of the Big Beehive. Views, however, are spectacular indeed. To take the option watch for the trail junction 1.4 kilometres below the teahouse. (See *Lake Agnes* trail.)

Saddleback

Lake Louise to Saddleback—3.7 kilometres (2.3 miles)

Day trip

Allow 1½-2 hours one way

Elevation gain: 580 metres (1,900 feet)

Maximum elevation: 2315 metres (7,600 feet)

Topo maps: Lake Louise, 82 N/8 East

Point of Departure: Drive to Lake Louise, following the 6 kilometre (3.7 mile) access road from its junction with the Trans-Canada Highway. A large parking area is available adjacent to the hotel. Walk to the lakeshore along the south bank of Louise Creek, and look for the trail sign between the pony corral and the boathouse.

0.0—Trail sign (1731 m).

0.3—Junction: Spur trail to Fairview Lookout cuts right. Moraine Lake trail branches left 100 metres farther along.

1.1—Avalanche slope.

—Steady uphill at moderate to steep grades.

3.7—Saddleback summit (2315 m).

"To see Mount Temple in its noblest grandeur I would take you to the Saddleback. This is a broad green alp, nearly 2000 feet above Lake Louise, a very favourite hour's ascent by trail, between Mount Fairview and the projecting 'horn' of the Saddle Peak. Crossing the plateau to the tree-fringed brink of the abyss beyond, our gaze is carried straight across the chasm, 1500 feet in depth, to the huge peak . . ."

James Outram, British mountaineer and explorer, wrote those words nearly 70 years ago, providing an apt description of the 3.7 kilometre hike from the shore of Lake Louise—a journey which also displays outstanding views down the broad Bow Valley.

In its early stages the trail travels steadily upward at a moderate to steep incline, passing through a closed forest of spruce and alpine fir. Beneath the steep slopes of Fairview Mountain, the route traverses the first of many avalanche paths which serve as excellent viewpoints for the Bow Valley. Openings continue and views improve with elevation, finally culminating beneath the Saddle with an exceptional panorama down the Bow Valley to the mountains near Banff.

As Outram noted, the summit of the Saddleback is a pleasant upland meadow, fringed by stands of alpine larch and, in early summer, covered with buttercups, western anemone, alpine speedwell and many other wildflowers. The broad peak of Mount Temple (3544 m) dominates the view from the summit of the pass, displaying its awesome 1200 metre north wall topped by a cap of ice and corniced snow.

Fairview and Saddle Mountain Options. The Saddleback is actually a pass situated between two low peaks—

Mount Temple from Saddle Peak

Fairview Mountain on the northwest and Saddle Mountain to the southeast. Both are easily ascended by strong hikers from the Saddleback summit. At an elevation of 2745 metres above sea level, the summit of Fairview offers the better views—a true alpine experience with the glacier-clad summits of Mount Victoria, Mount Temple and Sheol Mountain close-at-hand and the blue-green waters of Lake Louise over a vertical kilometre below. While one may scramble straight up to the summit (skirting steep snow-banks early in the year), a discernible trail switchbacks up the southeast slopes of the peak, leading off from the upper margin of alpine larch trees just above the crest of Saddle.

Sheol Valley Option. For hikers desiring a full day trip, an interesting extension of the Saddleback trail can be made by continuing down into the Sheol Valley. Lying directly beneath the brooding cliffs of Sheol Mountain, the valley was named in 1894 by the mountaineer S.E.S. Allen, who fancied its resemblance the "abode of the dead" in Hebrew mythology. Despite its gruesome name, the valley contains many pleasant glades which abound in wildflowers during the month of July. The trail finally emerges in Paradise Valley. From there the hiker may swing back around Saddle Mountain to Lake Louise via the Paradise and Moraine Lake trails. Total distance for the loop trip is 14.9 kilometres.

Paradise Valley

Moraine Lake Road to Lake Annette—5.6 kilometres (3.5 miles)
Paradise Valley Circuit—18.8 kilometres (11.7 miles)

Day trip

Allow 2 hours to Lake Annette

Elevation gain: 245 metres (800 feet)

Maximum elevation: 1980 metres (6,500 feet)

Topo maps: Lake Louise, 82 N/8 East

Point of Departure: Drive 2.4 kilometres (1.5 miles) south on the Moraine Lake Road from the junction with the 1-A Highway. A parking area is located at the trail head on the west side of the road.

0.0—Trail sign (1720 m).

—Uphill.

1.0—Junction: Keep right for Lake Annette and Paradise Valley.

1.3—Junction: Turn left for Lake Annette and Paradise Valley.

4.2—Junction: Lake Annette straight ahead. Sheol Valley and Saddleback to right.

5.2—Junction and bridge: Cross bridge for Lake Annette. Keep right for the valley trail to the Giant Steps.

—Moderate uphill on Lake Annette trail.

5.6—Lake Annette (1965 m).

—Trail climbs from lakeshore heading up the valley.

8.7—Junction: Sentinel Pass trail branches uphill to left. Paradise Valley and Giant Steps are downhill to right.

9.7—Meadow and bridge. Main trail cuts right back down the valley. Branch trail left leads to Giant Steps (1.1 kilometres).

—Valley trail follows back toward trail head along Paradise Creek.

18.8—Trail head and parking area.

When the mountaineer Walter Wilcox and his companions climbed to the summit of Mitre Pass in 1894, they looked into "a valley of surpassing beauty, wide and beautiful, with alternating open meadows and rich forests." They immediately named it Paradise Valley.

Today a trail ascends the valley from the Moraine Lake Road, branching to create a loop which passes by the shores of Lake Annette and the terraced falls of the Giant Steps.

From the trail parking lot, the first five kilometres of travel are rather uneventful as the trail is mainly enclosed within a forest of spruce and alpine fir. As one nears the end of this approach, however, Mount Temple comes into view and the trail drops down to the banks of Paradise Creek.

The trail to Lake Annette branches across the creek at the 5.2 kilometre mark and the lake itself is reached after a brief five minute climb.

The British mountaineer James Outram probably did the lake its greatest justice in his early description, comparing it to "a tiny bit of sky dropped from the heavens and almost lost in the depths of the sombre firs." The lake was named for Mrs. Annette Astley, the wife of the first manager at the Lake Louise chalet.

In its immediate surroundings, Annette is rather typical of many subalpine lakes, though its backdrop, the ice-capped 1200 metre north face of Mount Temple, is far from ordinary. This is by far the most impressive view of Banff's third highest mountain, though it is impossible to photograph the mountain from this viewpoint with anything more than an extreme wide angle lens. Long considered one of the most difficult faces in the Canadian Rockies, the rugged wall was first climbed in 1966.

For those making the valley circuit, the trail continues on, rising to a major

The Giant Steps

rockslide in just over one kilometre. At nearly 2200 metres above sea level the slide is the highest and best viewpoint on the trail. Even more so than Lake Annette, it is a good place to stop, rest and enjoy the many natural features in the valley. At the head of the valley is the Horseshoe Glacier and the Giant Steps area. Directly across from the viewpoint, to the northwest, is Mount Aberdeen (3152 m), where well-defined paths have been cleared through the lower forested slopes by avalanches from the cliffs above. Keep a close watch on the nearby boulders of the rockslide as well, since they conceal the burrows of both hoary marmots and pikas.

From its high traverse above the valley, the trail leads to the headwaters of Paradise Creek where a short side trail takes one to the tumbling cascades of the Giant Steps—a delicate series of water falls which can keep photographers occupied for an hour or more.

From its loop below the Giant Steps, the main trail heads back down the valley to eventually complete the upper valley circuit at the Lake Annette junction.

Sentinel Pass-Moraine Lake Option. An excellent day trip can be completed from Paradise Valley by taking the branch trail near the head of the valley over Sentinel Pass and down to Moraine Lake. Total distance for this trip is 16.9 kilometres, but you must either arrange transportation at Moraine Lake in advance or plan to hitchhike 10 kilometres back to your car. (See *Sentinel Pass* trail.)

Larch Valley—Sentinel Pass

Moraine Lake to Larch Valley—2.4 kilometres (1.5 miles)
Moraine Lake to Sentinel Pass—5.8 kilometres (3.6 miles)

Day trip

Allow 3 hours to Sentinel Pass

Elevation gain: 724 metres (2,376 feet)

Maximum elevation: 2611 metres (8,566 feet)

Topo maps: Lake Louise, 82 N/8 East

Point of Departure: Follow the Moraine Lake Road to its terminus at Moraine Lake Lodge, 12.4 kilometres (7.7 miles) from its junction with the 1-A Highway. There is a large parking area just north of the lodge. The trail begins just above the lakeshore and beyond the lodge.

0.0—Trail sign (1887 m).

—Within 50 metres the Larch Valley-Sentinel Pass trail branches to the right from the lakeshore trail.

1.1—Switchbacks begin.

—Steady uphill climb.

2.4—Junction: Larch Valley-Sentinel Pass to the right. Eiffel Lake straight ahead.

—Trail climbs into open meadows of Larch Valley.

4.7—Switchbacks up steep talus slope.

5.8—Sentinel Pass (2611 m).

Of the major trails in the mountain parks, the route through Sentinel Pass is the highest—a lofty 2611 metres above sea level. Approached through the delicate subalpine meadows of Larch Valley, the pass stands austerely amid stark pinnacles of rock and serves as an excellent viewpoint for the Valley of the Ten Peaks.

From Moraine Lake the trail switchbacks up through a forest of Engelmann spruce and alpine fir, splitting from the Eiffel Lake trail at Kilometre 2.4 and entering the meadows of Larch Valley. This high valley, named for the alpine larch which fringe the meadows, is as much a focal point for hikers as the rugged Sentinel Pass beyond. Particularly in autumn, when the needles on the larch have turned to gold, it becomes the most visited area in Banff Park. In midsummer, however, the larch needles are a pale green and the meadows are carpeted with the more showy varieties of wildflowers associated with a snowbed plant community.

As the trail emerges above the last of the trees, there are fine views back to the rugged Wenkchemna Peaks, the ice-draped summit of Mount Fay (3235 m) being the most prominent and striking. The small pools which dot the upper Larch Valley meadows were named the Minnestimma Lakes by the early mountaineer S. E. S. Allen. An Indian word meaning 'sleeping water,' this wonderful name has been all but forgotten by contemporary hikers and map makers.

Ahead, between the vertical walls of Pinnacle Mountain (3607 m) on the left and Mount Temple (3544 m) on the right, is the rugged summit of Sentinel Pass. While still over a kilometre away, the trail begins its climb up the steep talus to the pass—a vertical rise of nearly 200 metres.

Located near the axis of a syncline

Mount Fay from the Larch Valley meadows

(trough or downfold in the strata), the rocks surrounding Sentinel Pass lie nearly horizontal. Erosion of these flat-lying rock layers has created the weird spires and towers of nearby Pinnacle Mountain.

The pass was first ascended, from Paradise Valley, in 1894 by Samuel Allen and Yandell Henderson, both members of the Yale-Lake Louise Club which did much exploration in the region. Mount Temple, the third highest peak in Banff Park, was also climbed the same year by the Yale mountaineers—the first ascent of a Canadian peak above 11,000 feet.

Like most other trails in the Lake Louise-Moraine Lake region, the Larch Valley-Sentinel Pass route is heavily used throughout the summer and on weekends during the fall.

Paradise Valley Option. Strong hikers may wish to make a full day outing by continuing over Sentinel Pass and descending into Paradise Valley. The trail descends steeply from the pass (heavy snowdrifts often obscure the trail in this gully into July) and connects into the Paradise Valley circuit 2.3 kilometres below. From here you can take a right fork to Lake Annette or a left to the Giant Steps. Both trails join again lower in the valley and follow Paradise Creek to the Moraine Lake Road. Total distance for this option—from Moraine Lake to the Moraine Lake Road at Paradise Creek—is 16.7 kilometres. It is advisable to arrange transportation for the hike, however, or else be prepared for a 10 kilometre hitchhike or roadwalk back to Moraine Lake. (See *Paradise Valley* trail.)

Eiffel Lake—Wenkchemna Pass

Moraine Lake to Eiffel Lake—5.6 kilometres (3.5 miles)
Moraine Lake to Wenkchemna Pass—9.7 kilometres (6.0 miles)

Day trip

Allow 2-3 hours to Eiffel Lake

Elevation gain: 365 metres (1,200 feet)

Maximum elevation: 2255 metres (7,400 feet)

Topo maps: Lake Louise, 82 N/8 East

Point of Departure: Follow the Moraine Lake Road to its terminus at Moraine Lake Lodge, 12.4 kilometres (7.7 miles) from its junction with the 1-A Highway. There is a large parking area just north of the lodge. The trail begins just above the lakeshore and beyond the lodge.

0.0—Trail sign (1887 m).

—Within 50 metres the Larch Valley-Eiffel Lake trail branches to the right from the lakeshore trail.

1.1—Switchbacks begin.

—Steady uphill climb.

2.4—Junction: Eiffel Lake straight ahead. Larch Valley-Sentinel Pass to the right.

—Trail levels out contouring open slopes.

5.6—Eiffel Lake (2255 m), located 200 metres below trail.

—Moderate but steady uphill over alpine tundra and talus slopes.

9.7—Wenkchemna Pass (2600 m).

Exploring above Moraine Lake in 1899, Walter Wilcox and his companions were so impressed by the stark glaciated landscape they named the area Desolation Valley. In its deepest and most desolate heart lies Eiffel Lake.

The Eiffel Lake trail follows the same course as the Sentinel Pass trail for the first 2.4 kilometres, switchbacking upward through a closed, mature subalpine forest. Splitting near the edge of Larch Valley, the Eiffel Lake route continues on alone, emerging onto open slopes that reveal all summits in the Valley of the Ten Peaks as well as the brilliant blue waters of Moraine Lake.

As the trail continues through these flower-filled meadows the Wenkchemna Glacier can be seen stretching downvalley at the foot of the Ten Peaks. Heavy talus deposits from the cliffs above have completely covered over most of the glacier's surface, shielding the ice from the sun's rays and accounting in part for the relatively small recession in the past century.

At the 5.6 kilometre mark, the trail passes across a steep scree slope and skirts above the frigid waters of Eiffel Lake. Reflecting upon one of his first visits to the lake, Walter Wilcox wrote: "It would be difficult to find another lake of small size in a wilder setting, the shores being of great angular stones, perfectly in harmony with the wild range of mountains beyond. Except in one place where a green and inviting slope comes down to the water, this rough ground is utterly unsuitable for vegetation and nearly devoid of trees."

The main reason for Eiffel's rugged surroundings is that it was not created as most alpine lakes are. Instead of lying in a basin carved and dammed by the action of glaciers over many centuries, Eiffel is situated in a depression formed by a massive rockslide which broke away from

Valley of the Ten Peaks from the Eiffel Lake trail

Neptuak Mountain. Large boulders and piles of rock debris which spread across the valley from the base of the mountain provide mute testimony to the grand catastrophe which once shook this region.

Immediately above the lake and to the north is Eiffel Peak (3085 m), so named because of a huge rock pinnacle rising near its summit which is suggestive of the Parisian landmark. Looking at the peak from this angle the hiker can easily see the striking contrast between the light grey limestone composing the summit and the orangish quartzites of the lower cliffs.

An interesting extension of the hike can be made by continuing on for another four kilometres to the summit of Wenkchemna Pass (much of this last section of trail may be obscured by snowfields early in the summer). Standing at an elevation of 2600 metres above sea level, this high pass is an excellent viewpoint for the Valley of the Ten Peaks as well as the Eagle's Eyrie region of Yoho Park. Like nearby Sentinel Pass, it is one of the highest points serviced by trail in Banff Park.

Consolation Lakes

Moraine Lake to Lower Consolation Lake—2.9 kilometres (1.8 miles)

Half-day trip

Allow 1 hour one way

Elevation gain: 90 metres (300 feet)

Maximum elevation: 1950 metres (6,400 feet)

Topo maps: Lake Louise, 82 N/8 East

Point of Departure: Follow the Moraine Lake Road to its terminus at Moraine Lake Lodge, 12.4 kilometres (7.7 miles) from its junction with the 1-A Highway. There is a large parking area just north of the lodge and above the picnic area. Walk down through the picnic area to the bridge over Moraine Creek.

0.0—Trail head at Moraine Creek bridge (1887 m).

—Trail crosses boulder field then climbs gradually into forest.

1.3—Junction: Panorama Ridge trail to Taylor Lake branches left. Consolation Lakes lie straight ahead.

2.3—Open meadow.

2.9—Lower Consolation Lake (1950 m).

While it is the shortest of the many popular hikes in the Moraine Lake area, the outstanding alpine scenery surrounding the Consolation Lakes makes the trip well worth a half-day of modest effort.

The first 300 metres of trail pass over a substantial rockslide which descended from the Tower of Babel to create a natural dam for Moraine Lake. From this region of tumbled rock the trail rises into a pleasant forest of fir and spruce, levelling out along an open meadow just before reaching the lower lake. (To reach the water's edge you must pick a route through a large boulder field at the lake's northern end.)

Scramble onto one of the many prominent boulders for a relaxed view of the lake and Mounts Bident and Quadra beyond. Back to the north stands Mount Temple (3544 m), the third highest peak in Banff Park and the highest in the Lake Louise-Moraine Lake vicinity.

If you wish to spend a little more time in the area and are well shod, you can visit Upper Consolation Lake. Ford Babel Creek below the outlet of Lower Consolation (on rickety log booms) then follow a rough, wet track which follows along the lake's eastern shore. Climb over a low, narrow ridge of rock debris which separates the two lakes.

Walter Wilcox and Ross Peacock first explored the valley in 1899. Wilcox later wrote: "We are very much pleased with the place, and Ross suggested that, since the other was called Desolation Valley we might call this 'Consolation Valley,' a name that seems quite appropriate."

Today the valley offers consolation for those overwhelmed by the hordes of tourists at nearby Moraine Lake. But if you find the trail a bit too worn and overcrowded as well, you may be consoled by the knowledge that hikers have actually lost their way on this straightforward little trip and have had to be "rescued" by the Warden Service.

Lower Consolation Lake

Boulder Pass—Skoki Valley

Lake Louise Ski Area to Boulder Pass—8.6 kilometres (5.3 miles)

Lake Louise Ski Area to Skoki Lodge—14.4 kilometres (8.9 miles)

Day trip or backpack

Allow 3-4 hours to Boulder Pass
   5-6 hours to Skoki Valley

Elevation gain: 790 metres (2,600 feet)

Maximum elevation: 2475 metres (8,120 feet)

Topo maps: Lake Louise, 82 N/8 East
   Hector Lake, 82 N/9 East

Point of Departure: Drive to the Lake Louise Ski Area and follow the gravel access road which branches right just inside the entrance. Follow the access road for 2.0 kilometres (1.2 miles) to the right-hand junction with the Temple Lodge access road. Follow the Temple road for 1.1 kilometres (0.7 mile) to the Fish Creek access gate and parking area.

0.0—Access gate.

—Follow the Temple access road. Steady uphill climb.

3.9—Temple Lodge and ski slopes. Hike 200 metres up the ski run east of the lodge complex and pick-up the Boulder Pass trail.

—Trail rises gradually.

6.3—Opens into meadow.

7.1—Halfway Hut. Hidden Lake trail cuts left (1.3 kilometres). Boulder Pass straight ahead.

—Steady uphill.

8.6—Boulder Pass and Ptarmigan Lake (2308 m).

10.5—Junction: Deception Pass and Skoki Valley uphill to left. Baker Lake straight ahead (1.3 kilometres).

11.0—Deception Pass (2475 m).

—Steady downhill.

13.9—Junction: Red Deer Lakes trail branches right (4 kilometres). Skoki Lodge straight ahead.

14.4—Skoki Lodge (2165 m).

Hidden away behind the Lake Louise ski area, the high valleys, passes and lakes of the Slate Range create one of the exceptional hiking areas in Banff Park. And though the trip to Skoki Valley and return is popular as a weekend outing and Boulder Pass is often visited in a long day, one can only begin to explore the more than 200 square kilometres of rugged scenery in this region during an extended visit of several days.

While the initial four kilometres of slogging up the Temple access road will not bring joy to the hiker's heart, the drudgery of this section is a necessary prerequisite to the sublime countryside beyond. Once the Temple ski lodge and lift complex is passed, things improve rapidly: the road reverts to trail, albeit wide and often muddy, and the hiker enters a pleasant forest containing Engelmann spruce, alpine fir and the first scattered alpine larch.

Just 2.4 kilometres beyond Temple the trail opens into meadow with views ahead to Boulder Pass and the rugged summits of Mount Richardson (3086 m), Pika Peak (3033 m) and Ptarmigan Peak (3059 m)— the mountains that serve as the apex of the Slate Range. Over 15 kilometres away to the southwest stands glacier-topped Mount Temple (3544 m), the third highest peak in Banff Park. The meadow itself is filled with a wide variety of colourful wildflowers during the summer months—elephant's head and white paintbrush being most prominent.

The Halfway Hut is reached a short way into the meadow. A log cabin set on a low bluff above Corral Creek, the hut received its name during the early days of skiing in the Rockies when it served as accommodation for skiers travelling from the Lake Louise railway station to Skoki Lodge. Many legends have passed down through the years concerning this hut and the surrounding peaks, most

Ptarmigan Valley from Deception Pass

concerning the ghosts of skiers, lost in avalanches, which are said to haunt these valleys by night. In recent years the cabin has been used as a shelter by hikers, but its future role is uncertain.

From Halfway Hut the trail continues through relatively open country to the summit of Boulder Pass and the shore of Ptarmigan Lake, an ascending pathway which is usually fringed with giant tufts of blue forget-me-nots. Located at 2308 metres, just above the timberline, the broad tundra-carpeted pass is the home of the hoary marmot, pika, ptarmigan and Columbian ground squirrel.

The trail travels along the slopes above the north shore of Ptarmigan Lake, then cuts up to Deception Pass. From the Deception summit, the hiker can look back across the last two-and-a-half kilometres of travel, through Boulder Pass, and on to the jagged summits near Lake Louise. Ptarmigan Lake lies stretched out below and the cliffs of Redoubt Mountain rise beyond. Just over a kilometre east of Ptarmigan Lake an invisible but major thrust fault runs

across the valley separating the older rocks of the Main Ranges from the younger of the Front Ranges; in stepping over this fracture in the rock, one would be striding across a geological gap of nearly 200 million years.

From Deception Pass the trail drops steadily downward toward the Skoki Valley. Beneath Ptarmigan Peak to the west appear the milky blue waters of the Skoki Lakes—also known as Myosotis and Zigadenus, the genus names for the forget-me-not and the camus lily. Passing through a scattering of alpine larch as it re-enters timber, the trail eventually descends into a more defined subalpine forest of spruce and fir as it nears Skoki Lodge.

The name Skoki is supposedly an Indian word meaning "marsh" or "swamp" which aptly describes sections of the valley floor. Like many of the names found in the immediate area, it originates with the first party of mountaineers who visited the valley in 1911, one of the leaders being from the Skokie, Illinois vicinity.

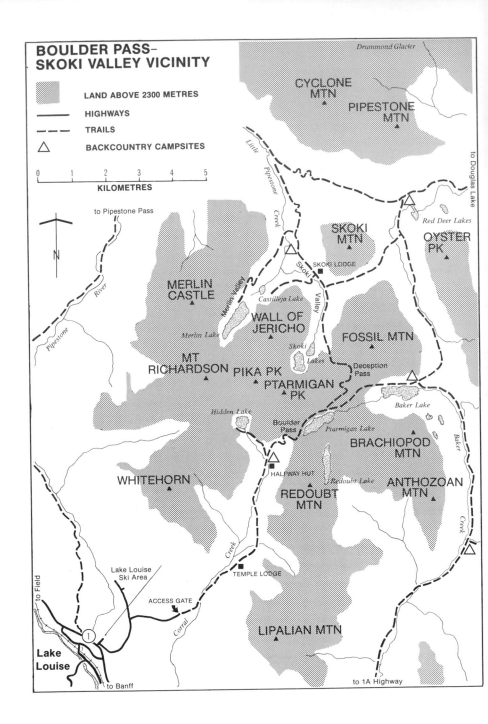

BOULDER PASS–
SKOKI VALLEY VICINITY

LAND ABOVE 2300 METRES

HIGHWAYS

TRAILS

BACKCOUNTRY CAMPSITES

0 1 2 3 4 5
KILOMETRES

N

to Pipestone Pass

Drummond Glacier

CYCLONE
MTN
▲

PIPESTONE
MTN
▲

Little Pipestone Creek

to Douglas Lake

Red Deer Lakes

SKOKI
MTN
▲

OYSTER
PK
▲

SKOKI LODGE

MERLIN
CASTLE
▲

Castilleja Lake

Merlin Valley

Merlin Lake

WALL OF
JERICHO
▲

Skoki Valley

Skoki Lakes

FOSSIL MTN
▲

MT
RICHARDSON
▲

PIKA PK
▲

PTARMIGAN
PK
▲

Deception
Pass

Pipestone River

Hidden Lake

Boulder
Pass

Ptarmigan Lake

Baker Lake

BRACHIOPOD
MTN
▲

Baker Creek

WHITEHORN
▲

HALFWAY HUT

Redoubt Lake

REDOUBT
MTN
▲

ANTHOZOAN
MTN
▲

to Field

Lake Louise
Ski Area

ACCESS GATE

Corral Creek

TEMPLE LODGE

LIPALIAN MTN
▲

1

Lake
Louise

to Banff

to 1A Highway

86

The first lodge in the valley was constructed in 1930 and it served as the centre of one of western Canada's first ski resorts. Of course, skiing was of the do-it-yourself variety then—without lifts. In recent years the lodge has experienced a resurgence in popularity with both hikers and cross-country skiers. (Information concerning lodge reservations and rates is available through the ski area office in Lake Louise.)

Boulder Pass Options. There are a number of short side trips radiating from the Boulder Pass-Ptarmigan Lake environs which offer pleasant half-day excursions to nearby lakes.

Lying in a pocket of alpine tundra beneath Mount Richardson and Pika Peak, Hidden Lake is only 1.3 kilometres north of Halfway Hut. The trail cuts away from the Boulder Pass route 100 metres north of the cabin.

Redoubt Lake is an easy 1.1 kilometres from either the west or east end of Ptarmigan Lake. There is no well-defined trail, but follow along the south shore of Ptarmigan for 800 metres or so, then cut straight up over open slopes toward the pocket at the foot of Redoubt Mountain.

Baker Lake can be reached by staying on the right fork at the Deception Pass junction and continuing on for 1.3 kilometres. Just above the inlet to Baker Lake a trail branches to three smaller lakes—Little Baker, Tilted and Brachiopod—about 2.5 kilometres distant.

Camping is permitted at Halfway Hut, Redoubt Lake and Baker Lake, but fires are not allowed.

Skoki Valley Options. The area surrounding Skoki Lodge and Valley also contains many interesting day trips—treks which run at somewhat lower elevations than those near Boulder Pass.

Set between the exotically-named Wall of Jericho and Merlin's Castle, Merlin Lake is one of the little known gems of the Rockies. The high route to the lake starts at the footbridge in front of the lodge. The first kilometre of trail is beautifully designed, constructed by the mountaineer and trail builder Lawrence Grassi. It traverses high onto the side of the Wall of Jericho and then, without ceremony, disappears. Unfortunately Grassi never had an opportunity to complete his work, so the remaining 2.1 kilometres to Merlin are for cairn-followers. The route drops to the shore of Castilleja Lake, then climbs to the steep cliff immediately below Merlin (pick the line of least resistance via the scree chute to the left of the cliff).

A horse trail also traverses the north side of the valley, starting up from the large, open meadow 1.1 kilometres below the lodge. Total distance from the lodge to Merlin is 4.5 kilometres, but the trail is rough in many places. Both routes are for good pathfinders, but the reward is one of the most beautiful lakes in the mountain parks.

The Red Deer Lakes can be reached over good trail that cuts off from the Skoki Valley trail 500 metres before the lodge. The lakes are approximately four kilometres beyond the junction and the campsite there is the only one in the Boulder Pass-Skoki Valley region where open fires are allowed. Travelling eastward from the lakes on the upper Red Deer River, there are several outstanding points of interest including the Natural Bridge, the Drummond Glacier and Douglas Lake (see *Red Deer River* trail).

Other interesting day trips in the Skoki Valley area include the circuit of Fossil Mountain and a jaunt to the Pipestone River on the Little Pipestone trail.

Red Deer River

Wilderness access

Maximum elevation: 2075 metres (6,800 feet)

Minimum elevation: 1770 metres (5,800 feet)

Topo maps: Hector Lake, 82 N/9 East
　　　　　　Barrier Mountain, 82 O/12 West

Point of Departure: Hike the Boulder Pass-Skoki Valley trail to the Red Deer Lakes—the headwaters of the Red Deer River. (See *Boulder Pass-Skoki Valley* trail description.)

*Distance approximate.

The Red Deer Valley is one of the great wilderness valleys in the park, and one of the few untouched by fire in over 100 years. While it provides a main access route to the far eastern wilderness of Banff Park, most backpackers will be content to visit some of the outstanding natural features near the river's headwaters on day hikes and short overnight trips from a base camp at Red Deer Lakes.

Usual access to the Red Deer River is from the west via the Boulder Pass-Skoki Valley trail, the headwaters at Red Deer Lakes being a total of 18 kilometres from the trail head at the Lake Louise ski area. From the Cyclone Warden Cabin at the Red Deer Lakes, the valley trail stays on the north bank of the river all the way to the Cascade Fire Road. The trail is in good shape throughout its length, though some tributary streams could cause problems early in the season.

The Natural Bridge is the first feature of interest in the upper valley. It is situated only five kilometres from Cyclone in a side valley between Oyster Peak and Mount Douglas (the Red Deer River must be crossed to gain access to the valley, but the ford should cause no great difficulties). Just 2.5 kilometres or so beyond the junction to the Natural Bridge the outlet stream from the Drummond Glacier enters from the north—an excellent viewpoint for this extensive body of ice.

Approximately seven kilometres below Cyclone and the Red Deer Lakes camp is the junction to Douglas Lake—a large and beautiful body of water set in yet another side valley beneath Mount Douglas. The lake can be reached by a 2.5 kilometre spur trail, but the ford across the Red Deer can be difficult.

Other landmarks in the lower Red Deer Valley include Horseshoe Lake (Kilometre 14) and the Divide Creek—Scotch Camp Junction (Kilometre 25.5). Fords across the Red Deer at these points are not recommended.

Pipestone River

Wilderness access

Maximum elevation: 2450 metres (8,036 feet)

Minimum elevation: 1555 metres (5,100 feet)

Topo maps: Lake Louise, 82 N/9 West
            Siffleur River, 82 N/16 West

Point of Departure: Hike the Boulder Pass-Skoki Valley trail to the Skoki Valley. Descend the Little Pipestone to its confluence with the Pipestone River. (See *Boulder Pass-Skoki Valley* trail description.)

*Distance approximate.

While the lower Pipestone River is of marginal value for backcountry travel, the upper half of the valley is surprisingly scenic and is emerging as an important access route to some interesting country in the northern Front Ranges of Banff Park.

The actual trail head for the Pipestone is situated on the north side of the Trans-Canada Highway approximately one kilometre west of the entrance to the Lake Louise ski area. While this trail up the lower half of the valley is a well-defined and much-used horse route, it probably should be avoided by all but the most experienced of backpackers since there is a very difficult ford approximately 13 kilometres up valley. Most travellers will want to join the Pipestone trail at the 20 kilometre mark by hiking the route to Skoki Valley and then descending the Little Pipestone.

The trail down the Little Pipestone is quite straightforward and reaches the Pipestone at a warden cabin. You must ford the Pipestone here to continue on up valley—a tricky, thigh-deep crossing. There is a good campsite on the opposite side.

Main objectives for those hiking the upper Pipestone Valley are probably either the Fish Lakes area or Pipestone Pass. (Molar Creek is a long, sloppy slog and has little to recommend it). There are lots of open meadows on the upper Pipestone and many excellent views. The trail is good.

The cutoff up to Fish Lakes is not signed, but there is a good campsite near the junction—an area known as the Singing Meadows. Just beyond, the trail swings to the east side of the Pipestone (either brave the ford or look for fallen trees upstream). The trail finally crosses Pipestone Pass as shown on the topo map and descends into the Siffleur drainage.

Fish Lakes—Molar Pass

Icefields Parkway to North Molar Pass—11.5 kilometres (7.1 miles)

Icefields Parkway to Upper Fish Lake—14.8 kilometres (9.2 miles)

Day trip or backpack

Allow 5-6 hours to Fish Lakes

Elevation gain: 760 metres (2,500 feet)

Maximum elevation: 2590 metres (8,500 feet)

Topo maps: Hector Lake, 82 N/9 West
Hector Lake, 82 N/9 East
(Fish Lakes trail not shown)

Point of Departure: Drive to the Mosquito Creek Campground, 24 kilometres (15.1 miles) north of Lake Louise on the Icefields Parkway. The trail sign is located on the east side of the highway while parking is available just below the bridge on the west side.

0.0—Trail sign (1830 m).

—Gradual uphill with many small side streams.

6.4—Last major stream crossing. Campsite.

6.9—Junction: Molar Pass trail cuts away to the right ascending to the summit in 3 kilometres. North Molar Pass-Fish Lakes trail continues ascent along left side of meadow.

8.0—Trail climbs above trees and levels out into alpine tundra.

8.8—Mosquito Lake.

10.5—Steep climb to North Molar Pass begins.

11.5—North Molar Pass (2590 m).

—Short, steep descent levelling out onto · alpine tundra.

14.8—Upper Fish Lake (2225 m). Campsite.

15.7—Lower Fish Lake.

The region surrounding the Molar Passes contains some of the finest alpine scenery in Banff Park—a land where views are limitless and options for exploration endless. Yet the vast rolling tundra which dominates this area is so fragile and easily damaged that future backcountry use will have to be controlled if the landscape is to survive unimpaired.

The most popular trip in the area is the 15 kilometre backpack over North Molar Pass to the Fish Lakes. Through its first seven kilometres, the trail rises gradually through the open, subalpine forest of the Mosquito Creek drainage then climbs onto the alpine meadowlands leading to North Molar Pass. Travel through the Mosquito Creek valley and the higher alplands is usually quite wet and boggy throughout the summer, and crossing some of the small tributary streams can be tricky (every stream of note is bridged, but expect wet boots anyway).

The alpine meadows below North Molar Pass are exceptionally beautiful—a wildflower garden which is dominated by the showy purple blooms of fleabane throughout late July and early August. Sharp fingers of rock and steep talus slopes form a huge amphitheatre enclosing this treeless terrain. And back to the west, the glacier-clad ramparts of the Mount Hector massif create a spectacular backdrop for tiny Mosquito Lake.

Beyond the ten kilometre mark, the gentle meadows are left behind and the stiff climb to North Molar Pass commences. Views westward from the summit of this narrow notch are extensive, stretching to the mountains of the Bow Valley and beyond. Ahead the trail descends into a more constricted and rolling alpine landscape enclosed by vertical walls and rockslide debris. The sharp summit of

The drop to Upper Fish Lake from North Molar is steep and quick, and the

lake can be seen when only a kilometre or so away cradled in a pretty basin amid open stands of Engelmann spruce and alpine fir. The trail finally reaches the lake's open shoreline and the valley campsite at the 14.8 kilometre mark, a peaceful spot but for the continual cascade of rock falling from rotten cliffs on the opposite shore.

The Upper Fish Lake area is an excellent centre for wandering and exploration. Lower Fish Lake is only a kilometre away, a much smaller body of water fringed by what is possibly the most northerly stand of alpine larch in North America. From the northeast corner of the lower lake, trails drop off into the Pipestone Valley.

Experienced backpackers capable of navigating moderately difficult fords can make a complete circuit to Dolomite Pass. The itinerary for this five-to-seven day trip includes the traverse of Pipestone Pass, a side-trip to Clearwater Pass, the descent of the Siffleur River to its confluence with Dolomite Creek and the ascent of Dolomite Creek to the Dolomite Pass country. (See *Dolomite Pass* trail.)

Because it is one of the highest passes in Banff Park and is situated in a region of heavy snowfall, North Molar is seldom open before late July. Be sure to check out trail conditions with parks' information before planning a trip to Fish Lakes.

Molar Pass. With an early start, day hikes can be made up Mosquito Creek to Molar Pass as well as to Mosquito Lake and the summit of North Molar Pass.

The trail to Molar Pass branches to the right from the more heavily travelled North Molar Pass route at Kilometre 6.9 (this junction has been poorly marked in the past and the trail is faint in its early stages). In another three kilometres the trail climbs out of the trees and onto the crest of the pass.

The alpine meadows on Molar Pass are just as impressive if not as extensive as those beneath North Molar. The pass also offers a much better view of Molar Mountain (3022 m) and the glaciated summits leading southward to the main peak of Mount Hector.

The trail over Molar Pass continues on in a southeasterly direction descending into the Pipestone Valley via Molar Creek—a route which is rough, wet, long, mundane and not recommended.

Helen Lake—Dolomite Pass

Crowfoot Glacier Viewpoint to Helen Lake—6.0 kilometres (3.7 miles)
Crowfoot Glacier Viewpoint to Dolomite Pass—8.9 kilometres (5.0 miles)

Day trip

Allow 3-4 hours to Dolomite Pass

Elevation gain: 575 metres (1,885 feet)
       loss: 127 metres (417 feet)

Maximum elevation: 2500 metres (8,200 feet)

Topo maps: Hector Lake, 82 N/9 West

Point of Departure: Drive the Icefields Parkway to the Crowfoot Glacier Viewpoint, 33.3 kilometres (20.7 miles) north of the Trans-Canada Highway and 7.7 kilometres (4.8 miles) south of Bow Summit. The trail sign and limited parking are on the northeast side of the road, opposite the viewpoint.

0.0—Trail sign (1945 m).

—Moderate climb through subalpine forest.

2.4—Avalanche slope. First good viewpoint.

2.9—Open views for remainder of hike.

3.4—Switchback on southeast end of Cirque Peak ridge. Grade moderates and trail begins contour toward Helen Lake.

4.5—Rockslide.

5.0—Helen Creek crossing.

6.0—Helen Lake (2405 m).

—Steep switchbacks.

6.9—Trail summit on high ridge (2500 m).

—Steep descent.

8.1—Katherine Lake (2373 m).

8.9—Dolomite Pass (2393 m).

Forest, meadow, lake and snow-peak provide a constant change of scene drawing the hiker onward toward Dolomite Pass. In addition to being one of the fine alpine hiking areas in the park, it has, in seasons past, boasted a rather large colony of hoary marmots and the occasional family of golden eagles—living in a state of not-too-peaceful coexistence.

Climbing from the Crowfoot Glacier Viewpoint, the trail traverses the west-facing slopes of the Bow Valley. At the end of three kilometres of steady ascent, it emerges from the forest of Engelmann spruce and alpine fir and onto steep, mountainside meadows. From this vantage point the Bow Valley falls away below with Crowfoot Mountain and Glacier visible to the southwest, Bow Peak (2869 m) next in line to the south, and the sharp peak of Mount Hector (3394 m) to the southeast.

Once the trail finally attains the shoulder of Cirque Peak it switches around 180 degrees and contours into the amphitheatre containing Helen Lake. A few stunted whitebark pine are scattered along the ridge at this switchback, indicators of the upper limits of tree growth.

At Kilometre 4.5 the trail drops around the toe of a relatively recent rockslide. In dipping below this pile of tumbled boulders, the route passes through a lush snowbed plant community filled with the colourful blooms of fleabane, paint-brush, ragwort and valerian in late July and early August. From here the trail climbs above the last trees, remaining above timberline for the duration of the trip to Dolomite Pass.

Helen Lake makes a pleasant resting spot in these harsh alpine surroundings. Near the shore and on the talus slopes above, hoary marmots whistle and romp. This large grey rodent is related to the

Dolomite Pass

eastern woodchuck. Because of a shrill whistle issued as a call of alarm, it is also known as the whistling marmot. The profusion of these chubby inhabitants is probably no small factor in the frequent appearance of golden eagles over this valley.

After a visit with the Helen Lake marmots, the hiker can continue up a steep series of switchbacks to the unnamed ridge which serves as the summit of the hike. At nearly 2500 metres above sea level, this spot provides views down to Katherine Lake and Dolomite Pass and back to a sea of peaks which compose the Waputik Mountains. For most day hikers this windswept vantage point is a good spot to stop and turn for home.

Beyond the ridge, the trail drops nearly 100 vertical metres to the level of Katherine Lake. The lake stretches beneath the castellate cliffs of Dolomite Peak to an opening that serves as a splendid window on the southern half of Banff Park. On a clear day the sharp horn of Mount Assiniboine can be seen nearly 100 kilometres away.

Though the trail is not well-defined beyond the north end of Katherine Lake, it is easy to climb over the spongy tundra to the crest of Dolomite Pass. A small lake near the summit provides an excellent resting spot.

The first reported crossing of the pass was made in 1898 by a party of American mountaineers led by the pioneer guide Ralph Edwards. Searching for the Saskatchewan River, the party mistakenly ascended Dolomite Creek and crossed over Dolomite Pass. The wayward mountaineers named lakes Helen and Katherine for the two daughters of one of their company, while the light grey limestone in the surrounding cliffs reminded them of the Swiss Dolomites.

Helen Creek Trail. Helen Lake and the country beyond can be reached via a trail which ascends directly up the Helen Creek drainage. Starting out from the Helen Creek bridge some 2.8 kilometres south of the Crowfoot Glacier Viewpoint on the Icefields Parkway, this route is often believed to be much shorter than the approach described above. In actuality, it saves only 200 metres to Helen Lake and offers fewer views along the way. It can be used as an optional exit, however, if you have two vehicles at your disposal.

Isabella Lake Option. Experienced backpackers can continue on through Dolomite Pass and descend Dolomite Creek to Isabella Lake—a trail which is much rougher and less defined than the first nine kilometres to the pass. Stay on the true left (west) bank of Dolomite Creek throughout the upper valley, avoiding branch trails which swing across to the right bank. Follow faint trail and cairns beside a waterfall, across a rockslide and down into the forest. A couple of moderately difficult fords must be made

on lower Dolomite Creek before finally reaching Isabella Lake. Total distance to the lake from Dolomite Pass is approximately 15 kilometres.

Of more interest than the rather lacklustre descent to Isabella is an extended trip of five or more days which can be made via Dolomite Creek, the upper Siffleur River, Pipestone Pass, the upper Pipestone River, Fish Lakes, North Molar Pass and Mosquito Creek, emerging on the Icefields Parkway nine kilometres south of the Dolomite Pass trail head. Total distance for this circuit is around 66 kilometres. The trail is well-defined throughout, but a major ford on Dolomite Creek just above its confluence with the Siffleur requires some experience and perseverance. (See *Fish Lakes* trail.)

Hector Lake

Icefields Parkway to Hector Lake—2.1 kilometres (1.3 miles)

Nature hike
Allow 1 hour one way
Elevation loss: 60 metres (200 feet)
Maximum elevation: 1830 metres (6,000 feet)
Topo maps: Hector Lake, 82 N/9 West

Point of Departure: Drive the Icefields Parkway 18.0 kilometres (11.2 miles) north from the Trans Canada Highway. The trail sign is on the west side of the highway just one kilometre beyond the Hector Lake viewpoint.

The Hector Lake trail is a short half-day excursion which is downhill all the way. Yet it is of limited use to casual hikers since a major ford of the Bow River must be made to reach the shore of the lake.

From the sign the trail travels due west to the floor of the Bow Valley through closed forest, reaching the Bow River at the 1.1 kilometre mark. While the ford across the Bow is not particularly difficult at low water, this could be a treacherous crossing whenever water levels are high. The trail picks up again on the opposite side of the river and reaches the shore of Hector Lake in another kilometre of level walking. It emerges at the site of an old cabin camp once operated by the pioneer guide and outfitter Jimmy Simpson.

It would appear that much of the use of this trail comes from fishermen who merely use the first half of the route as access to the river.

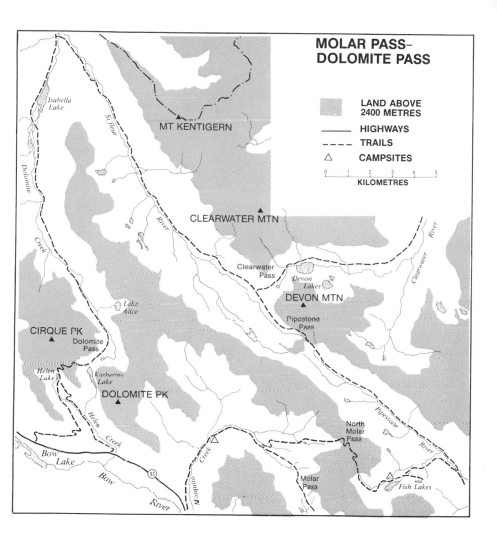

MOLAR PASS–
DOLOMITE PASS

LAND ABOVE
2400 METRES

—— HIGHWAYS

- - - TRAILS

△ CAMPSITES

0 1 2 3 4 5
KILOMETRES

Isabella
Lake

St. fleur

MT KENTIGERN ▲

Dolomite

Creek

River

CLEARWATER MTN ▲

Clearwater
Pass

Devon
Lakes

Lake
Alice

DEVON MTN ▲

Pipestone
Pass

CIRQUE PK ▲
Dolomite
Pass

Helen
Lake

Katherine
Lake

DOLOMITE PK ▲

Helen
Creek

Clearwater
River

Pipestone

North
Molar
Pass

River

Bow
Lake

Bow

93

Mosquito Creek

River

Molar
Pass

Fish Lakes

95

Bow Glacier Falls

Num-ti-jah Lodge to Bow Glacier Falls—4.3 kilometres (2.7 miles)

Half-day trip
Allow 1 - 2 hours to falls
Elevation gain: 150 metres (500 feet)
Maximum elevation: 2100 metres (6,900 feet)
Topo maps: Hector Lake, 82 N/9 West

Point of Departure: Drive to Bow Lake, 36.2 kilometres (22.5 miles) north of the Trans-Canada Highway on the Icefields Parkway. Turn off at Num-ti-jah Lodge and park at the trail head behind the lodge.

0.0—Trail starts behind lodge and angles across willow flats toward lakeshore.

—Trail follows lakeshore for 1.5 kilometres.

2.4—Broad gravel flats.

—Keep right of river as far as the mouth of a small canyon. Trail rises steeply along right edge of canyon (treacherous when wet).

3.2—Natural bridge.

3.4—Viewpoint on moraine.

—Pick route across outwash.

4.3—Bow Glacier Falls.

The Bow Glacier Falls trail presents an interesting half-day walk to the foot of an awesome cliff and waterfall. Featured along the way are the placid waters of Bow Lake, the gravel flats and moraines of the Bow Glacier outwash, and a narrow gorge spanned by a natural bridge.

From Num-ti-jah Lodge the trail leads along the shore of Bow Lake, offering reflected views of Crowfoot Mountain on the opposite side. Ahead the Bow Glacier lies amidst a sea of jagged peaks, the leaning pyramid of Saint Nicholas Peak rising most prominently on its southern edge.

After leaving the lake and travelling over outwash flats, the trail reaches a narrow gorge and begins a steep climb along its rim. Walter Wilcox noted the canyon during his exploration of 1895: "Where the canyon is deepest an immense block of limestone about twenty-five feet long has fallen down, and with either end resting on the canyon walls, it affords a natural bridge over the gloomy chasm. As probably no human being had ever crossed this bridge, we felt a slight hesitation in making the attempt."

Today's route does not cross the bridge, however, but continues upwards along the gorge, emerging onto the crest of a glacial moraine. Here lies the main outwash area for the Bow Glacier with the thundering Bow Glacier Falls beyond—the headwaters of the Bow River and the South Saskatchewan River system.

The base of the waterfall may be reached by picking a route across the 800 metres of gravel outwash (ptarmigan often seen along the way). The falls itself, tumbling through a break in the cliff, is the outlet for a small meltwater lake hidden above at the toe of the Bow Glacier.

Peyto Lake

Peyto Lake Viewpoint to Peyto Lake—2.4 kilometres (1.5 miles)

Half-day trip

Allow 2 hours round trip

Elevation loss: 275 metres (900 feet)

Maximum elevation: 2135 metres (7,000 feet)

Topo maps: Blaeberry River, 82 N/10 East
(trail not shown)

Point of Departure: Drive the Icefields Parkway to Bow Summit, 41.0 kilometres (25.5 miles) north of the Trans-Canada Highway. Follow the spur road which branches west to the Peyto Lake Viewpoint parking area. Walk to the overlook and watch for the trail sign at the uphill end of the guard railing near the forest edge.

Most travellers photograph this well-known lake from the viewpoint high above its turquoise waters, never realizing that a short trail leads from this overlook down to its shore. Others discover the trail and wander blithely downwards, not thinking about the 275 metre 'hole' they are descending into or the heart-pounding climb back to the viewpoint.

The trail from the viewpoint offers a couple of interesting options once the lake is reached, but it is not a trip for idle strollers. From the trail sign, the path dives down into a lush subalpine forest, switchbacking madly to the broad, gravel outwash flats at the head of Peyto Lake. From this point hikers can either roam at their leisure along the lakeshore or head off in the direction of Peyto Glacier to the south. On the latter option, walk across the flats parallel to the lake's main tributary stream to a point about 100 metres left of where the stream cuts through a forested morainal ridge. Find the trail which crosses this ridge, then follow cairns upstream through rocky terrain toward the toe of the glacier. Beware of ever-steepening terrain near the glacier. Anyone travelling onto the ice itself should be experienced, equipped with rope and ice axe and registered out with the Warden Service.

A shorter and less arduous trail leads down to Peyto Lake from the Icefields Parkway just 2.7 kilometres north of Bow Summit. Hikers should park their vehicles at the Peyto Glacier Viewpoint then walk up the highway (south) and cross to the trail sign on the west side of the road near the end of the guard railing. The trail leads down to a pleasant little beach on the east shore of Peyto Lake. Total distance to the lake from the highway is only 1.4 kilometres.

Chephren Lake—Cirque Lake

Waterfowl Lakes Campground to Chephren Lake—4.0 kilometres (2.5 miles)

Waterfowl Lakes Campground to Cirque Lake—4.7 kilometres (2.9 miles)

Half-day trip or day trip
Allow 1-2 hours to Chephren
Elevation gain: 150 metres (500 feet)
Maximum elevation: 1801 metres (5,910 feet)
Topo maps: Mistaya Lake, 82 N/15 East
(trail incorrectly marked)

Point of Departure: Drive to the Waterfowl Lake Campground, 58.1 kilometres (36.1 miles) north of the Trans-Canada Highway on the Icefields Parkway.

0.0—Trail head is located near where the Mistaya River enters the Lower Waterfowl Lake, at the far end of the lakeshore picnic area.

—Trail follows river upstream.

0.5—Bridge crosses Mistaya River.

—Moderate uphill grade.

1.8—Junction. Cirque Lake trail forks sharply to left (2.9 km). Keep right for Chephren Lake.

4.0—Chephren Lake (1713 m).

Chephren Lake. Hidden a short distance from the mainstream of traffic on the Icefields Parkway, beneath the sheer limestone walls of the Great Divide, Chephren Lake offers spectacular scenery and a restful quiet that can be reached with a minimum expenditure of time and energy.

Skirting the Waterfowl Lakes Campground, the trail crosses the Mistaya River and begins the gradual climb to Chephren Lake. The Cirque Lake junction is passed at Kilometre 1.8, and 400 metres later the forest thins, allowing occasional views of Howse Peak and Mount Chephren. Marshy meadows along the way provide prime moose habitat.

Despite its relatively low altitude, Chephren Lake gives the appearance of a higher alpine tarn. Howse Peak, the rugged, glacier-draped mountain which serves as the lake's backdrop, is named for the Hudson's Bay fur trader Joseph Howse, who crossed the Rockies in 1810 (the pass he travelled and which also bears his name lies just west of the peak). Mount Chephren (pronounced kefren) forms the lake's west shore and is named for the second of the three great pyramids of Egypt (its name changed from "Pyramid" in 1918).

Cirque Lake. Certainly no less scenic than its twin sister Chephren, Cirque Lake (1801 m) can be reached by taking the spur trail at Kilometre 1.8. The hike is pleasant, though slightly steeper, following a major stream through open glades and subalpine forest.

By hiking to Chephren in the morning then backtracking to Cirque in the afternoon, both lakes can be visited in one day. Total round trip distance for the twin lake excursion would be 13.8 kilometres.

Chephren Lake and Howse Peak

Sarbach Lookout

Icefields Parkway to Sarbach Lookout—5.2 kilometres (3.2 miles)

Day trip
Allow 2-3 hours to lookout
Elevation gain: 550 metres (1,800 feet)
Maximum elevation: 2075 metres (6,800 feet)
Topo maps: Mistaya Lake, 82 N/15 East
             Mistaya Lake, 82 N/15 West

Point of Departure: The trail head is situated on the west side of the Icefields Parkway 5.3 kilometres (3.3 miles) south of the Saskatchewan River Crossing highway junction and 71.9 kilometres (44.7 miles) north of the Trans-Canada Highway. Watch for a pull-off and trail sign on a long steep grade.

0.0—Trail sign.

—Trail descends on old road bed.

0.3—Mistaya Canyon and bridge. Branch off uphill from road after crossing bridge.

0.5—Junction. Sarbach Lookout trail cuts sharply back to left. Howse Pass trail 20 metres beyond.

—Gradual ascent.

3.1—Grade steepens.

5.2—Sarbach Lookout.

Like many other trails leading to fire lookouts, the Sarbach hike is an arduous uphill grind. Rising through a forest of fir, spruce and lodgepole pine, the trail does not emerge into the open until it reaches the lookout tower. From just above the tower, however, views encompass the confluence of three major rivers and a sea of massive peaks.

After crossing the Mistaya Canyon—a spectacular, potholed gorge that compares with the better-known canyons of Maligne and Marble—the trail begins its climb through the forest. The last two kilometres to the lookout are steep and switchbacking, but the ordeal is nearly over when the fresh cool smell of alpine fir and the bushy, five-needled whitebark pine are encountered—indicators of the upper subalpine forest.

Though trees surround the lookout, views incompassing an arc of 180 degrees may be obtained with a minor amount of scrambling up the mountainside beyond. Looming above the lookout to the east, directly across the Mistaya Valley, is the Mount Murchison massif, its highest summit rising to an elevation of 3333 metres above sea level. Dr. James Hector of the Palliser Expedition named the mountain in 1858 and indicated that the local Indians believed it to be the highest mountain in the Rockies.

Below the lookout to the north lies the junction of three rivers—the Howse and Mistaya feeding the North Saskatchewan which turns and flows eastward through an obvious gap in the mountains to the prairie beyond. The earliest fur traders to cross the main ranges of the Rockies between 1807 and 1810 used the valleys of the North Saskatchewan and the Howse as passages through the range.

Beyond Saskatchewan River Crossing stands Mount Wilson (3261 m), the first in a long line of peaks that stretches away toward the northwest and the headwaters of the North Saskatchewan.

100

Howse Pass

Icefields Parkway to Howse Pass—25.9 kilometres (16.1 miles)

Backpack
Allow 3 or more days
Elevation gain: 60 metres (200 feet)
Maximum elevation: 1585 metres (5,200 feet)
Topo maps: Mistaya Lake, 82 N/15 East
　　　　　　Mistaya Lake, 82 N/15 West

Point of Departure: The trail head is situated on the west side of the Icefields Parkway 5.3 kilometres (3.3 miles) south of the Saskatchewan River Crossing highway junction and 71.9 kilometres (44.7 miles) north of the Trans-Canada Highway. Watch for a pull-off and trail sign on a long steep grade.

0.0—Trail sign.

0.3—Mistaya Canyon and bridge.

0.5—Junction. Sarbach Lookout trail branches sharply to left. Howse Pass straight ahead.

　—Gradual descent through forest

4.0　Junction. Horse trail from Saskatchewan River Crossing joins from right.

4.2—Howse River flats.

　—Gentle rolling to flat walking.

7.7—Campsite and stream crossing.

14.0—Trail crosses broad dryas flats.

15.5—Trail climbs back into forest and away from river.

　—Boggy, rooty and rolling.

19.0—Junction. Spur trail to warden cabin and campsite (500 metres to right) and Lagoon Lake. Howse Pass straight ahead.

23.0—Junction. Forbes Brook trail to Freshfield Glacier branches right. Howse Pass to left. Confluence of Conway Creek and major tributary.

25.9—Howse Pass (1527 m).

The Howse River trail is significant in that it leads to a pass which served as the first regular fur trade route across the Rocky Mountains and it ascends a major wild valley which, in recent years, has seen the re-establishment of the grey wolf. Yet many hikers may find this 26 kilometre hike up a broad low-lying valley somewhat tedious.

For much of the way up the Howse, the trail swings in and out of a dense spruce forest with the river never more than 400 metres distant to the hiker's right. At Kilometre 9.0 the trail dips down to the edge of the river to afford an excellent view across-valley to a notch revealing the tumbled blue glaciers of the Lyell Icefield. It was just a short distance upstream from this viewpoint that David Thompson and his party of fur traders camped in June, 1807, "impatiently waiting the melting of the Snows" on Howse Pass.

After one more visit to the broad river flats at Kilometre 14.0, the trail climbs into the forest, never to see the light of day again—at least until the last two kilometres leading to the pass. The way is rough and rooty and rather depressing. The large marshy meadow surrounding the warden's cabin and campsite near Lagoon Lake does offer some respite, however, and is a good base from which to explore the upper valley.

While more open than much of the upper valley, views from the pass are rather unexceptional as they are limited by the walls of Mount Conway to the south and Howse Peak to the north. A fair trail is reported to descend the western slope of Howse Pass following the upper reaches of the Blaeberry for fifteen kilometres or so into British Columbia where it runs into a network of logging roads leading down to the Columbia River and the Trans-Canada Highway just north of Golden.

Glacier Lake

Day trip
Allow 3 hours one way
Elevation gain: 215 metres (700 feet)
Maximum elevation: 1645 metres (5,400 feet)
Topo maps: Mistaya Lake, 82 N/15 West

Point of Departure: The parking area for the trail is situated on the west side of the Icefields Parkway 1.1 kilometres (0.7 mile) north of the Saskatchewan River Crossing highway junction. Parking is well off the highway on the edge of an old roadside gravel pit.

0.0—Trail sign.

1.1—North Saskatchewan River. Crossed via a wooden footbridge.

2.3—Viewpoint overlooking the Howse River.

8.9—Eastern end of Glacier Lake.

9.2—Campsite.

12.6—Western end of Glacier Lake.

14.4—Trail becomes indistinct along glacial outwash stream.

In June of 1807, David Thompson, Canada's great pioneer surveyor and fur trader, and a group of companions entered the Howse River valley in hopes of finding a pass through the Rocky Mountains. Thompson discovered a good sized lake not far from one of his camps and marvelled that "all the Mountains in sight from the end of the Lake are seemingly of Ice." The body of water was named Glacier Lake 51 years later when Dr. James Hector, a member of another important exploratory expedition, John Palliser's, camped by the lake in the late fall of 1858.

The trail begins as an access road running to the southwest through a relatively recent burn with the expected growth of young lodgepole pine (also known as 'fire pine' since a temperature of around 45° Celsius is required for the tree's cones to release their seeds, and since the species thrives in the open environment created by a burn). The burn and the young forest allow good viewing of the surrounding terrain.

From the North Saskatchewan River bridge (1.1 kilometres) it is possible to study a total of nine peaks. Starting with the predominant peak to the southeast, they are Mount Murchison, Mount Chephren, Mount Sarbach, Mount Outram, Sullivan Peak, Survey Peak, Mount Erasmus, Mount Amery and, to the north, Mount Wilson. The main mass of rock in the mountains is Cambrian and Ordovician limestone and quartzite.

At the 2.3 kilometre mark the trail reaches the edge of a low bluff overlooking the Howse River—the valley leading to the historic Howse Pass. The trail to Glacier Lake, however, stays to the northwest side of the river and eventually cuts inland from the Howse. Beyond the bluff the trail runs through alternate patches of burn and mature forest with the burn eventually yielding to the

102

Glacier Lake

canopy of spruce and pine as the trail progresses.

Somewhat over six kilometres from the trail head the hiker attains maximum elevation (approximately 1645 metres); the remaining 2.4 kilometres descend rather steeply to the lake, which lies about 1435 metres above sea level.

The lake is one of the larger ones in Banff Park, somewhat over three kilometres long and nearly a kilometre wide. It is fed by the melting snow and ice of Mounts Outram, Lyell and Erasmus. The major tributary is the Glacier River, which the more adventuresome hiker can follow for some four kilometres beyond the western end of the lake toward the Southeast Lyell Glacier. However, beyond the end of Glacier Lake the trail soon becomes indistinct among the meanders and shifting gravels of the outwash stream.

A primitive campsite at Kilometre 9.2 on the shore of Glacier Lake provides a good springboard for backpackers wishing to spend a night in the area and do some exploring in the upper end of the valley.

Sunset Pass—Pinto Lake

Icefields Parkway to Sunset Lookout—4.5 kilometres (2.8 miles)
Icefields Parkway to Pinto Lake—13.7 kilometres (8.5 miles)

Day trip or backpack
Allow 3-4 hours to Sunset Pass
Elevation gain: 700 metres (2,300 feet)
Maximum elevation: 2165 metres (7,100 feet)
Topo maps: Cline River, 83 C/2 West

Point of Departure: Drive to Norman Creek, 16.9 kilometres (10.5 miles) north of the Saskatchewan River Crossing highway junction and 29.0 kilometres (18.0 miles) south of Sunwapta Pass on the Icefields Parkway. Watch for the trail sign on the east side of the highway just north of the creek.

0.0—Trail sign at the edge of the forest.

—Moderate uphill grade.

0.6—Grade becomes steep.

1.0—Norman Creek gorge viewpoint.

—Steady uphill with switchbacks.

2.9—Junction. Straight ahead to Sunset Pass and Pinto Lake. Left to Sunset Lookout (1.6 km).

4.0—Trail levels out. Open meadowland.

8.2—Sunset Pass. Park boundary.

—Steep descent.

13.7—Pinto Lake.

Located in the northern region of Banff Park, the Sunset Pass trail offers several exceptional, although arduous, hiking options. A steep walk of slightly less than five kilometres ascends to the Sunset Fire Lookout, where views stretch across the valleys of the North Saskatchewan and the Alexandra. The main trail climbs into the extensive meadowlands of Sunset Pass, beneath the cliffs of Mount Coleman, and eventually drops down to Pinto Lake on the edge of the White Goat Wilderness Area.

Sunset Lookout. As a day hike Sunset Lookout is the best choice. While the entire hike is steep, enclosed in forest and rather grim, the views at the lookout are worth the effort.

The fire lookout, which has not been manned in recent years, is a small white building perched precariously atop a sheer cliff. From this vantage point it is more than 450 vertical metres to the valley floor and the Icefields Parkway. Immediately across the valley to the south is Mount Amery (3329 m), while Mount Saskatchewan (3342 m) rises to the west.

The Alexandra River (from the west) and the North Saskatchewan River (from the north) meet directly beneath the lookout. Their waters, heavily laden with outwash from the Columbia Icefield, spread rock waste over the valley floor, creating gravel flats and a braided stream pattern.

The trail to the lookout is totally devoid of water, so remember to pack enough to quench your thirst for the day.

Sunset Pass. Most hikers prefer taking the Sunset Pass trip in conjunction with an overnight stay at Pinto Lake. Day hikers, however, may view this beautiful lake and the wild Cline River drainage from the lofty viewpoint just beyond the pass.

Sunset Pass

From the lookout trail junction, the Sunset Pass route climbs at a more moderate grade for another kilometre, emerging into the flat open meadowland which extends unbroken for over four kilometres to the park boundary. Mount Coleman, its nearly horizontal strata set within the axis of the Castle Mountain Syncline, stands on the left side of the meadow, while three lesser peaks in the 2800 metre range dominate the right. The massive summits of Mount Amery and Mount Saskatchewan are visible back to the west.

The park boundary is reached in an open subalpine area at Kilometre 8.2. Outstanding views open to Pinto Lake and the Cline Valley a kilometre beyond. Backpackers may continue down the deceptively long and steep 5.5 kilometres to spend the night at the lake.

Many of the features along the Sunset Pass route commemorate the first visitor to the area—A.P. Coleman, geologist and explorer, who travelled through in 1893. Mount Coleman was named in his honour in 1903 and Pinto Lake immortalizes one of the expedition's more troublesome packhorses.

From Pinto Lake two extended wilderness trips are available to backpackers willing to arrange transportation. A very straightforward 30 kilometre descent of the Cline Valley can be made by crossing to the south bank of the river just below the lake and following the horse trail to its junction with the David Thompson Highway. Another trail runs up Cataract Brook (on the east bank) to the foot of Cataract Pass, and while no trail presently exists over Cataract, experienced wilderness travellers armed with topo maps can easily make their own route through the treeless country to Nigel Pass—a total distance from Pinto Lake of approximately 26 kilometres.

Castleguard Meadows

Icefields Parkway to Castleguard Meadows—35 kilometres (22 miles)*

Wilderness access
Allow 1½ days to meadows
Elevation gain: 640 metres (2,100 feet)
Maximum elevation: 2135 metres (7,000 feet)
Topo maps: Cline River, 83 C/2 West
      Columbia Icefield, 83 C/3
      (last 24 kms not shown)

Point of Departure: The trail begins at a bridge across the North Saskatchewan River, 24.6 kilometres (15.3 miles) north of the Saskatchewan River Crossing highway junction. The bridge lies to the west and below the Icefields Parkway and is not directly visible from the road. (A short section of access road leads down to the bridge from a highway pulloff.)

*distances are approximate

Remote and rugged, the Castleguard Meadows lie high in the far northwestern corner of Banff Park. Bordering the southern reaches of the Columbia Icefield, the meadows offered early explorers and climbers the quickest access to the summits of the Columbia Icefield region.

The route to the meadows combines trails along both the Alexandra and Castleguard Rivers and represents a long hard slog, first up 22 kilometres of fire road along the north bank of the Alexandra to its confluence with the Castleguard, and then up some ten kilometres of rock and root-filled trail along the northeast bank of the Castleguard, topped off by a final three kilometres of steep climbing to the southern end of the meadows (and the only campsite) at 2100 metres. A bad wading of the Castleguard just below Castleguard Falls can be thigh deep and hard rolling in the early season and should discourage all but the very hardiest and experienced hikers. A map and compass will be useful on the trip.

An alternate alpinist's route to the meadows lies up the tongue of the Saskatchewan Glacier and thence into the northern end of the meadows. It is a shorter (13 kilometres) and more direct route but involves experience in glacier travel and a climbing permit.

Thompson Pass Option. The route to Watchman Lake, Cinema Lake and Thompson Pass begins on the southwest bank of the Castleguard just above Castleguard Falls and involves a full ford of the Castleguard, a major undertaking for a person on foot. The trail is rough but passable.

Parker's Ridge

Icefields Parkway to Glacier Viewpoint—2.4 kilometres (1.5 miles)

Half-day trip
Allow 45 minutes to viewpoint
Elevation gain: 275 metres (900 feet)
Maximum elevation: 2270 metres (7,450 feet)
Topo maps: Columbia Icefield, 83 C/3
    (trail not shown)

Point of Departure: Drive to the roadside parking .
area and sign, 4.2 kilometres (2.6 miles) south of
Sunwapta Pass and 41.7 kilometres (25.9 miles)
north of the Saskatchewan River Crossing
highway junction on the Icefields Parkway.

0.0—Trail sign.

    —Steady climb through scattered trees and
    along alpine slopes.

1.9—Crest of Parker's Ridge.

2.4—Saskatchewan Glacier Viewpoint.

This short hike is one of the few in the mountain parks which runs its total distance almost entirely within the alpine life zone. Starting from the roadside parking area the Parker's Ridge trail winds its way up and over a treeless windswept ridge—an area inhabited by mountain goats and supporting limited plant life of stunted willows, a few dwarfed woody plants, mosses, heather and several species of tiny alpine wildflowers. On the opposite side of the ridge and visible from the trail terminus lies the massive, 12 kilometre-long tongue of the Saskatchewan Glacier.

The lower reaches of the trail travel through the uppermost limits of the subalpine forest zone, where open meadowland and scattered stands of alpine fir prevail. Approximately halfway up the north-facing slope the trail passes above timberline. Here stunted fir scatter out into the low, clinging ground cover of alpine tundra at an elevation near 2100 metres.

After crossing the summit of the ridge, the trail gradually descends to the Saskatchewan Glacier viewpoint. Here the hiker has a panoramic view of the uppermost limits of the North Saskatchewan River valley, dominated by the Saskatchewan Glacier—a spur of ice flowing down from the continental divide and the Columbia Icefield.

While returning from the ridge summit, please heed the signs along the trail which discourage shortcutting. One would do well to consider the harshness of this climate and realize that these plants are surviving in an area where summer may be measured in days or a few short weeks. This trail is heavily used, and the damage done by less considerate hikers is obvious and will remain so for many decades to come.

Nigel Pass

Day trip

Allow 2 hours one way

Elevation gain: 275 metres (900 feet)

Maximum elevation: 2202 metres (7,225 feet)

Topo maps: Columbia Icefield, 83 C/3
(trail not shown)

Point of Departure: Drive the Icefields Parkway to the southern end of the old Camp Parker access road (an abandoned segment of the Banff-Jasper Highway), 8 kilometres (5 miles) south of the Banff-Jasper boundary at Sunwapta Pass. This gravel road branches down toward Nigel Creek from the northeast side of the highway and is closed by an access gate 100 metres inside the entrance. Park above the gate and walk the road for approximately 1.5 kilometres to Camp Parker—site of a small warden cabin and corral. The trail sign is on the edge of the forest to the right.

0.0—Camp Parker. Cabin and corral.

—Nigel Pass trail cuts north from fire road.

0.5—Nigel Creek bridge.

—After crossing the creek, keep on the trail which rises on its east bank.

3.1—Major rockslide above the trail.

5.2—Steady uphill for remainder of the hike.

6.1—Nigel Pass (2202 m) and park boundary.

6.4—Brazeau River south fork and viewpoint.

Nigel Pass is an excellent choice for anyone travelling in the Columbia Icefield vicinity and who would like to spend a day wandering through open subalpine meadows. Not only does the hike provide views of some of the more rugged peaks on the northeast edge of the Icefield and a glimpse into the remote southern wilderness of Jasper Park, but it does so with a minimal amount of effort, climbing less than 300 vertical metres in more than seven kilometres of travel.

After a brief walk on the old Banff-Jasper Highway to Camp Parker, the trail is gained and followed northward to a bridge on Nigel Creek. After the crossing, the route ascends to the east side of the creek where the country is gentle and open. Throughout this section of the valley there are good views back to Parker's Ridge and the 'horn' sub-peak of Mount Athabasca. The path runs straight and Nigel Pass is seldom out of sight ahead.

The trail climbs steadily for the last kilometre to the pass, levelling out where a cairn marks the boundary between Banff and Jasper parks. Forest cover is very sparse at the elevation of the pass, indicating the proximity of timberline. Back down the valley to the south, the ice-clad summit of Mount Saskatchewan (3342 m) is visible beyond Parker's Ridge. To the north the trail drops into the wild Brazeau River valley and the maze of peaks that comprise the southern edge of Jasper Park.

Directly west of the pass, rising above a large cirque, is Nigel Peak (3211 m), named in 1898 by the British mountaineers Hugh Stutfield and Norman Collie for their guide Nigel Vavasour. It was this expedition which discovered the Columbia Icefield.

By continuing beyond the pass and making a short descent of less than 500 metres, the hiker can cross the south fork of the Brazeau River to an open talus

The Parker's Ridge environs as viewed from Nigel Pass

slope where there are exceptional views down the main Brazeau Valley and back to the north side of Nigel Pass—a fine rock wall featuring several small waterfalls.

Lying some six kilometres southeast of Nigel Pass are the headwaters of the Brazeau River. While no defined trail leads in this direction, energetic explorers with a topographic map can strike out from the summit of the pass and pick a route through the open country to the foot of Cataract Pass—a fine area for wandering away an afternoon.

Cataract Pass Option. Strong, experienced backpackers can make an interesting trip from Nigel Pass to Pinto Lake via Cataract Pass. Follow up to the headwaters of the Brazeau River, cross Cataract Pass (2515 m) and descend Cataract Creek (trail picks up on the east side) to its junction with the Cline River just below Pinto Lake. This is a trip best reserved until late in the year since snowbanks often cover the very steep approaches to Cataract Pass into August. The distance from Nigel Pass to Pinto Lake is about 26 kilometres.

The Front Ranges

While Banff boasts more kilometres of trail and heavier backcountry visitation than any other park in the Canadian Rockies, one section of the park receives relatively light travel—that rather large territory to the north and east of the Trans-Canada Highway contained within the steeply tilted limestone mountains of the Front Ranges. This section of park encompasses an area of more than 2,000 square kilometres and can be considered a true wilderness in every sense of the word.

There are two main reasons why this part of Banff Park is seldom visited: it is so vast and remote that anyone wishing to penetrate into the heart of the region must plan a trip of a week or more; and many of the more interesting trails are rendered difficult and dangerous by unbridged streams and rivers.

Many backpackers would undoubtedly like to see this country "opened up"—to have trails upgraded and streams bridged. Yet there is a strong body of local opinion against any trail improvement in Banff's eastern wilderness, opinion based on the knowledge that this is one of the last strongholds of the grizzly bear in the southern Canadian Rockies. Considering the relatively high grizzly population, increased use of this area could only lead to bear-human conflicts—confrontations which might see some depletions in both the hiker and grizzly populations. As outdoorsman and naturalist Andy Russell has noted, "we have plenty of hikers, but not many grizzlies."

In writing this section, we would like to opt for the side of the grizzly. In the following chapter we provide a few abbreviated notes on the trails which should serve the more adventurous backpacker in good stead. It is our hope, however, that this section of the park will remain the domain of a few seasoned hikers, a controlled number of horseback parties and the grizzly bear.

One final note: with few exceptions, travel in this region of the park is best reserved until late in the season, i.e., September and October, since unbridged rivers are more easily crossed at that time.

Cascade Fire Road—72 kilometres (45 miles). This well-graded dirt road provides one of the primary means of access to the Front Ranges of Banff Park. Though a fire road does not yield the most aesthetic of hiking experiences, it is the one route in the eastern wilderness which presently guarantees the backpacker dry feet and a well-defined path.

Running north from the Minnewanka Road, just a kilometre west of Lake Minnewanka, the road bisects the Front Ranges district. It follows the Cascade River for nearly 25 kilometres, crosses Wigmore Summit, descends to the Panther River crossing, climbs again to Snow Creek Summit (2238 m) and finally joins the Red Deer River for the remainder of its journey to the park's east boundary. In addition to a half-dozen short side trips to alpine lakes in the vicinity of Wigmore and Snow Creek Summits, a number of major access trails branch from the fire road throughout its length.

Topo maps: Banff, 82 0/4 East; Mount Eisenhower, 82 0/5 East; Barrier Mountain, 82 0/12 East and West.

Dormer Pass—34 kilometres (21 miles). A major wilderness access trail that branches from the Cascade Fire Road 15 kilometres north of the Minnewanka Road (1.5 kilometres north of the Stoney Creek Warden Station). The main trail travels up Stoney Creek in a northerly direction, crosses Dormer Pass (2370 m) and descends the Dormer River to the eastern boundary of the park. The trail continues into the Bow River Provincial Forest as far as the Corners Cabin, the traditional wintering ranch for park outfitter's horses.

Thanks to heavy horse travel, the trail is well-defined its entire length, but major

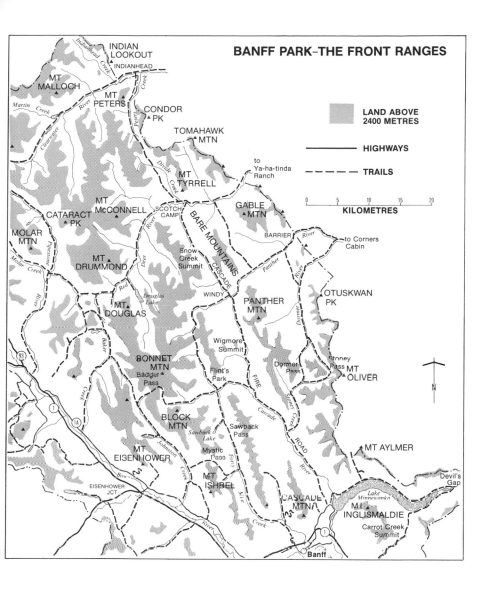

BANFF PARK–THE FRONT RANGES

INDIAN LOOKOUT

INDIANHEAD

MT MALLOCH

MT PETERS

CONDOR PK

TOMAHAWK MTN

to Ya-ha-tinda Ranch

MT TYRRELL

MT McCONNELL

SCOTCH CAMP

GABLE MTN

BARE MOUNTAINS

BARRIER

to Corners Cabin

CATARACT PK

MOLAR MTN

Snow Creek Summit

WINDY

OTUSKWAN PK

MT DRUMMOND

Douglas Lake

PANTHER MTN

MT DOUGLAS

Wigmore Summit

Dormer Pass

Stoney Pass

MT OLIVER

BONNET MTN

Badger Pass

Flint's Park

FIRE

BLOCK MTN

Sawback Lake

Sawback Pass

MT EISENHOWER

Johnston Creek

Mystic Pass

CASCADE

ROAD

MT AYLMER

Devil's Gap

EISENHOWER JCT

MT ISHBEL

Lake Minnewanka

CASCADE MTN

MT INGLISMALDIE

Carrot Creek Summit

Banff

LAND ABOVE 2400 METRES

HIGHWAYS

TRAILS

0 5 10 15 20
KILOMETRES

N

Indianhead Creek

Martin Creek

Clearwater River

Peters Creek

Divide Creek

River

Deer

Red

Baker Creek

Preston

Molar Creek

River

Panther

River

Dormer

River

Stoney Creek

Cascade

Bow River

Mile Creek

111

fords on Stoney Creek make the trip dangerous to early season backpackers (the first crossing has already claimed one life). As a result, trips into this area should be scheduled for late in the summer.

Another branch trail loops eastward from the Dormer route near the 11 kilometre mark, travels over Stoney Pass (the true headwaters of the Dormer River and Stoney Creek) and finally rejoins the main trail near the Dormer Warden Cabin about seven kilometres north of Dormer Pass. While the trail is reported as faint to nonexistent on Stoney Pass, the route should be obvious to anyone carrying topographic maps. Total distance for the optional loop is about 14 kilometres.

Yet another spur cuts north from the Dormer Pass trail some six kilometres west of the park boundary. Running along the western edge of Dormer Mountain for eight kilometres, this trail connects into the Panther River trail. The route sees regular horse use, but it is reported to be very boggy and sloppy through the narrow gorge just south of the Panther Valley. It also leads foot-travellers to problems on the Panther (see *Panther River*).

Topo maps: Mount Eisenhower, 82 0/5 East and Barrier Mountain, 82 0/12 East.

Flint's Park—8 kilometres (5 miles).

A short spur trail (restored fire road) cuts west from the Cascade Fire Road at Kilometre 25 and runs to a campsite and trail junction in the heart of the Flint's Park Valley. The trail is good—heavily used by horses—and there are three interesting options which branch south, west and north from the valley.

Climbing south from the Flint's Park trail junction, the Sawback Creek trail leads to Sawback Lake (7 kilometres) and Forty Mile Summit (8 kilometres). While the trail follows through an old burn for much of its distance, tracks to both the lake and pass are reported in good condition. South of Forty Mile Summit backpackers may continue down Forty Mile Creek to Mount Norquay or cross

over Mystic Summit into the Johnston's Creek drainage.

West from the trail fork the main valley route continues up the west fork of the Cascade, crosses Badger Pass (2539 m) and eventually joins up with the Johnston's Valley trail just south of Pulsatilla Pass. Total distance from Flint's Park to Johnston's Creek is around 19 kilometres. Again, the trail is reported to be in good shape.

Running north from the Flint's Park junction, up the north fork of the Cascade River, is another good trail which leads over a 2425 metre pass to the Panther River headwaters and then down the Panther to the Cascade Fire Road at Windy. The first three kilometres of travel is over an old logging road and the rest of the journey follows well-travelled horse trail. Total distance from Flint's Park to the Windy Warden Cabin is near 25 kilometres.

While all of these routes provide some of the best foot trail and scenery to be found in the Front Ranges, they also run through traditional grizzly territory. Furthermore, in recent years, Flint's Park has developed as a major centre for horseback outfitter's camps.

Topo maps: Mount Eisenhower, 82 0/5 East and West; Barrier Mountain, 82 0/12 East and West.

Panther River—16 kilometres (10 miles).

The horse trail down the lower Panther River cuts east from the Cascade Fire Road at the Windy Warden Cabin—approximately 45 kilometres north of the Minnewanka Road. The trail cuts through the Bare Range and follows the river to the park's east boundary. Three kilometres or so beyond the boundary, the trail joins a seismic road which leads into the Bow River Provincial Forest road network.

In addition to route-finding problems near the park boundary, difficult fords on the Panther make this a dangerous route for foot travellers through much of the summer. While crossing on the eastern three-quarters of the trail can be avoided by staying on the north side of the river, the fords in the Bare Range gorge are reported as difficult to avoid.

Six kilometres east of Windy, a 15 kilometre shortcut to the Red Deer Valley branches north from the Panther River trail. After crossing an open plateau between the Bare Range and Gable Mountain, it eventually connects in with the Cascade Fire Road just seven kilometres west of the park boundary, opposite Tyrrell Creek. The trail is obvious throughout most of its length and is considered excellent for hikers, yet there are fords to be contended with both on the Panther and Red Deer Rivers.

Topo maps: Barrier Mountain, 82 0/12 East and West.

Red Deer River—27 kilometres (17 miles). A major access route into the Front Ranges from the Lake Louise district. The trail reaches the Cascade Fire Road near Kilometre 63. (See *Red Deer River.*)

Divide Creek-Peter's Creek—26 kilometres (16 miles). Branching north from the Red Deer River trail less than two kilometres west of the Cascade Fire Road, this horse trail serves as the main connecting link between the Red Deer Valley and the Clearwater River to the north.

While the old Peter's Creek trail is in rough condition, a better route is reported to exist along the edge of the provincial forest to the east. The trail up Divide Creek is in reasonable condition and well-defined. (The telephone line marked on the topographic maps has been removed).

Topo maps: Barrier Mountain, 82 0/12 West and Scalp Creek, 82 0/13 West.

Clearwater River—32 kilometres (20 miles). The only major trail in the Front Ranges region which doesn't connect directly with the Cascade Fire Road, this is a backcountry segment servicing the remote Clearwater Valley in the park's far northeast corner. Main routes of access to the Clearwater Valley are from the Cascade Fire Road via Divide Creek and Peter's Creek, over Clearwater Pass from the Pipestone-Siffleur country, and via roads and trails in the Clearwater and Bow River Provincial Forests (fording problems are reported on the latter routes).

The Clearwater River trail, as it exists within Banff Park, runs along the north side of the river from the east park boundary (near the junction with the Peter's Creek trail) to Clearwater Pass. While the trail has been hiked successfully by experienced backpackers late in the season (September and October), some fords can cause problems earlier in the year, particularly at Martin Creek.

A spur route branches north from the Clearwater River trail approximately three kilometres west of the Indianhead Warden Cabin. This trail works its way northward and reaches Indianhead Creek five kilometres or so further along. It finally crosses over the park boundary and drops into the Clearwater Provincial Forest near the headwaters of the Ram River and Whiterabbit Creek. Conditions north of the park are unknown.

Topo maps: Scalp Creek, 82 0/13 West; Siffleur River, 82 N/16 East; and Hector Lake, 82 N/9 East and West.

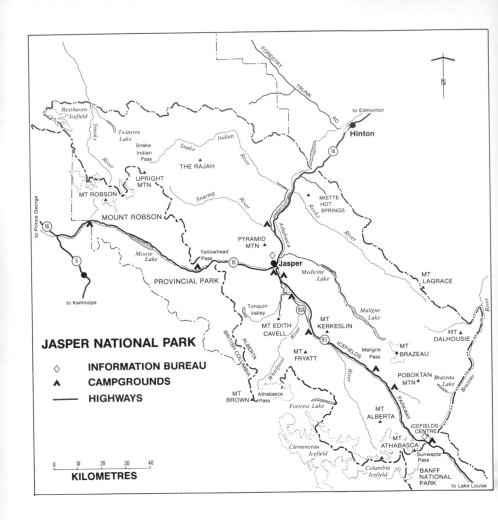

JASPER NATIONAL PARK

◊   **INFORMATION BUREAU**

▲   **CAMPGROUNDS**

—   **HIGHWAYS**

0   10   20   30   40

KILOMETRES

Jasper National Park

With an area of 10,878 square kilometres, Jasper is the largest of Canada's Rocky Mountain national parks. Lying along the eastern slope of the Rockies in western Alberta, the park is bordered on the west by the continental divide and Mount Robson Provincial Park, while to the south it shares a common boundary with Banff National Park. Access to the park is gained from the south via the Icefields Parkway (beginning just west of Lake Louise on the Trans-Canada Highway) and from the west and east via the Yellowhead Highway, running between Edmonton, Alberta and Kamloops, British Columbia.

Jasper contains close to 1,000 kilometres of trail, many of which run through areas of great historical significance (dating back to the early days of the fur trade) and always through some of the most colourful terrain in the Canadian Rockies. Despite a variety of day and half-day trips, such as those radiating from Jasper townsite, the park is known primarily as a backpacker's reserve, and boasts an extaordinarily well-developed and defined system of backcountry trails. Routes such as the North and South Boundary trails offer solitary rambles of over 160 kilometres each, while shorter trail segments such as Jonas Pass, Maligne Pass and the popular Skyline Trail can be linked together to form hikes ranging from three to nine days duration. Other areas, notably the Tonquin Valley and the meadows above Fryatt Creek, offer 'objective' hikes where a base camp can be established for further day hike exploration.

Because of the popularity of Jasper as a hiker's park, and because of the environmental fragility of many of the popular hiking areas, park officials have set a summer use quota for each of the park's trails, and anyone planning an overnight trip in Jasper must obtain a backcountry permit. The quota-permit system helps regulate the amount of use any given trail receives, an important and necessary safeguard. Quotas in popular areas tend to fill rapidly during the months of July and August, and hikers should come to the park with several options in mind. Restrictions concerning open wood fires also apply in certain areas, and hikers should check with park information people concerning the possibility of fires at their destination. The use of small camp stoves is encouraged. Permits and trail information can be obtained year round from the information bureau in Jasper townsite and at the Icefields Centre during the summer months.

The town of Jasper provides the full gamut of visitors' services, ranging from motels, gas stations and grocery stores to hiking and climbing specialty shops.

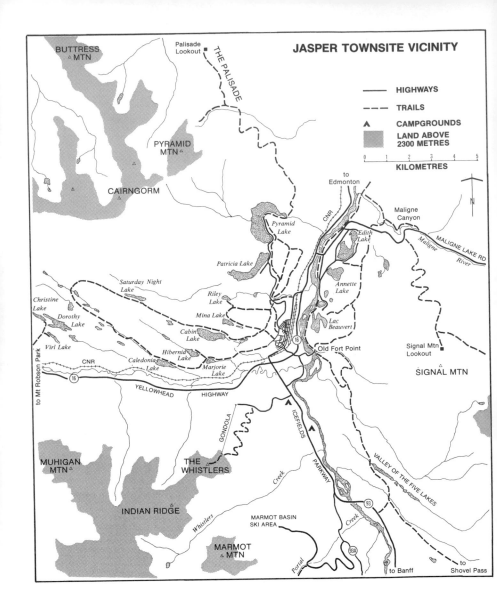

JASPER TOWNSITE VICINITY

HIGHWAYS
TRAILS
CAMPGROUNDS
LAND ABOVE
2300 METRES

0 1 2 3 4 5
KILOMETRES

N

BUTTRESS
MTN

Palisade
Lookout

THE PALISADE

PYRAMID
MTN

CAIRNGORM

to
Edmonton

CNR

Maligne
Canyon

Edith
Lake

MALIGNE LAKE RD

Maligne
River

Pyramid
Lake

Patricia Lake

Christine
Lake

Saturday Night
Lake

Riley
Lake

Annette
Lake

Dorothy
Lake

Mina Lake

Lac
Beauvert

Virl Lake

Cabin
Lake

16

Signal Mtn
Lookout

CNR

Hibernia
Lake

Old Fort Point

SIGNAL MTN

to Mt Robson Park

16

Caledonia
Lake

Marjorie
Lake

YELLOWHEAD HIGHWAY

GONDOLA

ICEFIELDS

PARKWAY

Creek

VALLEY OF THE FIVE LAKES

MUHIGAN
MTN

THE
WHISTLERS

Whistlers

INDIAN RIDGE

MARMOT BASIN
SKI AREA

Creek

93

MARMOT
MTN

Portal

93A

to Banff

to
Shovel Pass

Jasper Townsite Nature Trails

There are a number of trails in the Jasper townsite vicinity that provide an interesting array of hiking options for casual day hikers and park visitors restricted by time or limited to the immediate townsite area by lack of transportation. Most of the trails serve as access to a number of small lakes that lie to the north and west of the town and nearly all offer pleasant outings of the nature hike variety. Since most of the trails intersect, it is possible to tailor-fit hikes to the abilities and time available of nearly any party. Listed below are some of the popular excursions, most consisting of loop trips visiting two or more lakes. More information on the trails can be obtained from the park information office. *Topo maps: Jasper, D/16 East.*

Mina–Riley Lake Loop

9.2 kilometres (5.7 miles)

The trail to Mina and Riley Lakes offers an easy nature hike through a varied forest of lodgepole pine, spruce, aspen, cottonwood and Douglas fir. Though the two lakes receive heavy use, they manage to retain a certain serene charm.

The trail begins at the western edge of town on Pyramid Road (a sign between Maligne and Miette Avenues indicates the trail head). After crossing Cabin Lake Road 800 metres from the trail head, the path continues straight on to Mina Lake at Kilometre 2.0. The junction to Riley Lake lies 1.5 kilometres beyond Mina and an 800 metre spur trail descends to the lakeshore. After visiting Riley, the hiker returns to the Cabin Lake Road and follows it to the right. It is a little over a kilometre back to the original Cabin Lake Road crossing.

Marjorie, Hibernia and Caledonia Lakes

4.2 kilometres (2.6 miles)

A forest-enclosed trail to three peaceful lakes offers a pleasant half-day diversion for those staying in Jasper townsite. The lakes, however, are popular fishing spots and unfortunately show signs of heavy use.

The trail originates just beyond the Jasper trailer park at the west edge of town. A sign to the right of the road indicates the trail head. The trail grade is gentle throughout, penetrating a forest of lodgepole pine, aspen and spruce. Between the warden station and Marjorie Lake the path follows a low ridge, providing occasional views of the Miette and Athabasca valleys. The trail branches at the far end of Marjorie Lake, the right fork climbing to Hibernia Lake in 400 metres, the left travelling 1.6 kilometres farther to Caledonia Lake.

Saturday Night Loop

32.0 kilometres (20 miles)

The Saturday Night Loop provides a long day or overnight trip working out around a number of the small lakes in the hill country west of Jasper townsite.

From the trail sign on the Pyramid Lake Road, between Maligne and Miette Avenues, the trail heads uphill and turns left onto the Cabin Lake Road. The road ends at Cabin Lake, but the route continues as a well-defined trail that skirts the right side of the lake and then strikes out to the west. The circuit trip continues past Saturday Night Lake for somewhat over a kilometre and then arcs back toward town, passing close by Minnow Lake, High Lakes, Caledonia

Lake and Marjorie Lake. The route travels through dense forest the total distance, finally returning to the townsite area at the trailer park on the west edge of town.

Virl, Dorothy and Christine Lakes

4.2 kilometres (2.6 miles)

These three peaceful lakes, enclosed by a forest of pine, spruce, Douglas fir and aspen poplar, provide a pleasant half-day outing in the rolling country west of Jasper townsite. Though views from the lakeshores are limited, Virl, Dorothy and Christine have a quiet, reserved atmosphere which is an agreeable contrast to their more flamboyant alpine cousins.

The trail begins 11 kilometres (7 miles) west of the townsite just off the Yellowhead Highway. After crossing the Meadow Creek bridge, turn right onto a dirt road. About 400 metres down the road a sign indicates another small road which leads to a parking area within 50 metres.

From the trail head the path climbs over a ridge and descends to Minaga Creek at Kilometre 2.0. A gradual ascent over the next kilometre-and-a-half brings the hiker to the Virl Lake junction, where a short right hand spur leads to the lakeshore. Slightly more open than Dorothy and Christine, Virl reflects Indian Ridge and Muhigan Mountain to the south. Just 400 metres above the Virl Lake junction the main trail reaches Dorothy Lake, the largest of the three sisters. Tightly encircled by forest, it is quite similar in appearance to Virl. Christine Lake, featuring some unusual rock peninsulas, lies another 400 metres beyond.

Patricia Lake Circle

4.8 kilometres (3.0 miles)

A short and easy half-day trip, the Patricia Lake Circle starts on the Pyramid Lake Road opposite the Pyramid Lake riding stables, skirts the southern shore of Patricia Lake and arcs back to the starting point via Cottonwood Creek and the Cottonwood Slough, a prime area for beaver and moose.

Valley of the Five Lakes

Icefields Parkway to Lake Five—2.3 kilometres (1.4 miles)

Nature hike

Allow 2 hours for circuit

Elevation gain: 60 metres (200 feet)

Maximum elevation: 1095 metres (3,600 feet)

Topo maps: Jasper 83 D/16 East
(named Wabasso Lakes on map)

Point of Departure: The trail head is found on the east side of the Icefields Parkway 9.5 kilometres (5.9 miles) south of Jasper townsite. A trail sign indicates the starting point.

The Valley of the Five Lakes is a small open-forested valley at the foot of the Maligne Mountains. The five lakes, all of which are just over pond dimensions and of an exquisite jade green colour, can be visited in a two hour stroll, and the outing is a good family half-day trip.

The first kilometre of the journey is through open flat terrain, the predominant forest cover consisting of lodgepole pine. At the 800 metre mark the trail crosses a small stream and climbs a low ridge, where the hiker has a fine view back across the Athabasca Valley to Mount Edith Cavell (3363 m). From the top of the ridge the trail dips into the Valley of the Five Lakes, where one is able to visit any or all of the five within a very short time. A recommended route is to proceed to the fifth lake and pick up the trail running at the eastern side of the lake. This trail works down the valley and touches each lake, thus providing a loop circuit of the five.

Wabasso Lake

Icefields Parkway to Wabasso Lake—2.7 kilometres (1.7 miles)

Nature hike

Allow 1 hour round trip

Elevation gain: 45 metres (150 feet)

Maximum elevation: 1260 metres (3,700 feet)

Topo maps: Jasper, 83 D/16 East
Medicine Lake, 83 C/13 West

Point of Departure: The trail head is found 15.0 kilometres (9.3 miles) south of Jasper on the east side of the Icefields Parkway.

The Wabasso Lake trail is a very short, easy trail which takes the hiker across the Prairie de la Vache to a small lake on the western foot of Amber Mountain. The trail traverses quite level terrain through stands of lodgepole pine and aspen poplar, crossing a small stream at 1.4 kilometres and running past a pond at 2.4 kilometres. Wabasso Lake, its name derived from the Cree word for rabbit, lies in a small serene valley, providing a lovely setting for a peaceful body of water.

Palisade Lookout

Pyramid Lake to Palisade Lookout—10.8 kilometres (6.7 miles)

Day trip
Allow 4-5 hours to lookout
Elevation gain: 915 metres (3,000 feet)
Maximum elevation: 2075 metres (6,800 feet)
Topo maps: Jasper, 83 D/16 East

Point of Departure: Drive to Pyramid Lake, 6.6 kilometres (4.1 miles) north of Jasper townsite on the Pyramid Lake Drive. Continue on around the lake to where the road ends at a small picnic area just west of a fire road gate.

0.0—Trail begins at the fire road gate.

—Route follows fire road at a gradual to moderate grade.

1.1—Pyramid Lake outlet and bridge.

7.6—Road junction. Keep right for Palisade Lookout.

10.8—Palisade Lookout.

Though the trip to Palisade Lookout is a long, grim trek over wide, well-graded fire road, the views from the summit are probably the most rewarding in the Jasper vicinity. Perched on the edge of a sheer escarpment over 1000 vertical metres above the Athabasca River, the lookout scans a broad area stretching from Roche Miette and Jasper Lake to the towering summit of Mount Edith Cavell.

From the picnic area at Pyramid Lake, the fire road rolls relentlessly through a forest of spruce, aspen and lodgepole pine. The only break in the cover occurs at Kilometre 2.1 where a grove of old Douglas fir trees with charred bark appears to the left above the road—survivors of a forest fire that swept the area many years ago.

As the road rises to the seven kilometre mark, the first views begin to open on the surrounding countryside. At Kilometre 7.6 the road forks: the right spur leads to Palisade Lookout, while the left continues on to the Pyramid Mountain telecommunications station.

Arriving at the lookout, views suddenly open to the north and east. Across the Athabasca Valley are the grey limestone mountains of the Colin Range with strata tilted nearly vertical and eroded into a series of "sawtooth" peaks. The range was named by the explorer-geologist Dr. James Hector for Colin Fraser, an employee of the Hudson's Bay Company who tended Jasper's House in the 1830's and 40's.

Roche Miette dominates the distant opening of the Athabasca Valley to the northeast. The butte-like mountain of Palliser limestone rises to the right of Jasper Lake. It was several kilometres north of its cliffs that the Jasper's House fur trading post was located. In 1846 the Canadian artist Paul Kane made a few observations concerning this colourful hostelry: ". . . it consists of only three

Palisade Lookout and the Colin Range

miserable log huts. The dwelling-house is composed of two rooms . . . one of them is used by all comers and goers: Indians, voyageurs, and traders, men, women, and children being huddled together indiscriminately."

A short climb to an open knoll behind the lookout provides excellent views southward to Pyramid Mountain (2766 m). Located in the Main Ranges of the Rockies, it is composed of red and orange quartzites and argillites deposited under Precambrian and Cambrian seas. Today its summit is unceremoniously crowned by a telecommunications tower.

The rock comprising the Palisade ridge is Devonian limestone, the same formation found in Roche Miette. Rock of this age is conspicuous throughout the Front Ranges of the Canadian Rockies, and in fact, the Palisade serves as the western boundary of the Front Ranges in this area.

Keep a close watch around the lookout for mountain sheep which visit this open ridge. Red fox have been known to frequent the lookout during past seasons as well. And remember to pack water on the hike, since there is no dependable supply along the way.

Tonquin Valley

Amethyst Lakes via Astoria River—19.0 kilometres (11.8 miles)
Amethyst Lakes via Maccarib Pass—21.3 kilometres (13.2 miles)

Maccarib Pass Route:

Backpack

Allow 7-9 hours to Amethyst Lakes

Elevation gain: 700 metres (2,300 feet)

Maximum elevation: 2210 metres (7,250 feet)

Topo maps: Amethyst Lakes, 83 D/9
              Jasper, 83 D/16 East

Point of Departure: Drive to the 93-A Highway, 7.4 kilometres (4.6 miles) south of Jasper townsite on the Icefields Parkway. Follow the 93-A south for 2.4 kilometres (1.5 miles) to the junction with the Marmot Basin ski area access road. Follow the Marmot Basin Road for 6.3 kilometres (3.9 miles) to the point where it crosses Portal Creek. Park in the large gravel pulloff beside the creek.

0.0—Trail head at rear of gravel parking lot.

0.5—Bridge. Trail crosses to north side of Portal Creek.

—Ascend Portal Creek canyon.

4.0—Bridge. Circus Creek.

5.0—Trail emerges onto open rockslides.

7.7—Portal Campground.

10.1—Grade steepens on climb to pass.

12.4—Maccarib Pass (2210 m).

12.9—First views into Tonquin Valley.

18.5—Tonquin Valley viewpoint.

19.5—Maccarib Campground and Maccarib Creek Bridge.

20.4—Junction: Amethyst Lakes to left. Moat Lake straight ahead.

21.3—Amethyst Lakes (north end).

22.9—12½ Mile Campground (1965 m).

Dr. J. Monroe Thorington, a well known mountaineer and historian who has devoted many years of his life to rambling about the Canadian Rockies, writes eloquently of the Tonquin Valley and how its "unique combination of lake, precipice, and ice . . . presents itself with a singular beauty almost unequalled in alpine regions of North America." For anyone who has visited this area after a spell of good weather, and particularly late in the year when the crowds have dispersed and the air is crisp and clear, it would be hard to dispute that this is one of the truly spectacular hiking areas in the mountain west. But in the midst of summer, when the rains are pelting down, the mosquitoes, black flies and no-see-ums are swarming, the campgrounds are all filled to capacity, and the trails have been churned to mush by heavy horse use, this lovely area comes very close to a backpacker's definition of hell; at such times it is better to forget the Tonquin's reputation and to go in search of less travelled ways.

Two trails of almost equal length lead to the valley—one running up the Astoria River from near the base of Mount Edith Cavell, the other travelling via Portal Creek and Maccarib Pass from the Marmot Basin Road.

Maccarib Pass Route. Of the two main access trails into the Tonquin Valley, Maccarib Pass is slightly longer and more arduous, yet it holds a definite scenic edge.

Striking off from the Marmot Basin Road, the trail over Maccarib ascends the narrow canyon of Portal Creek, and by climbing high onto the north side of the valley and traversing rock slides below Peveril Peak it soon provides excellent views to the head of the valley and the peaks surrounding the pass. After descending back to the valley floor, the last

Amethyst Lakes and the Ramparts

five kilometres to the Maccarib crest
climb through an open subalpine forest of
spruce and fir. The trail finally emerges
above the last of the trees less than two
kilometres from the top.

While the approach to Maccarib Pass
offers some fine views, particularly to the
jagged summit of Old Horn Mountain
rising above a col to the south, the trail's
true reward lies on the western slope of
the pass. From the first glimpse of The
Ramparts and Moat Pass obtained near
the summit, each succeeding kilometre
across the open alpine tundra brings an
ever-broadening perspective of the Tonquin Valley and its surrounding peaks.

The Maccarib Pass trail reaches the
floor of the Tonquin Valley at Kilometre
20.4 where the trail forks, the right
branch leading to Moat Lake and the left
to the Amethyst Lakes and the 12½ Mile
Campground just 2.4 kilometres distant.

Astoria River Route. From the bridge
at the outlet to Cavell Lake, this popular
route to the Tonquin Valley makes a very
straightforward ascent of the Astoria
Valley for its first ten kilometres or so,

then switchbacks up the southern flank of
Old Horn Mountain to emerge onto the
open alpine meadows overlooking the
Eremite Valley. After attaining this lofty
viewpoint at near 2100 metres above sea
level, the trail wanders across the meadows for another four kilometres providing ever-improving views of the Tonquin
Valley and The Ramparts before making
the descent to Amethyst Lakes.

The Tonquin Valley more closely
resembles a high, five kilometre-long
pass than a true valley. Its broad crest
cradles the Amethyst Lakes, a pair of
beautiful interconnected lakes which lie
at the base of a 1000 metre wall of
Precambrian quartzite called The Ramparts. The wall is actually composed of
ten spectacular castellate peaks which are
certainly worthy of names such as
Bastion, Drawbridge, Redoubt, Dun-
geon and Paragon—a glowering collection of towers and turrets which the
Indians once thought to be inhabited by
huge and horrible beasts possessed of
supernatural powers.

Once the Tonquin Valley is reached, by
either Maccarib Pass or the Astoria

125

Astoria River Route:

Backpack

Allow 6-8 hours to Amethyst Lakes

Elevation gain: 395 metres (1,300 feet)

Maximum elevation: 2105 metres (6,900 feet)

Topo maps: Amethyst Lakes, 83 D/9
(trail not shown)

Point of Departure: Drive to the 93-A Highway, 7.4 kilometres (4.6 miles) south of Jasper townsite on the Icefields Parkway. Follow the 93-A south for 5.3 kilometres (3.3 miles) to the junction with the Mount Edith Cavell Road. Continue on the Mount Edith Cavell Road for 12.7 kilometres (7.9 miles) to the roadside pulloff above Cavell Lake. Leave your vehicle in one of the pulloff parking areas and hike down to the Astoria River trail head at the outlet to Cavell Lake.

0.0—Cavell Lake and bridge (1720 m).

5.0—Astoria River bridge.

6.8—Old Horn Campground.

8.2—Junction: Tonquin Valley straight ahead. Shortcut trail to Chrome Lake crosses log bridge to left.

10.6—Trail fork. Stay right on well-defined high trail.

12.9—Maximum elevation (2105 m). High subalpine meadows.

13.7—8½ Mile Campground.

16.8—10½ Mile Campground and junction. Right hand branch leads to 12½ Mile Campground. Left hand branch leads to Surprise Point Campground.

19.0—Tonquin Valley Lodge.

—Veer right just before reaching the lodge. Trail continues between lagoon and lake.

20.1—12½ Mile Campground (1965 m).

River, the hiker can travel along the length of the Amethyst Lakes by means of trails which follow above the eastern shoreline. A well-defined trail skirts above the shore of the northern-most lake, but south of the Tonquin Valley Lodge and the Narrows a number of poor tracks lead out across marshy flats. In travelling along the southern Amethyst Lake, it's best to stay on the higher and drier ground about 500 metres above the shore. Good trail picks up again at the end of the southern lake where a bridge spans the outlet stream to the Surprise Point Campground.

Access to Surprise Point can also be made from the 10½ Mile Campground on the Astoria River trail by taking the left hand spur which leads downhill toward the southern tip of the lakes, past the warden cabin and across the boggy valley flats to the outlet bridge. As has been suggested, the Tonquin Valley is a very soggy region, and regular horse travel to and from the two lodges on the lakes helps to transform trails into a quagmire during rainy weather. This perpetual dampness also helps to create one of the healthiest mosquito populations found anywhere in the Rockies.

Chrome Lake-Eremite Valley Option. While the Amethyst Lakes and The Ramparts serve as the scenic focal point of the region, the Tonquin Valley is open-ended with trails leading both north and south to lakes and mountains of equal grandeur. One of the more popular day trips which can be taken from campsites in the Tonquin Valley runs south from the Surprise Point Campground to Chrome Lake—a rough and rocky 2.4 kilometre trek. Chrome Lake is a small but beautiful sheet of turquoise water which reflects the mountains surrounding the head of the Eremite Valley to the south.

In an open meadow just 300 metres before Chrome Lake, another trail branches to the west. Following this spur for 500 metres, the hiker arrives at yet another junction just a short distance above Penstock Creek. The left hand branch from this fork leads south to

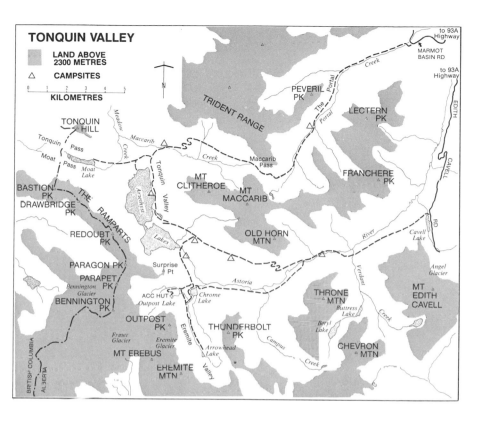

TONQUIN VALLEY

LAND ABOVE 2300 METRES

△ CAMPSITES

0 1 2 3 4 5
KILOMETRES

to 93A Highway
MARMOT BASIN RD
to 93A Highway

Creek

The Portal

PEVERIL PK

LECTERN PK

TRIDENT RANGE

TONQUIN HILL

Meadow Creek

Maccarib Creek

Tonquin Pass

Moat Pass

Moat Lake

Maccarib Pass

FRANCHERE PK

BASTION PK

DRAWBRIDGE PK

THE RAMPARTS

Amethyst

Tonquin Valley

MT CLITHEROE

MT MACCARIB

REDOUBT PK

Lakes

OLD HORN MTN

River

Cavell Lake

CAVELL

EDITH

RD

PARAGON PK

Surprise Pt

Astoria

Verdant

Angel Glacier

PARAPET PK

Bennington Glacier

ACC HUT

Chrome Lake

Outpost Lake

THRONE MTN

Buttress Lake

MT EDITH CAVELL

BENNINGTON PK

OUTPOST PK

Fraser Glacier

Eremite Glacier

Eremite Valley

THUNDERBOLT PK

Arrowhead Lake

Campus

Beryl Lake

Creek

CHEVRON MTN

MT EREBUS

EREMITE MTN

BRITISH COLUMBIA
ALBERTA

Arrowhead Lake (4.0 kilometres) and the head of the Eremite Valley—a spectacular alpine region where glaciers crown almost every peak and which has been a popular haunt of climbers for many decades; the right hand branch follows upstream along Penstock Creek, crosses to the true right bank of the creek at the foot of a steep forested slope, and then climbs to the shores of tiny Outpost Lake—a total distance of only 1.1 kilometres from the junction with the Eremite Valley trail.

All trails in the Chrome Lake-Eremite Valley vicinity are rough, rocky, usually muddy and sometimes poorly defined. Hikers should take their time and work with a topographical map.

Moat Lake Option. This is a short side trip branching from the Maccarib Pass trail just beyond the north end of Amethyst Lakes. The trail is boggy in the beginning but can be followed across open meadows to where it enters the trees and becomes well defined. A spur trail cuts left at Kilometre 1.3 and leads to a small fishing camp and the north end of the Amethyst Lakes—a very pretty viewpoint. Moat Lake is reached just three kilometres from the Maccarib trail junction. The perpendicular cliffs of the northern Ramparts rise above the lake's southern shoreline, while its waters stretch for more than a kilometre toward the nearby twin passes of Moat and Tonquin on the Alberta-B.C. boundary.

127

Angel Glacier

Cavell Parking Lot to Angel Glacier Viewpoint—3.2 kilometres (2.0 miles)

Half-day trip
Allow 1 hour to viewpoint
Elevation gain: 305 metres (1,000 feet)
Maximum elevation: 2135 metres (7,000 feet)
Topo maps: Amethyst Lake, 83 D/9
    (trail not shown)

Point of Departure: Drive to the 93-A Highway, 7.4 kilometres (4.6 miles) south of Jasper townsite on the Icefields Parkway. Follow the 93-A south for 5.3 kilometres (3.3 miles) to the junction with the Mount Edith Cavell Road. Drive the Cavell Road 14.5 kilometres (9 miles) to its terminus—the parking area at the foot of the mountain.

0.0—Trail sign at south edge of parking lot.

    —Paved trail.

0.6—Junction. Switchback left for main trail to upper meadows.

    —Steady uphill.

3.2—Angel Glacier viewpoint.

    —Trail makes an extended loop into the upper meadows.

The Angel Glacier trail climbs high above the usual tourist viewpoint for this spectacular hanging glacier and loops through a beautiful alpine meadow which provides an outstanding perspective of the glacier and the east wall of Mount Edith Cavell—the highest peak in this section of the park. The trail is heavily travelled, however, so hikers can usually forget about solitude on this short outing.

Starting from the parking area on a broad, paved trail, the hiker quickly leaves the asphalt behind as he switchbacks up and over the sharp ridge of a lateral moraine. Following along the base of this glacial debris, he should be watchful for hoary marmots and pikas, both of these wary animals finding a safe habitat amidst this rocky jumble.

After climbing through a subalpine forest of spruce and alpine fir, the trail emerges near timberline to face the magnificent Mount Edith Cavell and Angel Glacier. The mountain is composed primarily of Precambrian and Cambrian quartzites, and the head of the Angel Glacier is slowly grinding a huge amphitheatre into the uppermost reaches of the east face. The toe of the glacier, cascading over a 300 metre cliff in a spectacular series of icefalls, is its most visible part from this angle.

From the overlook, the trail continues to the south, then loops upward to even higher viewpoints in the flower filled alpine meadows above. The loop is finally closed by dropping back down to join the approach trail near the first viewpoint. Hikers should stay on the trail in the upper meadows, since indiscriminate wandering by the large numbers of people who visit here could quickly make a hash of this beautiful but fragile landscape.

128

Athabasca Pass

Moab Lake to Athabasca Pass—47 kilometres (29 miles)*

Backpack

Allow 2 days one way

Elevation gain: 560 metres (1,836 feet)

Maximum elevation: 1748 metres (5,736 feet)

Topo maps: Athabasca Falls, 83 C/12
　　　　　Amethyst Lakes, 83 D/9
　　　　　Athabasca Pass, 83 D/8
　　　　　(last 32 kms not shown)

Point of Departure: From the junction of the Icefields Parkway and Highway 93-A at Athabasca Falls, drive north on the 93-A for 9.0 kilometres (5.6 miles) to the Whirlpool Fire Road. Follow the fire road to the Moab Lake parking area 7.0 kilometres (4.3 miles) distant. The traffic control gate on the fire road at the parking area represents the Athabasca Pass trail head.

*Distance approximate.

Although much of the 47 kilometre hike to Athabasca Pass is along a low valley bottom and is rather monotonous, the route itself is one of such historical significance that many people follow it each year despite the long approach.

The trail begins as a fire road, working to the southwest from the Moab Lake parking area. It follows the road to its end at a backcountry warden cabin some 16 kilometres beyond Moab Lake. From the end of the road the route continues as an old horse trail, staying close to the north bank of the Whirlpool River. Although several kilometres of trail have been brushed out between the Scott Creek flats and the Kane Meadows, the last eight kilometres or so to the pass are poorly defined and usually quite boggy. The general direction is obvious, however.

During the winter of 1811, David Thompson, Canada's foremost surveyor and fur trader, made the first recorded crossing of the pass. The pass subsequently became the main fur trade route across the Rockies and it was here that the voyageurs of the famous North West Company and the Hudson's Bay Company would transport 90-pound packs of beaver pelts from the Pacific drainage of the Columbia River to the waterways leading east to Hudson's Bay and Montreal. In 1824 the Governor of the Hudson's Bay Company, George Simpson, crossed the pass and named a small lake on its summit The Committee's Punchbowl, in honour of the officers of the company.

As yet, no trail has been developed down the western slope from the pass, and access from the old Boat Encampment at the bend of the Columbia via the Wood River has been flooded by the Mica Creek Dam.

Geraldine Lakes

Geraldine Road to Second Geraldine Lake—5.9 kilometres (3.7 miles)

Half-day or day trip

Allow 2 hours to second lake

Elevation gain: 350 metres (1,150 feet)

Maximum elevation: 1875 metres (6,150 feet)

Topo maps: Athabasca Falls, 83 C/12
(last 4 kms not shown)

Point of Departure: Follow alternate route 93-A to the Geraldine Lookout Fire Road, 1.1 kilometres (0.7 mile) north of 93-A's junction with the Icefields Parkway at Athabasca Falls. Follow this dirt road for approximately six kilometres to the marked Geraldine Lakes trail head.

0.0—Trail sign.

—Moderate uphill climb.

1.8—First Geraldine Lake.

2.7—Southern end of first lake.

—Steep 90 metre climb.

3.8—Small tarn between first and second lakes.

—Very steep 150 metre climb.

5.0—Viewpoint on ridge above second lake.

5.9—Campsite at south end of second lake.

Lying high between the steep slopes of Mount Fryatt and Whirlpool Peak, the three Geraldine Lakes offer hiking options that range from a few hours' stroll to a full day of rock scrambling and exploring. The first lake is an easy 45 minute trek from the trail head; the second lake is a longer and tougher scrambled over a rough-hewn trail; and the third lake is a hike for adventurers who need no trail and are well-accustomed to the rigours of bushwhacking. The upper two lakes are situated in wild rocky environs and give an impression of remote wilderness, even though they lie only a few kilometres from the trail head.

The initial two kilometres of trail to the lowest lake are well-travelled. The lake itself, popular with fishermen, shows signs of heavy use, and the shoreline litter speaks poorly of thoughtless visitors. The lake, however, is serene, enclosed by a thick forest of lodgepole pine and spruce, and reflects the flanks of Mount Fryatt (3361 m) to the south.

From the north end of the lake the trail continues along the west shore, reaching the far end of the lake at Kilometre 1.7. From here it climbs steeply for 300 metres, paralleling a 90 metre waterfall that cascades over high rock steps to the lake below. The trail here is quite rough, filled with rocks and roots, and strong boots (and legs) are recommended.

At the top of the falls the trail enters a short valley and angles off to its eastern side, crossing a large boulder field and bypassing a diminutive tarn at Kilometre 3.8. Much of the trail over the boulder field is marked only by cairns, and the hiker will have to watch closely for them if he wishes to follow the easiest route up the valley. At the end of the valley the trail climbs steeply, again beside a waterfall, but this second climb is steeper and longer than the first.

A rocky ridge at the top of the climb is a

good viewpoint. From here the hiker can best appreciate the geological nature of the Geraldine Lakes as he sees the way the higher lakes feed into the lower. Known as *pater noster* lakes, the Geraldine Lakes form a chain of small tarns occupying depressions in a glacially-carved stairway. The rocks rising on either side are Cambrian in age, with strata dipping to the southwest at an angle of ten to twenty-five degrees.

Although the ridge will probably represent the culmination of the day's efforts for many hikers, the trail does continue, descending into the basin of the second lake and following close to its eastern shore. It ends at a primitive campsite at the southern end of the lake. For particularly ambitious hikers, well-experienced in route-finding, a third lake lies some 3.2 kilometres beyond the second. No trail has been cut to the third lake as of this writing.

Fryatt Creek

Geraldine Road to Fryatt Creek Falls—19.6 kilometres (13.4 miles)

Backpack

Allow 7 hours one way

Elevation gain: 760 metres (2,500 feet)

Maximum elevation: 1980 metres (6,500 feet)

Topo maps: Athabasca Falls, 83 C/12
           Fortress Lake, 83 C/5
           (last 5 kms not shown)

Point of Departure: Follow alternate route 93-A to the Geraldine Lookout Fire Road, 1.1 kilometres (0.7 mile) north of the 93-A's junction with the Icefields Parkway at Athabasca Falls. Follow this dirt road for 1.8 kilometres (1.1 miles). A trail sign and small parking area on the left side of the road indicate the trail head.

0.0—Trail sign.

   —Route follows old fire road track.

1.9—Stream and bridges.

4.1—Trail crosses through an old pole fence.

4.9—Stream crossing.

5.3—Athabasca River. Packer's corral.

7.2—Trail turns south toward Fryatt Valley.

7.8—Junction: Fryatt Creek straight ahead. Lick Creek to the left.

9.0—Trail fork. Stay straight ahead.

9.8—Trail crosses Fryatt Creek.

14.0—Trail recrosses Fryatt Creek. Stay with creek bed to the right.

17.0—North end of Fryatt Lake.

17.8—South end of Fryatt Lake.

19.6—Meadows below Fryatt Creek Falls. Steep access trail continues up the headwall to the right of the falls. Alpinist's hut just beyond the top of the wall.

The 20 kilometre trail stretching from the Geraldine Lookout road to the upper reaches of the Fryatt Valley represents an ideal hike for backpackers looking for something a bit more challenging than the casual hiker's day trip. It is a recommended overnight trip, not only because it is 40 kilometres return, but because the trail runs through one of the more spectacularly rugged valleys in Jasper Park and deserves a few hours exploration time.

However, a certain price must be paid to enjoy the sheer rock and cascading water of the upper Fryatt Valley or the rolling meadows below the Belanger Glacier, a toll exacted by some nine kilometres of quite monotonous hiking: from the trail head to the point at which it veers south up Fryatt Creek, the trail wanders interminably across the flats of the Athabasca River, offering little more than lodgepole pine as scenery. Furthermore, this initial portion of trail is often crossed by small paths, all unmarked, which can lead to some confusion. But a general southeasterly orientation should carry the hiker through an old pole fence (4.1 kilometres), across a small stream (4.9 kilometres), past an abandoned packer's corral (5.3 kilometres), and finally across a low ridge to a bluff overlooking the Athabasca (7.2 kilometres).

From the bluff the hiker gets his first real chance to view the surrounding country. Directly to the east lies the uniformly dipping Precambrian quartzite of the Endless Chain Ridge, representing the easterly slope of a great syncline, or trough-like downfold in the rock formation. The Athabasca runs down the axis of the syncline, while the bluff the hiker stands on is part of the western slope. To the south one sees the entrance to Fryatt Valley, watched over by Mount Fryatt (3308 m) on the right and Mount Christie (3032 m) on the left.

Fryatt Lake

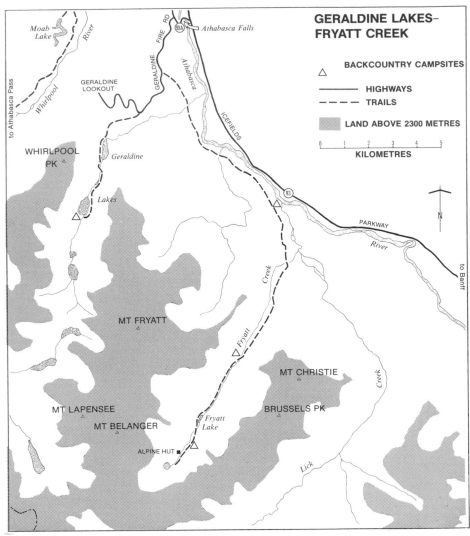

GERALDINE LAKES–FRYATT CREEK

△   **BACKCOUNTRY CAMPSITES**

———   **HIGHWAYS**

- - - -   **TRAILS**

▓   **LAND ABOVE 2300 METRES**

0   1   2   3   4   5

KILOMETRES

of Brussels Peak (3111 m). All of these mountains are composed of Precambrian and Cambrian sedimentary rock, and Mount Fryatt stands as the highest peak in the southwest angle between the Whirlpool and Athabasca Rivers.

Turning south at the bluff the trail starts toward Fryatt Valley, reaching Fryatt Creek at Kilometre 9.8. Crossing the creek via a wooden footbridge (a good place to fill a canteen, particularly in the late season), the trail begins to gain altitude rapidly, climbing across the western flank of Mount Christie through a mature forest of spruce and fir.

A little over four kilometres beyond the first crossing of Fryatt Creek the trail recrosses the stream to the western side of the valley. At this point the trail becomes rather erratic and often non-existent. The crossing itself is achieved by means of a few old logs and is indicative of the interesting hiking ahead. For a little over three kilometres the hiker must pick his way along the edge of the creek bed, crossing a large and wildly jumbled glacial moraine—interesting terrain but hard on the

134

ankles. At the 16 kilometre mark are the remains of an old campsite, and at Kilometre 17.0 the trail reaches the northern end of Fryatt Lake. Here the trail becomes clearly marked again, running along the western side of the lake through heavy timber. From the far (southern) end of the lake the trail offers one of the more rewarding views of the hike as one looks back across the lake and down the narrow steep-walled valley toward Mount Kerkeslin (2819 m) in the distance.

A little over a kilometre beyond the southern shore of the lake the main trail enters a lush meadow at the foot of a rock wall which abruptly closes off the valley, creating a 'box-canyon' effect. Runoff from the Belanger Glacier (not visible from the meadow) tumbles down across the rock in a spectacular cascade, adding a prismatic touch to the already colourful surroundings, and the heights of Mount Christie, Mount Fryatt, Mount Belanger and Brussels Peak sweep up steeply from the narrow valley bottom.

The trail does, in fact, continue, and sure-footed hikers will gain much by scrambling up the steep, rough track to the right of the falls. An alpinist's hut lies just a short distance along the stream at the top of the wall and serves as a centre for climbing activity in the area. From the hut hikers can explore to the upper headwall of the valley, an area ringed by vertical cliffs, and visit the beautiful alpine lake beneath the Belanger Glacier. It is a world apart from the forested drudgery of the lower valley, and well worth the toil of the trip.

Fortress Lake

Sunwapta Canyon to Fortress Lake—23 kilometres (14 miles)*

Backpack

Allow 8 hours one way

Elevation gain: nil

Maximum elevation: 1370 metres (4,500 feet)

Topo maps: Athabasca Falls, 83 C/12
          Fortress Lake, 83 C/5
          (last 11 kms not shown)

Point of Departure: The trail begins at Sunwapta Falls, 55 kilometres (34.2 miles) south of Jasper on the Icefields Parkway. From the south side of the bridge across the falls the trail runs south along the east bank of the Athabasca River.

*Distance approximate.

Although the trail to Fortress Lake is not long and traverses nearly level terrain, two treacherous fords make it all but impassable for the person on foot. As a hike the complete trip should be attempted only very late in the season and then only by experienced, strong backpackers.

From Sunwapta Falls the route follows a horse trail up the south side of the Athabasca River for a little over 14 kilometres. A campsite near the ford on the Athabasca signifies the end of the trail for most travellers.

Beyond the thigh-deep ford of the Athabasca, the trail loses definition on extensive gravel flats, and hikers must pay attention to a series of cairns and blazes to keep on course. Another ford a few kilometres distant, this time of the Chaba River, creates a second major hazard for hikers. All in all, a trip to be avoided by all but the most experienced.

Jonas Pass

Backpack

Allow 3 days minimum

Elevation gain: 932 metres (3,058 feet)
loss: 995 metres (3,262 feet)

Maximum elevation: 2440 metres (8,000 feet)

Topo maps: Columbia Icefield, 83 C/3
Sunwapta, 83 C/6

Point of Departure: The initial portion of the Jonas Pass trail coincides with the Nigel Pass trail. For point of departure and route description, see *Nigel Pass* in Banff Park.

0.0—Camp Parker (1920 m).

6.1—Nigel Pass (2202 m).

6.4—Brazeau south fork ford.

—Brazeau River Valley overlook.

9.3—Bridge across the Brazeau and campsite.

10.4—Bridge over Boulder Creek.

12.9—Jonas Cutoff campsite and trail junction. Jonas Pass to the left. Brazeau Lake straight ahead.

—Trail climbs steeply for 2 kilometres.

22.7—Crest of Jonas Pass (2235 m).

25.9—Trail swings right toward the Jonas Shoulder.

28.5—Jonas Shoulder summit (2440 m).

31.7—Trail crosses Poboktan Creek. Turn downstream.

32.7—Campsite.

34.6—Trail fork. Hikers stay right, above creek.

39.0—Waterfalls Warden Cabin.

41.0—Cataract and campsite.

45.5—Poboktan tributary ford and outfitter's camp.

46.8—Major trail junction. Poboktan Warden Station to left, Maligne Pass to right.

53.0—Parking area across creek from warden station.

The 53.0 kilometre trail from Camp Parker in Banff National Park to the Poboktan Warden Station in Jasper National Park constitutes a three-day trek through a most impressive array of subalpine and alpine terrain. The route features two passes above timberline, one of them nearly 13 kilometres long, plus an assortment of glaciated peaks, lush river valleys, waterfalls and wildlife. Despite the ruggedness of the landscape, the hike is not difficult and anyone with some mountain backpacking experience and in good shape should fare well on the trip. However, because of the altitude of the trail, snow often lies deep in the passes until well into July, and prospective hikers should consult with park officials before beginning the expedition.

Starting at Camp Parker the trail climbs gradually toward Nigel Pass and the Jasper Park boundary (see *Nigel Pass* in Banff Park). From the Nigel meadows the trail descends to the floor of the Brazeau Valley, crossing the river's south fork tributary along the way.

Once the trail reaches the valley floor it is a little over a kilometre to a bridge across the Brazeau and, just beyond the bridge, a small campsite. From the campsite the trail leaves the open meadows of the upper valley and enters a spruce and pine forest, crossing a major tributary of the Brazeau, Boulder Creek (bridged), at Kilometre 10.4. Past the creek the trail works out of the forest and onto the open Brazeau River flats, reaching the Jonas Cutoff campsite at the 12.9 kilometre mark. This is a good stopping point for the day since the next campsite is 19.8 kilometres beyond: the park requests that all hikers move through the Jonas Pass area in one day in order to protect delicate alpine environment.

136

The campsite represents the cutoff for Jonas Pass and the trail veers left at a marked junction to start a vigorous climb toward the pass. The trail rises through a beautiful open forest, climbing 210 metres in less than two kilometres. A series of small streams coming down from the left heralds the approach of timberline, and within a few minutes hiking the trail levels off, leaving the last of the alpine fir behind. Ahead the trail works gradually up the southwest side of the broad ravine that constitutes the pass, maintaining an elevation some 30 metres above the small creek that fills the valley's bottom. The pass is as long as it is beautiful, and it isn't until the 22.7 kilometre mark that its crest is reached.

Beyond the pass the trail maintains its altitude for about 1.5 kilometres, bypassing a small alpine tarn, and then gradually descends a similar distance, angling off toward the north. Just beyond a large, distinctive talus slope the trail swings to the right and begins a steep ascent to the Jonas Shoulder, the high ridge that separates the Jonas and Poboktan drainages. The first portion of

the climb is steep and the trail is sketchy in places; most hikers will want to keep an eye open for stone cairns to lead them up the initial 1.5 kilometres. The trail becomes more distinct with altitude, however, and hikers should soon find a well-marked path making a long and more gradual traverse toward the ridge above.

The scenery along the Jonas Shoulder climb is spectacular, and frequent rest stops with map, compass and camera are highly rewarding. There is also a chance of sighting some of the caribou that make the Jonas-Poboktan area their summer residence (the park asks that they not be disturbed). Mountain goat, grizzly bear and a variety of smaller mammals also frequent the region.

From the Jonas Shoulder crest, barren, desolate and beautiful at 2400 metres, the trail descends a steep talus slope and then veers left across spongy meadows. Again the trail is indistinct, and once hikers are working their way north down the meadows they should angle off toward the east side of the obvious gorge a short distance ahead.

137

The trail becomes well-defined again just before it reaches timberline and then descends rapidly into the valley of Poboktan Creek. At the valley floor the trail cuts across the creek to join the Poboktan Pass trail. A campsite a kilometre downstream offers a second night's rest.

From the campsite the trail makes a long and gradual descent of the Poboktan drainage. The general route is obvious, although there are some specific points of indecision. Within two kilometres of the campsite the trail forks and hikers should follow the right, higher, branch; the lower trail is an old horse trail and is now all but impassable.

At the 39.0 kilometre mark the trail bypasses the Waterfalls Warden Cabin (obviously and aptly named) and moves on without problems to a beautiful cataract and campsite at Kilometre 41.0. A tributary at the cataract could cause a troublesome ford before midsummer, as could a similar tributary 4.5 kilometres further down the trail.

The latter ford, however, is the last major obstacle of the trip. Across the stream the trail runs through an outfitter's camp (follow the main path through the centre of the camp; minor trails branch left and right) and proceeds to a major marked intersection just across Poligne Creek at Kilometre 46.8. The Poboktan Warden Station and the Icefields Parkway lie an easy 6.2 kilometres down Poboktan Creek.

Jonas Pass-Brazeau Lake Loop. One very popular variation of the Jonas Pass trip, especially for hikers with limited transportation, is the loop trip of Nigel Pass, Brazeau Lake, Poboktan Pass, Jonas Pass and thence back to Camp Parker via Nigel Pass. The total circuit is just under 80 kilometres (50 miles) and divides itself nicely into five days hiking: Camp Parker to the Jonas Cutoff (12.9 kilometres); to Brazeau Lake (16.0 kilometres); over Poboktan Pass (17.2 kilometres); over Jonas Pass (19.8 kilometres); and back to Camp Parker.

The only tricky part of the hike is in finding the trail up to the Jonas Shoulder: from the Jonas-Poboktan junction at the western end of Poboktan Pass the trail switchbacks steeply uphill, rising above timberline and into the spongy meadows below Jonas Shoulder. Here the trail becomes indistinct and the hiker should proceed up the valley keeping a close eye on the talus slope to the right. A switchbacking path up the slope leads to Jonas Shoulder. (A map and compass will come in handy.)

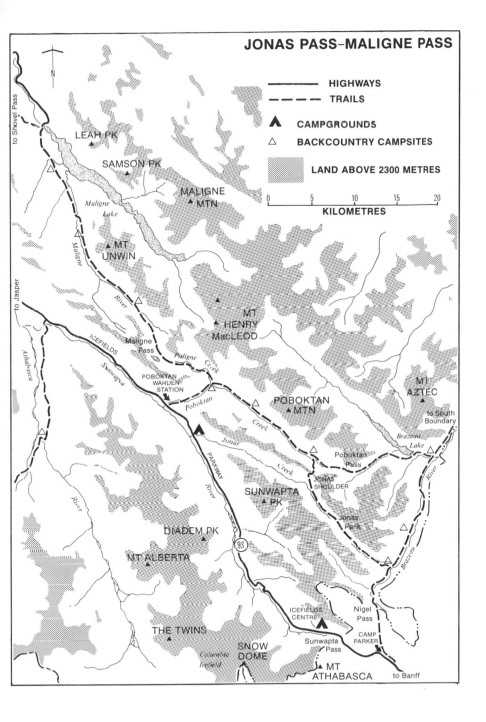

JONAS PASS-MALIGNE PASS

———————	HIGHWAYS
— — — —	TRAILS
▲	CAMPGROUNDS
△	BACKCOUNTRY CAMPSITES
▓	LAND ABOVE 2300 METRES

0   5   10   15   20
KILOMETRES

to Shovel Pass

LEAH PK ▲

SAMSON PK ▲

Maligne Lake

MALIGNE ▲ MTN

Maligne River

▲ MT UNWIN

to Jasper

ICEFIELDS

Sunwapta

Maligne Pass

Padigne Creek

MT ▲ HENRY MacLEOD

POBOKTAN WAHDEN STATION

Poboktan

Creek

MT AZTEC

to South Boundary

POBOKTAN ▲ MTN

Athabasca River

PARKWAY

River

Jonas

Creek

SUNWAPTA ▲ PK

JONAS SHOULDER

Poboktan Pass

Brazeau Lake

△

△

Jonas Park

Brazeau River

DIADEM PK ▲

93

MT ALBERTA ▲

THE TWINS ▲

SNOW DOME

Columbia Icefield

ICEFIELDS CENTRE ▲

Sunwapta Pass

MT ▲ ATHABASCA

Nigel Pass

CAMP PARKER

to Banff

Maligne Pass

Poboktan Creek Warden Station to Maligne Lake—47.9 kilometres (29.7 miles)

Backpack

Allow 2 days minimum

Elevation gain: 680 metres (2,240 feet)

Maximum elevation: 2235 metres (7,340 feet)

Topo maps: Sunwapta, 83 C/6
              Southesk, 83 C/11
              Athabasca Falls, 83 C/12

Point of Departure: Drive to the Poboktan Warden Station, 72.4 kilometres (45 miles) south of Jasper townsite on the Icefields Parkway. The trail begins from the parking area across the creek from the station.

0.0—Trail sign (1555 m).

6.2—Maligne Pass-Poboktan Creek junction. Take the left fork.

—Trail climbs steadily for 4.8 kilometres. Six fords.

11.0—Trail levels off at timberline.

13.5—Maximum elevation on southeast side of pass.

15.2—Maligne Pass (2235 m).

—Gradual descent through open meadows.

17.8—Maligne River ford.

19.6—Campsite.

—Trail passes through alternate sections of forest and willow flats; several small stream fords.

34.4—Suspension bridge across Maligne River.

38.8—Trail fork. Stay right.

40.8—Extensive meadows; bridge over Trapper Creek.

42.2—Campsite.

47.3—Moose Lake junction. Stay left.

47.7—Bald Hills Fire Road. Turn right down road.

47.9—Parking area (1675 m).

The Maligne Pass trail is a challenging 47.7 kilometres of mountain track that can be hiked either by itself or in combination with the Jonas Pass trail to the south and the Jasper Skyline to the north. While not as spectacular as either the Jonas Pass or Skyline route, Maligne Pass does offer much in the way of beautiful scenery, especially in the alpine meadows stretching out from the pass. The entire distance is prime habitat for the larger mammals of the Canadian Rockies and with luck hikers might spot elk, moose, mountain goat, caribou or grizzly bear.

Like its companion trails to the north and south, Maligne Pass often lies buried under deep snow until the latter part of July, and hikers should inquire about snow conditions and water runoff before starting the trek. In fact, since the trail features a number of unbridged stream crossings and several kilometres of boggy meadows, it is recommended that the hike be made only in August or early September when most creeks are low.

From the sign at the Poboktan Warden Cabin the trail ascends the Poboktan Creek drainage, gaining 210 metres of altitude in the 6.2 kilometres to the Poboktan Creek-Maligne Pass junction. The trail cuts left (north) at the junction and begins what can be a long wet climb toward the Maligne Pass meadows.

Working through heavy spruce and pine forest the trail crosses and recrosses Poligne Creek six times in less than five kilometres. Late season hikers will probably keep their feet dry during the 240 metre ascent, but for early summer travellers it will be a rather aquatic journey. One solution to the problem is to bushwhack up one side of the creek, but deadfall and avalanche debris make for hard-won headway.

At the 11.0 kilometre mark the trail reaches timberline and follows a more

Nearing Maligne Pass from Poligne Creek

gradual grade toward the pass, working through boggy meadows and making two more fords of Poligne Creek before finally heading for higher, drier ground on the east side of the pass. At Kilometre 15.2 the trail traces the eastern shore of a small but lovely lake that drains both north and south from the summit of the pass.

Beyond the lake the trail drops gradually toward timberline, passing through magnificent alpine meadows which present a rich variety of wildflowers during the summer months. With timberline comes another series of stream fords and, although less numerous than those on the other side of the pass, they will again constitute a problem for early summer hikers.

Passing a campsite at Kilometre 19.6,

the trail moves through alternate sections of forest and large open willow flats that provide excellent scenic relief for what otherwise would be a very long stretch of enclosed hiking. Another campsite is passed at the 30.5 kilometre mark and the Maligne River is crossed some four kilometers beyond—this time via a sturdy cable suspension bridge.

Beyond the Maligne River the trail continues as before, a relatively level path through forest and meadows. There is another campsite just beyond Trapper Creek (bridged) and a rather long final five kilometres of hiking as the trail refuses to swing toward Maligne Lake, and there is one last stout climb and descent before the trail exits on the Bald Hills Fire Road just above the Maligne Lake parking area.

141

The Skyline Trail

Maligne Lake to Maligne Lake Road—44.1 kilometres (27.4 miles)

Backpack
Allow 2 or 3 days
Elevation gain: 1400 metres (4,600 feet)
    loss: 1920 metres (6,300 feet)
Maximum elevation: 2530 metres (8,300 feet)
Topo maps: Medicine Lake, 83 C/13 West
    Athabasca Falls, 83 C/12

Point of Departure: Drive the Maligne Lake Road to its terminus at Maligne Lake, 44.6 kilometres (27.7 miles) southeast of its junction with the Yellowhead Highway. Upon reaching the lake, keep right and cross the lake's outlet to the parking area near the warden station.

0.0—Trail sign above parking lot.

2.1—Junction. Lorraine Lake left 200 metres.

2.4—Junction. Mona Lake right 200 metres.

4.8—Evelyn Creek and bridge. Campsite.

8.3—Campsite.

10.3—Little Shovel Pass (2225 m).

12.2—Campsite.

17.5—Big Shovel Pass (2285 m).

19.5—Junction. Left branch descends to campsite (200 m) and Icefields Parkway via Wabasso Lake (14.5 km). Skyline route continues to right.

20.4—Curator Lake.

22.1—The Notch (2530 m).

28.3—Centre Lakes, 200 metres to right of trail.

30.4—Tekarra Lake and campsite.

34.5—Junction. Main trail branches downhill to the right.

35.6—Junction with Signal Mountain Fire Road. Campsite.

44.1—Fire road gate and Maligne Lake Road.

Ambling along the ridges of the Maligne Range, the Skyline is one of the exceptional backpacks in Jasper Park. Approximately 25 of its 44 kilometres travel at or above timberline and its highest summits provide expansive views over a good portion of the park's 10,900 square kilometres. In its meadowed valleys live marmots, pikas, ground squirrels, voles and, at certain times, grizzly bear and woodland caribou. Its Snowbowl is one of the most pleasing subalpine meadowlands in the mountain parks; its Notch, one of the most barren and forlorn cols. But the hiking season on this popular route is short, and because of the fragile nature of the terrain use is carefully controlled.

The easiest way to take this one way backpack is from Maligne Lake, starting 520 metres higher than the northwest end of the trail near Maligne Canyon. From the sign above the northwest end of Maligne Lake, the trail strikes off through a fire succession forest of lodgepole pine. Within the first three kilometres it passes two small forest-enclosed lakes—Lorraine and Mona, both noted for their brook trout. Throughout the first five kilometres the grade remains gentle.

At Kilometre 4.8 the trail crosses Evelyn Creek (an excellent spot to rest and fill water bottles), then begins to switchback upward to Little Shovel Pass. Views continue to improve from this point on as the hiker climbs into open subalpine terrain. Off to the left are the rounded Bald Hills. Back beyond the eastern shore of Maligne Lake stand the sharp peaks Leah (2801 m) and Samson (3081 m). Near the pass the glaciered twin summits of Mount Unwin (3268 m) and Mount Charlton (3217 m) appear above the Bald Hills to the south.

From the treeless summit of Little Shovel Pass the trail descends into the beautiful subalpine meadowland of the

142

Snowbowl. Alpine fir and Engelmann spruce finger out into the tundra vegetation of the bowl, and even during the driest summers fresh streams tumble through from the heights above, a factor which adds to the general sogginess of the area. The passing of horses and hikers has worn deep ruts into the soft ground, and were this route forsaken for a 100 years the scars would likely remain.

Ascending from the Snowbowl, the trail reaches the crest of the Shovel Pass at Kilometre 17.5. Far above the last vestiges of forest, the pass is nestled against Curator Mountain while the other barren, rounded summits of the

Maligne Range stand near at hand. Composed of highly weathered and eroded Precambrian and Cambrian quartzites and argillites, the range lies on the eastern extreme of the Rockies' Main Ranges.

Shovel Pass gains its name from an incident which occurred in 1911. The Otto brothers, pioneer outfitters in the Jasper area, were attempting to transport a boat to Maligne Lake via this improbable route. Finding the snows so deep their horses could not pass, they ingeniously hacked a pair of shovels out of the native timber below and managed to scratch a trail through the snowbanks. One of these shovels supposedly remained along the trail for several years, testifying to the Ottos' arduous haul.

At Kilometre 19.5 the Wabasso Lake trail intersects the Skyline. From the junction one can look down the narrow defile to the Athabasca Valley. Serving as an optional route, the trail emerges on the Icefields Parkway 14.5 kilometres away. The trail is very steep, however, and is seldom used as an access to the Skyline.

From the Wabasso Lake junction the Skyline climbs to the shores of Curator Lake, a stark, rockbound tarn set within a steep-walled cirque. From the lake the trail begins its steep climb to the summit of the journey—the Notch—nearly two kilometres and 260 vertical metres away. (Snow hangs in this area into mid-summer and a cornice on the Notch often blocks the way.)

At a height of 2530 metres above sea level, the Notch provides extraordinary views. For the next five kilometres the hiker remains near its elevation, wandering along barren ridges with range upon range of mountains for company on either side. To the southwest and across the Athabasca Valley, Mount Edith Cavell is the most noticeable peak, rising to an elevation of 3363 metres. Nearly 1500 vertical metres below this vantage point the Athabasca River rolls toward Jasper townsite. A small white pyramid jutting above the northwestern skyline eighty aerial kilometres away, is Mount Robson (3954 m), the highest mountain in the Canadian Rockies.

Beyond the summit of Amber Mountain the trail begins a gradual switchbacking descent, levelling off near the Centre Lakes and entering the first scattered alpine fir above Tekarra Lake. Immediately behind the lake is Mount Tekarra, named by the explorer Dr. James Hector for an Iroquois who accompanied him up the Athabasca River in 1859.

Crossing the outlet stream below the lake, the trail climbs onto the lower slopes of Mount Tekarra and begins a traverse around to a more northerly exposure. Ahead views slowly open to the Colin Range, Pyramid Mountain and other familiar peaks near Jasper townsite. Rolling along through open tundra, the trail finally emerges on the Signal Mountain Fire Road at Kilometre 35.6. The lookout is visible from the junction, just 500 metres up the road. From here, 8.5 kilometres of downhill fire road hiking bring the traveller to the Maligne Lake Road near Maligne Canyon.

Since the start and finish of the hike are nearly forty kilometres apart by highway, transportation should be arranged in advance.

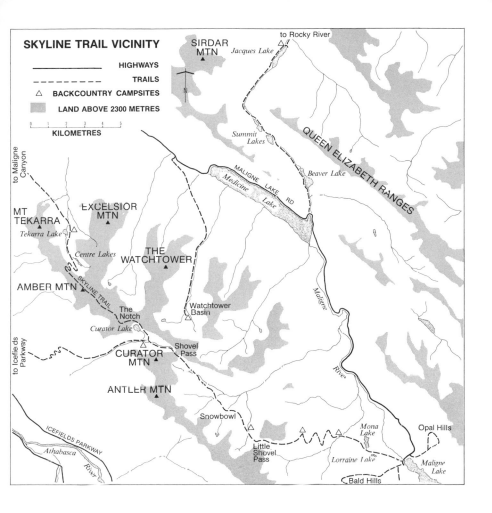

Bald Hills Lookout

Maligne Lake to Bald Hills Lookout—5.2 kilometres (3.2 miles)

Day trip
Allow 2 hours to lookout
Elevation gain: 490 metres (1,600 feet)
Maximum elevation: 2165 metres (7,100 feet)
Topo maps: Athabasca Falls, 83 C/12
        (trail not shown)

Point of Departure: Drive the Maligne Lake Road to its terminus at Maligne Lake, 44.6 kilometres (27.7 miles) southeast of its junction with the Yellowhead Highway. Upon reaching the lake, keep right and cross the lake's outlet to the parking area near the warden station.

0.0—Trail sign located just above the parking area at the fire road gate.

   —Steady uphill on moderate grade.

3.2—Junction. Stay on fire road.

3.4—Maligne Valley views.

5.2—Bald Hills Lookout.

Reached by a rather uninspiring trudge on "improved" fire road, the Bald Hills Fire Lookout provides an exceptional overview of Maligne Lake and its surrounding peaks. The subalpine meadows around the lookout are carpeted with wildflowers in July and early August, providing a colourful foreground for the lake and mountains and an ideal environment for aimless wandering.

The route to the lookout rises from the parking area at Maligne Lake on a broad, well-kept gravel fire road, travelling through a fire succession forest of lodgepole pine. Near Kilometre 2.5, however, scattered spruce begin to appear and ahead the environment becomes pronouncedly subalpine in character, with pleasant open meadows and stands of stunted alpine fir and Engelmann spruce gradually disappearing into the barren tundra above.

Views from the open slopes near the lookout encompass nearly 360 degrees. Below the greenish-blue waters of Maligne Lake stretch to the Narrows, with Leah Peak (2801 m) and Samson Peak (3081 m) rising beyond. The prominent glacier-clad summits that peek above the tundra to the south are Mounts Unwin and Charlton, both well in excess of 3000 metres above sea level.

In 1908, Mary Schaffer, the Rockies' first lady of exploration, and her companions reached Maligne Lake—its first recorded visit in over thirty years. Describing their journey down the lake and through the Narrows by raft, Mary Schaffer later wrote: "There burst upon us that which, all in our little company agreed, was the finest view any of us had ever beheld in the Rockies . . . Yet there it lay, for the time being all ours—those miles and miles of lake, the unnamed peaks rising above us, one following the other, each more beautiful than the last."

Maligne Lake from Bald Hills

Since that day thousands have marvelled at the beauties of Maligne.

The panorama from the north side of the lookout is no less interesting. To the northwest stand the rounded summits of the Maligne Mountains, a 45 kilometre long chain that stretches to Jasper townsite. To the north the Maligne River rolls away to the foot of the Queen Elizabeth Range. The bedding of the range, composed of a light grey Devonian limestone, has been tilted nearly vertical by the forces of mountain building and eroded to form a series of sharp, sawtoothed peaks.

Hikers should be forewarned that there is no reliable water supply on the trail, so take a canteen along.

Opal Hills

Opal Hills Loop—8.2 kilometres (5.1 miles)

Half-day trip
Allow 4 hours round trip
Elevation gain: 305 metres (1,000 feet)
Maximum elevation: 1980 metres (6,500 feet)
Topo maps: Athabasca Falls, 83 C/12
          (Trail not shown)

Point of Departure: Drive the Maligne Lake Road to its terminus at Maligne Lake, 44.6 kilometres (27.7 miles) southeast of its junction with the Yellowhead Highway. Upon reaching the lake, keep left and drive to the uppermost parking lot above the boat dock.

0.0—Trail sign at east edge of parking area.

0.2—Trail branches left.

  —Very steep uphill.

1.6—Trail split. Trail loops around into meadows above, returning to this point. Keep right.

  —Steady uphill.

2.6—Trail emerges into meadow.

  —Levels out into meadows behind hills.

4.7—Emerges from behind hills, dropping back into forest.

  —Moderate downhill.

6.6—Trail split junction.

8.2—Trail head at parking area.

Despite a steep initial climb, the Opal Hills loop is one of the more pleasant half-day hikes in Jasper Park. A short jaunt to the top of the grassy hillocks near the trail summit offers a fine view of Maligne Lake and the surrounding peaks. Travelling through high subalpine meadowland, the trip allows excellent opportunities for a day of nature-browsing, or just lying back on a hillside and snoozing in the sun.

There is no fooling about on the Opal Hills trail as it heads grimly upward with hardly a switchback, gaining elevation at a heart-pounding rate. The first two kilometres are through a dense forest of lodgepole pine, the creation of some past forest fire. Splitting at Kilometre 1.6, the trail loops up into an open bowl beneath the Opal Hills. Either branch will bring the hiker to the same point, but the right-hand option reaches the objective in far less time.

Keeping to the right at the junction, the trail enters spruce forest for a short stretch, then climbs back into the pine and finally out into open meadow at Kilometre 2.6. Once into the meadow, the trail levels off, crosses through a draw to the left and circles into a basin behind low hills. Any of these grassy knolls provides an excellent view out across the upper Maligne Valley. Maligne Lake stretches away to the southeast and disappears beneath the twin peaks of Mount Unwin (3268 m) and Mount Charlton (3217 m); across the valley lie the rolling Bald Hills; farther to the northwest are the rounded summits of the Maligne Range.

The first recorded journey to Maligne Lake was made in 1875 by the railroad surveyor Henry MacLeod, who was so disappointed by his long and fruitless slog to this cul de sac that he named it Sorefoot Lake. The Stoney Indians knew of the lake by the name "Chaba Imne," or Great Beaver Lake. In 1908 the lake was explored by an expedition mounted by

Opal Hills

Mary Schaffer, who was responsible for naming most of the mountains in the vicinity.

The trail continues its run through the open basin. The area provides excellent big game habitat, and moose are often seen browsing the scrub willow on the broad flats.

After travelling through the basin for two kilometres, the trail emerges from behind the meadowed knolls and makes a gradual descent through pleasant forest back to the loop junction.

Jacques Lake

Beaver Creek Picnic Area to Jacques Lake —11.6 kilometres (7.2 miles)

Day trip or backpack
Allow 4-5 hours to Jacques Lake
Elevation gain: 60 metres (200 feet)
Maximum elevation: 1555 metres (5,100 feet)
Topo maps: Medicine Lake, 83 C/13 East
            Medicine Lake, 83 C/13 West

Point of Departure: Drive the Maligne Lake Road to the Beaver Creek Picnic Area, 28.3 kilometres (17.6 miles) southeast from its junction with the Yellowhead Highway. The picnic area is near the southeast end of Medicine Lake at a point where the road makes a bend away from the lake.

0.0—Trail sign on fire road beside picnic area.

—Flat fire road walking.

1.6—Beaver Lake.

4.8—First Summit Lake.

6.0—Second Summit Lake.

7.4—Small lake.

—Area of many small stream crossings.

11.6—Jacques Lake (south end).

12.2—Jacques Lake Campsite.

12.4—Warden cabin. North end of Jacques Lake.

Lying beneath the severely faulted limestone mountains of the Front Ranges and surrounded by a luxuriant forest, Jacques Lake is an excellent destination for either strong day hikers or casual backpackers. The trail to the lake is unusual in that it travels through a narrow mountain valley, past four lakes and over a watershed divide—all within less than twelve kilometres and with little appreciable gain or loss of elevation.

After a pleasant fire road walk of 1.6 kilometres the first point of interest on the hike is reached—Beaver Lake. The lake receives heavy summer use by fishermen angling for the elusive brook trout which inhabit its depths. The surface of its still green waters is often visited by loon and other waterfowl. It is far too pleasant a stop for so early in the day.

The fire road continues, entering more open country. The sheer walls of the Queen Elizabeth Range appear to the right, the mountains' light grey slabs of Devonian limestone tilted nearly vertical and eroded to form a jagged sawtooth ridge.

At Kilometre 4.8 the hiker comes upon the first Summit Lake, a small body of water ringed by a forest of spruce, lodgepole pine and cottonwood poplar. Here the fire road reverts to foot trail and continues on past two more small lakes in the next three kilometres. Notice that the first two of these lakes have no visible outlet; lakes of this type are known as "sinks" and generally drain through subterranean passages in the limestone bedrock.

The last four kilometres to Jacques Lake are through a dense forest filled with streams. The main creek running down to the lake is crossed at least three times, while numerous small tributaries tumble in along the way. Needless to say, this is not a dry hike.

150

Jacques Lake

Though strong hikers can make the round trip in a day, the peaceful scene at Jacques Lake is not conducive to leaping up and racing back on the return trek. Better to backpack and stay at the small campground near the lake's outlet.

The best area for a good view is the north end of the lake, either by the campground or from the open meadow in front of the warden cabin. Looking back across the lake from north to south, the mountain standing to the far right is Sirdar (2808 m). Beyond the far end of the lake are the peaks of the Queen Elizabeth Range, looking quite different from their northern exposure.

It is probable that the name Jacques, which is used for not only the lake but also the mountain range to the northeast, came from Jacques Cardinal, a horse-tender for the North West Company on the Athabasca Trail during the early 19th Century.

The Watchtower

Maligne Lake Road to Campsite—9.8 kilometres (6.1 miles)

Day trip or backpack

Allow 3 hours one way

Elevation gain: 670 metres (2,200 feet)

Maximum elevation: 2075 metres (6,800 feet)

Topo maps: Medicine Lake, 83 C/13 West
(trail not shown)

Point of Departure: Drive to the marked
Watchtower turnoff, 18.5 kilometres (11.5 miles)
up the Maligne Lake Road. The trail head is at
the parking lot.

0.0—Trail sign.

—Trail splits immediately. Stay right and
cross bridge. Keep to the right beyond
the bridge.

0.2—Trail forks. Stay left.

0.5—Trail swings to the east and levels off.

2.6—Trail veers south, begins a moderate
climb up the Watchtower drainage.

5.6—Trail forks. Stay right, following the west
bank of the stream.

—Trail opens onto the Watchtower Valley
bottom.

9.6—Campsite across stream on east bank.
Ford stream.

9.8—Campsite. (The Watchtower Cabin burn-
ed down in 1977).

As a first backpack trip of the season,
the ten kilometre trek to the Watchtower
Valley is nearly ideal: it is relatively short
and of moderate gradient, but long
enough and in places steep enough to
remind dormant muscles just what
backpacking is all about. The upper
valley is beautiful and the high meadows
and passes visible from the campsite
offer interesting exploratory possibilities
for anyone able to spend more than one
night in the area.

From the sign at the parking lot the
trail heads south into a dense forest of
pine, spruce and fir. The trail forks
almost immediately and the hiker should
stick with the more recently cut path to
the right, crossing the river via a sturdy
footbridge. Although the river here is
hardly more than a stream for most of
the year, its turbulant nature 20
kilometres downstream, where it joins
the Athabasca, caused the early French
voyageurs such problems that they called
it the Maligne ('evil').

Across the river, the trail turns
downstream for a short distance before
swinging south again and beginning a
short but steep climb up the northern
flank of the Watchtower. After the trail
has gained enough elevation to leave
most hikers slightly winded, it angles off
toward the east and the next two
kilometres run gradually uphill, traversing numerous marshy areas, most of
which are bridged with corduroy
walkways of lodgepole pine.

At the 2.5 kilometre mark the trail
gradually veers back to the south and
begins the major climbing portion of the
hike. The grade, however, is rarely so
steep that the hiker can't put his heel
down, and the following three kilometres
pass quickly, even though the scenery is
restricted to the immediate forest.

At Kilometre 5.8 the trail suddenly
levels off and the hiker trades the forest
for the semi-open meadows of the

The Upper Watchtower Valley

Watchtower Valley. The trail forks here and the hiker is advised to stay to the right, above the stream that drains from the upper valley. The last four kilometres follow the west bank of the stream and are usually very boggy until late in the summer. The trail can also be sketchy in places, but the terrain is open and the general route obvious.

For hikers travelling to the campsite, some additional information is necessary. As the trail approaches the upper end of the valley a large and convoluted mountain looms up to the east, across the stream. A glacier-carved cirque sweeps down from the west face of the peak to the valley bottom and it is at the foot of this cirque that the campsite is found. For those good at estimating hiking distances, the site is roughly four kilometres from the point where the trail opens into the valley bottom and slightly less than three kilometres from the alpine passes at the valley's southern end.

From the campsite the hiker has several options. He can explore the cirque behind the campsite or he can wander off in the opposite direction to scramble up the lower sections of the 2791 metre Watchtower (so named in 1916 for its general appearance). Or he can head up toward the high meadows that blanket the far end of the valley. A scramble of less than three kilometres (approximately 1½ hours) up and over the middle of the three passes at the end of the valley will put the hiker in the Shovel Pass area of the Skyline Trail.

Sulphur Skyline

Miette Hot Springs to Sulphur Summit—4.0 kilometres (2.5 miles)

Half-day trip
Allow 2 hours to summit
Elevation gain: 670 metres (2,200 feet)
Maximum elevation: 2069 metres (6,788 feet)
Topo maps: Miette, 83 F/4 West
              Miette, 83 F/4 East
              (last 1.8 km not shown)

Point of Departure: Drive to Pocahontas, 7.0 kilometres (4.4 miles) west of Jasper East Gate on the Yellowhead Highway. Turn south onto the Miette Hot Springs Road and follow it 17.4 kilometres (10.9 miles) to a parking area across from the Miette Hot Springs Campground.

0.0—Trail sign at the rear of the campground.

—Trail climbs at moderate but steady grade on access road.

0.8—Road narrows to trail width.

—Ascends through old burn dotted with spruce and pine.

2.2—Pass and junction. Sulphur Skyline cuts uphill to right. Trail to Mystery Lake continues straight ahead.

—Grade steepens and views open.

3.4—Trail climbs above last stunted trees.

4.0—Sulphur Skyline summit (2069 m).

The short but steep trail leading to the summit of Sulphur Ridge is one of the truly fine day hikes in Jasper Park. Not only does it offer excellent close-up views of sawtoothed mountain ranges, but it is also an exceptional vantage point for several remote wilderness valleys—the most prominent being the Fiddle River drainage which snakes southwest for over 24 kilometres to its headwaters on a high rockbound pass. But be forewarned, this is a steep dry hike. Take water along.

Beginning at the rear of the Miette Hot Springs Campground, the trail climbs steadily to a low pass 2.2 kilometres distant. Immediately upon cresting the pass, the Sulphur Skyline trail branches up and to the right, beginning an even steeper ascent into the alpine environs of this small mountain overlooking the hot springs complex. The laboured breathing ends on the highest point of the ridge and expansive views spread out below.

In addition to the southerly vistas of the Fiddle River valley and the rocky pyramid of Utopia Mountain (2563 m), there are equally impressive valleys and mountains stretching away to the north. Just a few kilometres below Miette Hot Springs, beyond the confluence of Sulphur Creek and the lower Fiddle River, are the jagged summits of Ashlar Ridge— the layers of grey limestone having been uplifted and steeply tilted to erode into a typical sawtooth mountain formation. The valleys running on either side of Ashlar Ridge descend to the broad Athabasca Valley, and further north the broad U-shaped Moosehorn Valley disappears into the distant haze.

For those with a little time and energy left to spare, the Skyline Ridge can be traversed along its length toward the hot springs. With some bushwhacking and careful route-finding, hikers can descend near the end of the ridge to the trail just above the campground.

Fiddle River from Sulphur Skyline

Mystery Lake

Day trip or backpack

Allow 4 hours one way

Elevation gain: 455 metres (1,500 feet)

        loss: 275 metres (900 feet)

Maximum elevation: 1645 metres (5,400 feet)

Topo maps: Miette, 83 F/4 East

        Miette, 83 F/4 West

        (last 6 kms not shown)

Point of Departure: Drive to Pocahontas, 7.0 kilometres (4.4 miles) west of Jasper East Gate on the Yellowhead Highway. Turn south onto the Miette Hot Springs Road and follow it 17.4 kilometres (10.9 miles) to a parking area across from the Miette Hot Springs Campground.

0.0—Trail sign at rear of campground.

—Trail follows access road.

0.8—Road narrows to trail width.

—Switchbacks up through short willow meadows.

2.2—Top of pass. Sulphur Skyline trail branches to the right. Mystery Lake straight ahead.

—Trail begins steep descent.

4.5—Fiddle River. Keep to west bank, travelling north.

4.8—Fiddle River ford.

6.8—Trail leaves river bank, begins ascent to Mystery Lake.

7.1—Junction. Take left fork.

9.8—Jasper Park boundary.

10.5—Mystery Lake.

11.7—Mystery Lake campsite.

Mystery Lake is a small, peaceful body of water lying just beyond the eastern boundary of Jasper National Park. Below treeline, the lake offers a gentle solitude for backpackers desiring a protected retreat combined with a day or two of trout fishing. The trail to the lake is an interesting one, offering several types of challenge and a variety of terrain. Because of a major ford of the Fiddle River, it is recommended that the trail be hiked only after midsummer.

The trail begins at the upper edge of the Miette Hot Springs Campground and gradually climbs to a low pass at the 2.2 kilometre mark. This first section of trail is frequently intersected by smaller trails running in from left and right, but the main route is easily discernible. The trail switchbacks through some willow meadows just before the pass summit is reached, granting the hiker an opportunity to look back down the Sulphur Creek valley.

From the top of the pass the trail begins a gradual descent through coniferous forest to Kilometre 3.9, where a viewpoint reveals the rapids of the Fiddle River 300 metres below. Beyond the viewpoint the trail drops rapidly toward the river and into the narrow canyon of the Fiddle.

At the 4.5 kilometre mark the trail reaches the river's edge and swings to the north, toward a narrow notch in the canyon's high limestone cliffs. The hiker must ford the river before reaching the notch and should watch closely for a likely spot as he moves downstream. The ford, nearly impossible for the hiker in early summer, is usually not difficult after the first week of August.

Once across the river the hiker should stay on the east bank, even though the horse trail wanders back and forth across the river four or five times in the following 2.3 kilometres. Staying on the east bank will necessitate some bush-

156

Fiddle River crossing

whacking and riverside boulder hopping whenever the horse trail is on the opposite side, but it does save several tricky fordings.

At Kilometre 6.8 the trail cuts away from the river to the east and begins a short but steep climb to Mystery Lake. Keeping to the left at the 7.1 kilometre trail junction, the hiker walks through alternating sections of forest and willow, the latter often over his head (and thus miserable on a wet day), to the western end of Mystery Lake at Kilometre 10.5. Although there is evidence of a packer's camp at the lakeshore, the designated campsite is at the far end of the lake, reached by following the lake's south shore.

Fiddle River

Miette Hot Springs to Whitehorse Pass—24 kilometres (15 miles)*

Wilderness access

Allow 2 days to the pass

Elevation gain: 745 metres (2,450 feet)

Maximum elevation: 2120 metres (6,950 feet)

Topo maps: Miette, 83 F/4 West
            Miette, 83 F/4 East
            (last 19 kms not shown)

Point of Departure: Drive the Yellowhead Highway to the Pocahontas service centre, 7.1 kilometres (4.4 miles) west of Jasper Park East Gate and 41.2 kilometres (25.6 miles) northeast of Jasper townsite. Follow the Miette Hot Springs Road 17.5 kilometres to its terminus at the hot springs complex. Park opposite the campground and hike down to the pool. The trail strikes off up Sulphur Creek from the pool facility.

*Distance approximate.

Striking off to the southeast from Miette Hot Springs, the Fiddle River trail runs through remote country which is gradually being discovered by experienced backpackers. While most travellers terminate their journey on Whitehorse Pass, it is possible to continue the trip on provincial forest lands, continuing down Whitehorse Creek and emerging on the forestry road just south of Cadomin.

The first five kilometres of trail running up Sulphur Creek and down to the Fiddle River are quite well developed and, in fact, often very muddy as they are used regularly by the horse outfitter from Miette Hot Springs. But the track running up the Fiddle is not as well defined and can be confusing in sections, particularly when it swings across the stream in typical horse-trail fashion as it does near the Fiddle River Warden Cabin. Experienced route finders who are used to travelling through rough country should have no problem in the valley, however, nor should they be thwarted by the fords (though this hike is best attacked later in the season).

Approximately 19 kilometres from Miette Hot Springs, the trail branches left up the north tributary stream and climbs to the narrow notch of Whitehorse Pass—a treeless summit situated at 2120 metres above sea level which marks the park boundary. A campsite near the pass offers an excellent base for exploration, while more adventuresome backpackers may continue on to the mining centre of Cadomin 18 kilometres distant—14 kilometres down the Whitehorse Creek trail and four kilometres north on the forestry road.

Moosehorn Creek

Celestine Road to Moosehorn Lakes—36 kilometres (22 miles)*

Wilderness access

Allow 2 days to Moosehorn Lakes

Elevation gain: 550 metres (1,800 feet)

Maximum elevation: 1615 metres (5,300 feet)

Topo maps: Snaring, 83 E/1 East
      Miette, 83 F/4 West
      Entrance, 83 F/5 West
      Rock Lake, 83 E/8 East
      Rock Lake, 83 E/8 West

Point of Departure: Drive the Yellowhead Highway east from Jasper townsite 11.6 kilometres (7.2 miles) to the junction with the Celestine Lake Road. Follow the Celestine Road through the Snaring Campground 6.4 kilometres (4.0 miles) to the controlled access gravel road. Check one way travel restrictions listed on the sign and abide strictly to the hours of travel. Follow the road 18 kilometres (11 miles) to where the Devona Flats road branches to the right.

*Distances approximate.

This route runs up a seldom visited valley at the eastern edge of the Front Ranges to a pair of low elevation lakes just beyond the park's north boundary. The trip is a fine choice for experienced backpackers who want to 'get away from it all,' and by continuing beyond the Moosehorn Lakes a circuit of the Bosche Range can be completed—an extended journey of some five to seven days.

After reaching the Devona cutoff on the Celestine Lake Road, backpackers descend to Devona Flats and join the CNR tracks. Follow the railroad northward for eleven kilometres to the Miette Warden Cabin, just beyond the mouth of Ronde Creek. Here the Moosehorn Valley trail branches north across the lower slopes of the Bosche Range to Moosehorn Creek and reaches the park boundary and Upper Moosehorn Lake in another twelve kilometres.

For hikers who wish to complete the Moosehorn Snake Indian loop, the trail continues west into the Bosche Range from Lower Moosehorn Lake, then veers north to re-enter Jasper Park. From the park boundary the trail skirts the northern end of the Bosche Range just south of Rock Creek and follows the Rock Creek trail southward to intersect with the North Boundary Trail at Kilometre 20.0, just east of Willow Creek Campground. (See *North Boundary Trail*.)

Total distance for the loop option—from the head of the Devona Flats road and return—is approximately 102 kilometres. While exact conditions are unknown, this trail is often used by park warden patrols, and the route should be obvious to experienced wilderness travellers armed with topo maps.

Devona Lookout

Half-day trip

Allow 1½ hours one way

Elevation gain: 150 metres (500 feet)

Maximum elevation: 1404 metres (4,605 feet)

Topo maps: Snaring, 83 E/1 East

Point of Departure: Drive the Yellowhead Highway east from Jasper townsite 11.6 kilometres (7.2 miles) to the junction with the Celestine Lake Road. Follow the Celestine Road through the Snaring Campground 6.4 kilometres (4.0 miles) to the controlled access gravel road. Check one way travel restrictions listed on the sign and abide strictly to the hours of travel. Follow the road 27 kilometres (17 miles) to its terminus at the Celestine Lake parking area.

Despite outstanding views of the lower Athabasca Valley, the hike to the Devona Fire Lookout can only be considered a bonus for those who have driven the Celestine Lake Fire Road—a one way track which is rough and quite exposed in places.

From the Celestine Lake parking area, hikers can continue on to the fire lookout over the final 4.2 kilometres of road which are closed to motor vehicles. Two lakes are passed in the first two kilometres, Princess and Celestine, both very popular for their rainbow trout fishing.

After reaching the lookout tower, continue out along the ridge for another 200 metres to an open point of land where there is an excellent panorama of the Athabasca Valley.

Vine Creek

Wilderness access

Allow 4 hours one way

Elevation gain: 640 metres (2,100 feet)

Maximum elevation: 1675 metres (5,500 feet)

Topo maps: Snaring, 83 E/1 East
(trail not shown)

Point of Departure: Drive the Yellowhead Highway east from Jasper townsite 11.6 kilometres (7.2 miles) to the junction with the Celestine Lake Road. Follow the Celestine Road through the Snaring Campground 6.4 kilometres (4.0 miles) to the controlled access gravel road. Check one way travel restrictions listed on the sign and abide strictly to the hours of travel. Follow the road 10 kilometres (6 miles) to where Vine Creek intersects from the northwest.

*Distance approximate.

Vine Creek is a trail which is difficult to get to and of marginal interest once it is reached. Yet, for experienced hikers who would like to do some exploring beyond the headwaters of this little-used valley, the trip may be worthwhile.

From the trail head on the Celestine Lake Road, the route makes a straightforward ascent of the narrow Vine Creek drainage. There is a campsite near the headwaters, and the 1675 metre divide, while still below timberline, serves as a good springboard for those who would climb Roche DeSmet. While travel may be rough, there are numerous exploration opportunities for another ten kilometres beyond the Vine Creek headwaters provided by the many low passes and side valleys of the DeSmet Range.

160

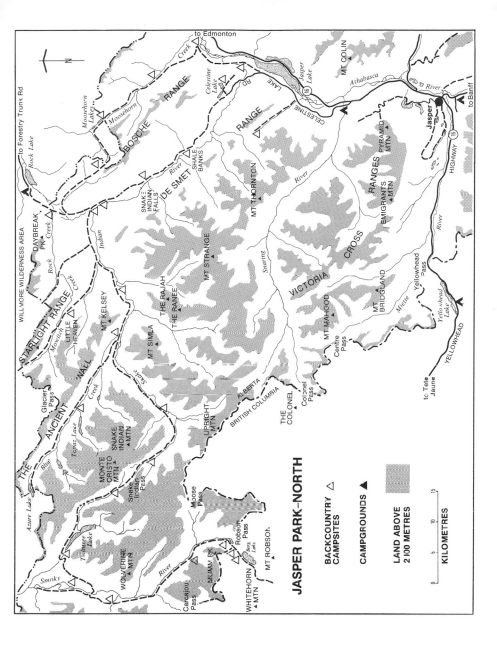

JASPER PARK—NORTH

BACKCOUNTRY CAMPSITES △

CAMPGROUNDS ▲

LAND ABOVE 2100 METRES

KILOMETRES
0   5   10   15

161

North Boundary Trail

Celestine Lake to Robson Park—151.5 kilometres (94.1 miles)

Backpack
Allow 8 days to two weeks
Elevation gain: 1055 metres (3,465 feet)
     loss: 1445 metres (4,740 feet)
Maximum elevation: 2019 metres (6,625 feet)
Topo maps: Snaring, 83 E/1 East
    Rock Lake, 83 E/8 East
    Rock Lake, 83 E/8 West
    Blue Creek, 83 E/7 East
    Blue Creek, 83 E/7 West
    Twintree Lake, 83 E/6 East
    Twintree Lake, 83 E/6 West
    Mount Robson, 83 E/3 East

Point of Departure: Drive east from Jasper townsite on the Yellowhead Highway 11.6 kilometres (7.2 miles) to the Celestine Lake Road. Follow the Celestine Road past the Snaring Campground. At Kilometre 6.4 (Mile 4.0) the road becomes limited to one way traffic. A sign indicates the hours of travel to and from Celestine Lake (travellers can also find a list of these times at the park information office in Jasper townsite). The restricted access road winds for another 27 kilometres (17 miles) along the Athabasca Valley to a small parking area 1.6 kilometres from Celestine Lake. The North Boundary Trail strikes off from the north edge of the parking lot. (For point of departure directions to the western terminus of the trail, see *Berg Lake*.)

0.0—Celestine Lake Parking Lot.

12.1—Shalebanks Campground.

19.8—Seldom Inn Campground.

21.3—Snake Indian Falls (200 metres off trail to left).

22.1—Trail branches right from fire road.

30.4—Horseshoe Campground.

32.2—Junction. Rock Creek and Willow Creek Warden Station to right. North Boundary Trail to left.

32.7—Willow Creek Campground.

34.1—Junction. Rock Creek and Eagle's Nest Pass to right. North Boundary Trail straight ahead.

38.3—Mud Creek.

In the summer of 1910, a small party of European alpinists exploring the slopes of Mount Robson heard of an old Indian trail which led down the Smoky River, over a high pass and eastward along the Snake Indian River to its mouth in the Athabasca Valley. Thinking the route might offer a quick exit from the mountains, the group set off down the Smoky under the guidance of outfitter John Yates. With some expert route-finding by this veteran guide, the party made the first traverse of today's North Boundary Trail.

Visits to the northern wilds of Jasper Park were fairly few and sporadic over the next few decades. Even in the 1960's the North Boundary country was well known to only a few wardens and a handful of horsemen and adventuresome hikers. But today, probably because it is one of the best maintained wilderness trails in western Canada, the North Boundary is visited by hundreds of backpackers every summer.

Hikers should be forwarned that, except for the country near Mount Robson and a brief interval on Snake Indian Pass, the North Boundary Trail is not noted for its spectacular alpine scenery. In fact, many travellers find the trail quite tedious, particularly when the weather is wet and the trail has been churned up by horses' hooves. Yet, if one appreciates wild, remote country without river fords and bushwhacking, where pleasant campsites await the weary hiker at the end of every day's journey, then the trail is ideal.

Certainly the North Boundary country possesses its own unique and subdued brand of beauty. It is a wilderness inhabited by moose, bear and one of the largest wolf populations in the mountain parks (as well as porcupines which will munch on your pack at night if you leave it sitting on the ground). We've known many a park warden who would quite

Snake Indian Falls

40.9—Junction. Little Heaven and Glacier Pass to right. North Boundary Trail straight ahead.

41.7—Deer Creek.

45.4—Welbourne Campground and Warden Cabin.

50.1—Milk Creek.

52.2—Nellie Lake.

56.4—Blue Creek Warden Station.

57.3—Blue Creek Campground.

57.8—Blue Creek Suspension Bridge.

58.1—Junction. Blue Creek trail to Topaz and Indigo Lakes to right. North Boundary Trail straight ahead.

69.6—Three Slides Warden Cabin.

72.3—Three Slides Campground.

80.5—Hoodoo Warden Cabin (200 metres off trail to left).

85.0—Oatmeal Campground.

91.3—Snake Indian Pass (2019 m).

97.2—Byng Campground.

97.6—Byng Warden Cabin.

105.5—Twintree Lake.

106.7—Twintree Lake Warden Cabin.

108.4—Twintree Lake Campground.

110.6—Twintree Creek bridge.

117.7—Donaldson Creek Campground.

120.3—Smoky River bridge.

120.8—Junction. Short River and park boundary to right. North Boundary Trail straight ahead.

121.2—Smoky River Warden Station.

124.9—Chown Creek Campground and bridge.

132.0—Warden Cabin.

133.1—Carcajou Creek.

136.0—Wolverine Campground.

148.9—Adolphus Campground and Warden Station.

150.7—Adolphus Lake.

151.5—Robson Pass (1651 m). Alberta-B.C. boundary.

173.4—Berg Lake trail head.

happily live out his days riding through these wild valleys.

The eastern terminus of this long wilderness trek is at Celestine Lake, just 53 kilometres east of Jasper townsite via the Yellowhead Highway and the Celestine Lake Fire Road. From rather inauspicious beginnings in the forest-enclosed Celestine Lake parking area, the trail follows the Snake Indian River to its source on Snake Indian Pass, descends past Twintree Lake to the Smoky River, ascends the Smoky to its headwaters on the glacier-clad slopes of Mount Robson and finally emerges near the Yellowhead Highway at the Berg Lake trail head in Robson Park, B.C. Though popularly known as the 100 mile North Boundary Trail, the distance from Celestine Lake to Robson Pass measures out to 94.1 miles; tacking on the last segment of trail through Robson Park, the total trip is 107.7 miles, or 173.4 kilometres.

As might be suspected, the hiking options in so vast a country are endless. Many backpackers only penetrate this wilderness for a day or two before retracing their steps, but to most the attraction lies in traversing the entire trail. While some hike the North Boundary Trail from west to east, our preference is from east to west—a choice which allows a gradual improvement in scenery day by day culminating in the spectacular Mount Robson environs near the end of the journey. Elevation gain is spread out over many miles on the east to west option and is hardly noticeable, while eastbound travellers face two long gruelling climbs on the first half of their journey and an uninspiring 22 kilometre fire road walk on the final day.

Travelling from east to west the North Boundary Trail can be divided up into six more or less defined sections, each one around 25 to 33 kilometres in length.

The Lower Snake Indian River (Celestine Lake to Willow Creek)—32.7 kilometres. Starting from the trail head near Celestine Lake, the first 22.1 kilometres of the trail follow a relatively level, well-graded fire road. Travel is

Snake Indian Pass

fairly tedious along this first section except for the Snake Indian Falls, a most impressive waterfall which thunders over a sheer cliff of limestone. Just under a kilometre beyond Snake Indian Falls the trail branches away from the fire road, and at Kilometre 29.8 it opens out into broad meadowlands as it nears the point where the Snake Indian River makes a major bend toward the south. Willow Creek flows into the Snake Indian from the north at this bend, and the country surrounding this junction is particularly beautiful as the meadows offer expansive views up the course of the river to the west and to the Daybreak Peak country in the north.

The Middle Snake Indian River (Willow Creek to Blue Creek)—25.1 kilometres. From Willow Creek the trail turns westward on its long journey toward the Great Divide. The country remains pleasant and open, the trail winding through stands of aspen and lodgepole pine and along meadows laced with scrub birch, willow and shrubby cinquefoil. Continuing westward the valley narrows as the hiker draws nearer to the rugged peaks which serve as the gateway to Blue Creek and the upper Snake Indian Valley. At Kilometre 52.2 one of the gems of the North Boundary Trail is encountered—Nellie Lake, reflecting the jagged summit of 2786 metre Mount Simla. From this point there is a true sense of having entered the mountains.

The Upper Snake Indian River (Blue Creek to Snake Indian Pass)—33.5 kilometres. Blue Creek is a significant landmark on the North Boundary Trail for several reasons: it serves as the gateway to some very remote country on the park's northern border, the nearby warden station is 'home base' for much of the patrol activity in the northern section of the park; and for the westbound hiker it is the beginning of more serious mountain travel. The first six kilometres of hiking west of Blue Creek are quite beautiful as views often stretch across the Snake Indian Valley and its marshy, lake-dotted overflow plain. At Three Slides the first major glacier of the trip can be seen covering the slopes of Upright Mountain at the head of a valley to the south (not Mount Robson as some folks believe). At Kilometre 80.5 the Hoodoo Warden Cabin is passed and the climb to Snake Indian Pass begins, a moderate but steady uphill which breaks out of the trees at Kilometre 86.5 to allow an unobstructed view to the narrow gap of Snake Indian Pass straight ahead.

Twintree Creek (Snake Indian Pass to Smoky River)—29.0 kilometres. At 2019 metres above sea level, Snake Indian Pass is set in rolling alpine terrain. Paralleling the pass to the north are steeply tilted slabs of limestone which form the most spectacular peaks of the region—Snake Indian Mountain and Monte Cristo Mountain. From this pleasant summit the trail descends Twintree Creek to the shores of Twintree Lake—a silty, forest-enclosed body of water which was named by outfitter John Yates and company in 1910 for two lone pine trees situated on two small islands of rock near the lake's outlet. From Twintree Lake the trail descends Twintree Creek a distance before crossing the stream and climbing over a ridge of Twintree Mountain. From the forested crest of the ridge, a stiff descent of 300 metres is made in eight kilometres to the crossing on the Smoky River. It is a rocky, rooty and often boggy track that is easily the toughest section of trail on the entire hike.

Smoky River (Smoky River Crossing to Robson Pass)—31.2 kilometres. A new world is entered once the traveller reaches the Smoky River. Here are rugged mountains and rocky river flats where glaciers are close at hand and hard at work. The valley of Chown Creek running away to the west at Kilometre 124.9 is particularly spectacular, dominated as it is by the cold

grey ramparts of 3216 metre Mount Bess. The climb up the Smoky is relatively gradual though rough and rocky in sections, and the scenery continues to improve. At Kilometre 139.3 the trail travels beneath the Mural Glacier as it begins a somewhat more serious ascent toward Robson Pass. Finally the long-awaited view of Mount Robson (weather permitting) is obtained as the traveller crosses the open meadow below Adolphus Lake. The lake lies about 1500 metres into the trees beyond this willow-covered valley, but its western shore opens out onto the broad flats of Robson Pass where the monarch of the Rockies towers in all its majesty.

Robson Park (Robson Pass to Berg Lake trail head)—21.9 kilometres. When the weary traveller reaches the boundary to Robson Park, he might well consider that he has returned to civilization. Within the space of a few kilometres the hiker passes from a relatively peaceful and primitive land into one of the busiest backcountry areas in the mountain parks. The scenery, however, is exceptional. (For a detailed description, see *Berg Lake*.)

Our division of the North Boundary Trail into six sections is a subjective one, and by no means is it a suggestion that the trip be undertaken in only six days. It is merely an attempt to identify significant changes in topography encountered along the way. Indeed, it would be a bit of a chore for even the strongest hiker to complete this traverse in six or seven days. The Warden Service recommends 10 days to two weeks be spent on the journey and by placing campsites at approximately 10 to 13 kilometre intervals, it has encouraged this pace (though strong backpackers can jump campsites to average around 25 kilometres a day).

Finally, cabins situated along the trail are strictly for warden patrol use. While they are all interconnected by telephone (this phone line is a constant companion throughout the trip), the cabins should only be entered in the direst emergency.

Rock Lake-Willow Creek Option.
From the junction at Kilometre 32.2, a 13 kilometre branch trail runs north to Rock Lake, just beyond the park boundary on provincial forest lands. The trail follows Willow Creek for approximately half the distance before crossing a low divide to the Rock Creek valley. The route is well-defined, but there is a ford on Rock Creek. Because Rock Lake can be reached by a good branch road off the Grand Cache Forestry Road this trail is most often used as optional access to the North Boundary Trail.

Rock Creek-Eagle's Nest Pass Option.
From the junction at Kilometre 34.1, a 19 kilometre branch trail runs northwest to the park boundary and the southern edge of the Willmore Wilderness. The route makes a long gradual crossing of a low watershed divide to Rock Creek, ascends that drainage to the park boundary and eventually crosses Eagle's Nest Pass in the Willmore. Trail conditions are reported as good to Rock Creek but deteriorating near the park boundary.

Little Heaven-Glacier Pass Option.
From the junction at Kilometre 40.9, a 26 kilometre branch trail runs northwest to 2075 metre Glacier Pass. Again, the trail is reported good in the south, deteriorating near the boundary.

Blue Creek Option. Considered by many to be the most worthwhile option off the North Boundary Trail, this 32 kilometre branch forks northwest from the North Boundary at Kilometre 58.1 and runs up the Blue Creek valley to Azure (Indigo) Lake on the park's boundary with the Willmore Wilderness. The trail is reported in good condition with bridges up to the Natural Arch area around Kilometre 25, but supposedly deteriorates on the last section to Azure Lake. There is excellent Dolly Varden fishing reported in Topaz and other major lakes along the valley, and the scenery is considered to be superior to anything on the main North Boundary route.

Smoky River Option. From the junction at Kilometre 120.8, a 15 kilometre segment runs north along the Smoky to the park boundary. The trail is reported in good condition and is used primarily as an access route to the Willmore Wilderness. The branch trail east to Azure Lake is not recommended because of a very difficult ford on the Smoky.

Chown Creek Option. A short eight kilometre branch cuts west from the North Boundary route at Kilometre 124.9 and runs out to the summit of Bess Pass. Though a bit rough, the route is easily followed and provides some excellent scenery near the foot of Mount Bess.

Berg Lake

Robson River Parking Area to Kinney Lake—4.2 kilometres (2.6 miles)
Robson River Parking Area to Berg Lake—17.4 kilometres (10.8 miles)

Backpack
Allow 8-10 hours to Berg Lake
Elevation gain: 790 metres (2,600 feet)
Maximum elevation: 1638 metres (5,375 feet)
Topo maps: Mount Robson, 83 E/3 East

Point of Departure: Drive the Yellowhead Highway to the Mount Robson service centre, 58 kilometres (36 miles) west of the Alberta-B.C. Boundary (Yellowhead Pass). Take the dirt road which cuts off to the north (by the service station) and follow to its terminus at the Robson River parking area, approximately 2½ kilometres distant.

0.0—Robson River bridge.

4.2—Kinney Lake (outlet bridge). Campsite.

4.5—Kinney Lake (shore viewpoint).

6.1—Avalanche area.

6.9—Junction. Foot trail stays to right.

8.2—Robson River and bridges. Outwash flats above Kinney Lake.

10.3—Suspension bridge over Robson River.

10.5—Campground.

11.3—Suspension bridge over Robson River. Steep switchbacks begin.

11.8—White Falls viewpoint.

12.7—Falls-of-the-Pool viewpoint.

14.3—Emperor Falls (200 metres to right).

15.0—Campsite. Trail flattens out.

16.9—Outwash stream and bridges.

17.4—Berg Lake (northwest shore).

19.3—Berg Lake Chalet.

19.6—Campsite.

20.9—Warden Cabin.

21.6—Shelter and campsite.

21.9—Robson Pass. Alberta-B.C. boundary.

"On every side the snowy heads of mighty hills crowded round, whilst, immediately behind us, a giant among giants, and immeasurably supreme, rose Robson's peak . . . We saw its upper portion dimmed by a necklace of light, feathery clouds, beyond which its pointed apex of ice, glittering in the morning sun, shot up far into the blue heaven above."

So reflected Viscount Milton and W.B. Cheadle, two young British adventurers who passed Mount Robson on their way from Jasper House to Tete Jaune Cache in 1863. One can only tremble to think to what heights their prose might have risen had they journeyed via Robson Pass and Berg Lake, beneath the awesome, ice-bound north wall of the highest peak in the Canadian Rockies. There can be little dispute that this area is one of the gems of the mountain world. There is even less doubt that it is the most heavily travelled backpacking trail in the mountain parks.

From the trail head parking area, the trail climbs gradually along the torrent of the Robson River and through a micro-rain forest of Douglas fir, cedar, spruce and hemlock. The lush forest, which is very out-of-place in the Rocky Mountains, is in part created by Mount Robson. Rather than spreading over the broader band of the Rockies, as is usual, rain concentrates in this valley when Pacific weather systems run afoul of this huge mountain.

Kinney Lake, located 4.2 kilometres from the trail head, is an excellent example of a glacially fed lake. Its waters are milky blue, the result of great quantities of finely ground rock material fed into the Robson River by glaciers on Mount Robson and its neighbouring peaks. The lake is named for the Reverend George B. Kinney, a Canadian mountaineer who made the first attempts to scale Mount Robson in 1907, 1908 and 1909.

Mount Robson and Berg Lake

From the southeast end of Kinney Lake the trail is not so easy as before. It ascends a short series of switchbacks and traverses above the northeast side of the lake, just a little warm-up for the rigors ahead.

At Kilometre 6.1 the hiker comes upon an extraordinary scene of devastation. In the early spring of 1968 a spectacular avalanche rolled down from the western slopes of Mount Robson. In its wake huge cedar trees have been left splintered and crushed. Many of these once magnificent trees are still standing, but their tops have been snapped off thirty or more feet above the ground.

At Kilometre 7.2 there is an excellent view of Kinney Lake and the gravel outwash area at its head. The waters of the Robson River deposit rock and silt over the valley floor creating an outwash plain. The hiker has an opportunity to examine the phenomenon at closer quarters when he crosses the broad flats at Kilometre 8.2.

After a short steep climb up from the Kinney Lake outwash flats and two more crossings of the Robson River on suspension bridges, the trail begins it tortuous rise up the spectacular Valley-of-a-Thousand Falls. In the next 3.5 kilometres the hiker climbs over 450 vertical metres, ascending near the narrow gorge which contains the thundering Robson River. Three major waterfalls are viewed on the ascent—White Falls, the Falls-of-the-Pool and Emperor Falls.

After levelling off above the Valley-of-a-Thousand Falls, the trail dips down along the river again, offering the first glimpse of the majestic, snow-crusted north wall of Mount Robson. Views of the wall and its glaciers become increasingly spectacular beyond.

The view across the powder-blue waters of Berg Lake to Mount Robson is exceptional to say the least. Two rivers of ice cascade down from the uppermost reaches of the mountain—Mist Glacier and Berg Glacier. The latter terminates in the lake. The groan and rumble of these two overburdened bodies is constant, with chunks of ice calving from Berg Glacier and drifting into the lake.

The summit of Mount Robson lies more than two vertical kilometres above the lake, at an elevation of 3854 metres above sea level. First climbed in 1913 by a party led by Conrad Kain, it has been the object of many subsequent expeditions and is still considered one of the most difficult ascents in Canada. The mountain also contains the greatest section of Cambrian rock known in Canada—some 400 metres thick.

Robson Pass lies just over two kilometres beyond the northeast end of Berg Lake and serves as the gateway to the remote northwest corner of Jasper National Park. The trail runs through the pass to Adolphus Lake and the Smoky River valley beyond. There are three campsites in Robson Pass vicinity: the first and most popular lies just beyond Berg Lake Chalet along the edge of the lake's broad gravel beach; another provincial park campsite is situated on the open flats just 300 metres west of the pass; and there is a more secluded national park campsite just over a kilometre east of Adolphus Lake. As of this writing, future accommodation or services at Berg Lake Chalet are doubtful.

There are a number of interesting explorations which can be made by hikers staying in the Berg Lake-Robson Pass vicinity. The toe of the Robson Glacier can be visited in an easy half-day trip and there are routes leading up from the chalet area to the open slopes below Mumm Peak that offer outstanding aerial views of Berg Lake and Mount Robson. More energetic souls can backpack further into the wilderness by continuing into Jasper Park along the North Boundary Trail for another day to Chown Creek; there are short but interesting side trips which can be made up both Mural Creek and Chown Creek along the way.

Those planning a trip to Berg Lake should consider, however, an entry in the journal of J.M. Sellar, who travelled down the Fraser River in 1862: ". . . the guide told us that out of twenty-nine times that he had passed it (Mount Robson) he had only seen the top once before . . ."

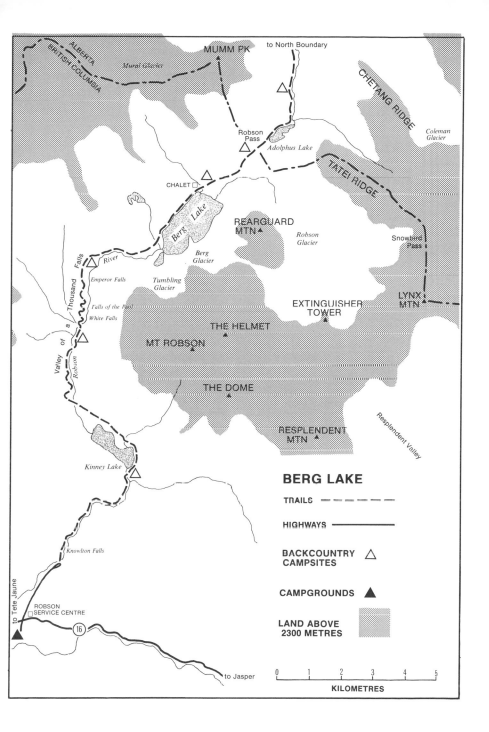

ALBERTA
BRITISH COLUMBIA

Mural Glacier

MUMM PK

to North Boundary

CHETANG RIDGE

*Coleman
Glacier*

Robson
Pass

Adolphus Lake

CHALET □

Berg Lake

TATEI RIDGE

REARGUARD
MTN ▲

*Robson
Glacier*

Snowbird
Pass

LYNX
MTN ▲

Falls

River

Emperor Falls

*Berg
Glacier*

*Tumbling
Glacier*

Falls of the Pool

White Falls

THE HELMET ▲

EXTINGUISHER
TOWER

MT ROBSON ▲

Valley of a Thousand

Robson

THE DOME ▲

RESPLENDENT
MTN ▲

Resplendent Valley

Kinney Lake

BERG LAKE

TRAILS — — — —

HIGHWAYS ————

BACKCOUNTRY △
CAMPSITES

CAMPGROUNDS ▲

LAND ABOVE
2300 METRES

Knowlton Falls

to Tete Jaune

ROBSON
□ SERVICE CENTRE

16

to Jasper

0 1 2 3 4 5

KILOMETRES

South Boundary Trail

Backpack
Allow 10-14 days
Maximum elevation: 2255 metres (7,400 feet)
Minimum elevation: 1465 metres (4,800 feet)
Topo maps: Columbia Icefield, 83 C/3†
      Sunwapta, 83 C/6
      Job Creek, 83 C/7 West
      George Creek, 83 C/10 West
      Southesk, 83 C/11†
      Mountain Park, 83 C/14
      Medicine Lake, 83 C/13 East
      Medicine Lake, 83 C/13 West
      †trail not shown

Point of Departure: The southern terminus of the route is at the Nigel Pass trail head in Banff Park. The northern terminus is at the Jacques Lake trail head in Jasper.

0—Camp Parker (1920 m).

6—Nigel Pass (2202 m).

9—Boulder Creek campsite.

13—Jonas Cutoff campsite.

19—Afternoon Peak campsite.

29—Brazeau campsite.

42—Arete campsite.

57—Isaac Creek campsite.

71—Southesk campsite.

81—Cairn River campsite.

95—Cairn Pass campsite.

100—Cairn (Southesk) Pass (2255 m).

108—Lagrace campsite.

117—Medicine-tent campsite.

127—Rocky Forks campsite.

138—Climax campsite.

151—Grizzly campsite.

164—Jacques Lake campsite.

176—Beaver Creek picnic area (1465 m).

*Distances are approximate.

Of all Jasper's backcountry trails, the South Boundary provides the best opportunity for an extended wilderness sojourn. The trail is long—over 170 kilometres, and in some spots difficult to follow. There are several unbridged river crossings which are tricky any time of the summer or fall, and there are no easy "escape" routes back to creature comforts.

Despite the difficulties, the trail passes through some areas of great beauty, and anyone with a substantial amount of wilderness backpacking experience and capable of organizing a ten to twelve day trip will find the journey rewarding in terms of challenge, solitude and scenery.

From its southern terminus, Camp Parker in Banff Park, the trail follows the Nigel Pass route to the headwaters of the Brazeau River. Working down the Brazeau in a northerly direction, the trail crosses and recrosses the river before reaching the Brazeau campsite around Kilometre 29. The Brazeau camp lies just below Brazeau Lake, and hikers may want to take a short side trip to the lake—the largest found along the South Boundary route. This first section of trail is well-defined and, with the exception of a shallow ford of the south fork of the Brazeau just beyond Nigel Pass, presents no problems.

From the Brazeau campsite the trail continues its journey along the northwest side of the Brazeau River, skirting the eastern flanks of Mount Aztec, Arete Mountain, Valley Head Mountain and Mount Isaac. The trail bypasses the Isaac Creek Warden Cabin to the west and reaches the Isaac Creek campsite near Kilometre 57. From the campsite area hikers have a clear view of Tarpeian Rock with its sheer 1300 metre face, one of the top two or three scenic highlights of the entire South Boundary Trail. On the west side of the valley, opposite Tarpeian, is the massif of Mount Dalhousie, such an extensive collection of summits and outriding peaks that it nearly constitutes a mountain range in itself.

After crossing Isaac Creek (an ankle to calf-deep ford), the trail contours around the base of Mount Dalhousie, leaving the northerly running waters of the Brazeau to find the Southesk River flowing from the west. A little beyond the 70 kilometre mark the trail angles off to the northwest passing the Southesk campsite at a small lake and reaching the south bank of the Southesk River about two kilometres further along. The route turns upstream, and hikers will have to rely on blazes and bits of orange flagging to find the Southesk bridge some 300 metres distant.

Once across the Southesk, more flagging leads the hiker up a short incline and then off to the west. Two seismic lines will be encountered and in each case hikers should turn left down the line, where, in a matter of one or two hundred metres, more flagging on the right will pull the traveller back into the forest. Good trail lies just beyond the second seismic line. Needless to say, this section of trail can be confusing (the foot trail does not coincide with that marked on the George Creek map), and some parties have turned back at this point; however, a little intuition and perseverance should see hikers through to the Cairn River campsite at Kilometre 81. (Expect upgrading or route changes which may have taken place since this writing.)

From the Cairn River campsite hikers must make two thigh-deep fords of the Cairn, one at the campsite and one a little under three kilometres distant. After the second crossing, the traveller continues up the northeast side of the Cairn River. The trail is good up the river, and a little over six kilometres from the second ford it bypasses a bridge on the left (leading to a warden cabin) and proceeds to the Cairn Pass campsite at the 95 kilometre mark. The campsite is located in a grove of trees at the edge of high open meadows, marking the end of the forested Cairn River trail and heralding the approach of Cairn Pass (marked Southesk Pass on the map)—a spectacular alpine area

which is the high point of the trip, both in terms of scenery and altitude.

On the north side of the pass the trail descends to the Medicine-tent River, skirting the Medicine-tent Lakes to reach the Lagrace campsite near Kilometre 108. Continuing another nine kilometres or so down the northeast side of the river, the hiker comes upon the Medicine-tent campsite. Just 400 metres above the campsite hikers have the opportunity for a quick exit from the trail; cutting north between Mount Cardinal and Mount MacKenzie a good trail leads over Rocky Pass to a forestry road just south of Mountain Park.

From the Medicine-tent campsite hikers have the option of fording the river (and then fording it again 2.5 kilometres downstream) or staying on the northeast bank and bushwhacking downstream to the spot where the trail recrosses to the true right bank. From the second ford the trail stays on the northeast bank to the Rocky Forks campsite.

As the trail nears the confluence of the Rocky and Medicine-tent, the hiker's route becomes a bit tricky to follow again. Instead of following the horse trail, which crosses the Rocky River to the warden cabin a little over two kilometres above the forks, hikers should stay on the north side of the river and watch for blazes which lead to the Rocky Forks campsite—situated just a short distance north of the actual river junction. (Coming from the north blazes start about 60 metres below the campsite.)

From Rocky Forks a well-defined trail stays on the northeast side of the Rocky River, and an outstanding waterfall on the Rocky just south of Blackface Creek adds a very pleasant diversion. Climax campsite is reached around the 138 kilometre mark, and just over four kilometres beyond a suspension bridge takes the hiker to the true left bank of the river (the bridge is just a short distance upstream from the horse crossing).

Around eight kilometres below the crossing, the trail passes Grizzly campsite and begins its climb away from the Rocky River, contouring around into the

Jacques Creek canyon. The ascent of Jacques Creek is straightforward, the trail zig-zagging back and forth across four good horse bridges, and Jacques Lake is attained at the 164 kilometre mark. From there it is an easy 12.2 kilometre stroll out to the Maligne Lake Road via the popular Jacques Lake trail.

The last 38 kilometres of the South Boundary Trail, from Climax campsite to the Maligne Lake Road, is all quite well-defined, but since most of the route is forest-enclosed, it can become quite tedious.

One final reminder: anyone planning to hike the South Boundary Trail should carry all the 1:50,000 maps covering the route and know how to read them. Any travel through country as wild and removed as this requires a good sense of direction and a fair measure of horse sense.

Southesk Lake. More adventuresome backpackers examining the Southesk sheet will no doubt be attracted to the possibilities of an optional trip to the headwaters of the Southesk and Rocky Rivers via Southesk Lake. In addition to poor trail conditions along this route, Jasper Park has designated this a "special area" and travel into the region is restricted.

Yoho National Park

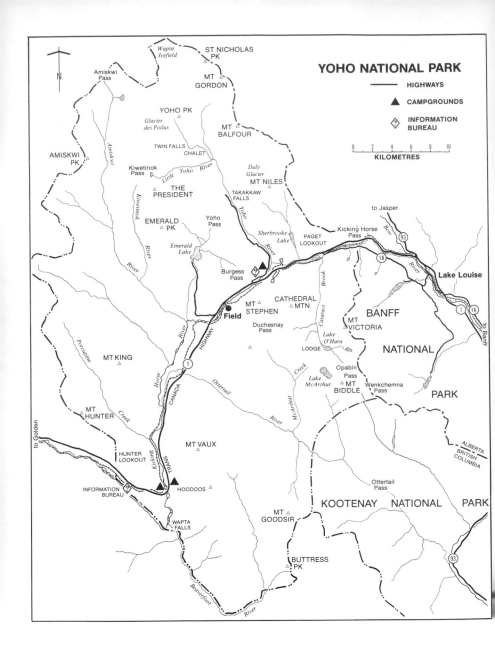

YOHO NATIONAL PARK

Yoho National Park

Yoho National Park lies on the western slope of the Great Divide, bordered by Banff Park on the east and Kootenay Park on the south. Covering 1,313 square kilometres of rugged mountain terrain, Yoho is the smallest of the four contiguous parks. The only highway access to the park is via the Trans-Canada, a journey west from Calgary, Alberta, of some 210 kilometres or east from Golden, B.C., of 32 kilometres. Within the park, two short side roads branch north from the Trans-Canada to Emerald Lake and Takakkaw Falls.

Yoho's 400 kilometre trail system extends into nearly every corner of the park, and while the majority of these trails are well-constructed and maintained, most hiking centres around the two backcountry recreation areas of Lake O'Hara and the Yoho Valley. The overwhelming popularity of these two areas is a result of spectacular alpine terrain coupled with excellent trail systems which allow backpackers to set up a central camp and range out in many directions on scenic day trips. Needless to say, neither area offers much in the way of solitude.

Running directly through the heartland of the park, sharing the valley bottom with the Kicking Horse River and the Canadian Pacific Railroad, the Trans-Canada Highway serves as access to a number of short but scenic day trips, the most popular being Sherbrooke Lake, Paget Lookout and Wapta Falls. Longer trails also ascend seldom travelled but major Kicking Horse tributary valleys such as the Ottertail, the Amiskwi and the Beaverfoot.

Emerald Lake is also a much used hub for day hikes. Trails radiate from the lake to the lofty heights of Yoho and Burgess Passes as well as beautiful Hamilton Lake. The area's adjacency to the Yoho and Little Yoho Valleys makes it a natural extension for hikes to and from that region.

Situated 16.5 kilometres (10.2 miles) west of the continental divide, the small railway town of Field is the only service centre in the park. A gift shop, gas station, grocery store and hotel offer the barest of essential services. There is also a small camp store located a few kilometres to the east of Field, next to the Cathedral Mountain Campground. Field houses the warden service and park administration offices.

Backpackers must obtain a backcountry use permit, specifying their destination, before setting out on any overnight trip. Since the major campsites have restricted user quotas, popular areas are often filled to capacity during the peak season and hikers would do well to keep several options in mind. Permits are available from the information office just east of the Yoho West Gate, the park operations centre (5 kilometres west of Field) and the information bureau near the Cathedral Mountain Campground (a short distance up the Yoho Valley Road). Off-trail trips and climbing expeditions must register with the warden service.

Paget Lookout

Wapta Picnic Area to Paget Lookout—3.5 kilometres (2.2 miles)

Half-day trip
Allow 1½-2 hours to lookout
Elevation gain: 760 metres (2,500 feet)
Maximum elevation: 2375 metres (7,800 feet)
Topo maps: Lake Louise, 82 N/8 West

Point of Departure: Drive to the Wapta Lake Picnic Area, 5.2 kilometres (3.2 miles) west of the Great Divide. The picnic area is on the north side of the highway just 300 metres west of Wapta Lake Lodge.

0.0—Trail sign located upslope from picnic shelter.

0.2—Junction. Keep left.

—Steady uphill.

1.4—Junction. Sherbrooke Lake straight ahead. Paget Lookout to the right.

—Trail begins steep ascent.

3.5—Paget Lookout.

The Paget Lookout hike is short but rugged, climbing 760 vertical metres in less than four kilometres. Despite the rigorous nature of the hike, however, the vantage point of the lookout offers such extensive views of the Kicking Horse Valley and the Cataract Valley in Yoho Park, and of the Bow Valley and the Slate Range in Banff Park, that the trip is highly recommended to anyone who enjoys first-rate mountain sightseeing.

The first half-hour or so of travel takes the hiker up and across the southern flank of Paget Peak (named for the Reverend Dean Paget of Calgary who made the first ascent of the mountain), running through a predominant forest cover of lodgepole pine, Engelmann spruce and alpine fir. At the 1.4 kilometre mark the trail splits and the hiker bound for the lookout should follow the right hand fork; Sherbrooke Lake lies to the left.

Not far beyond the Sherbrooke Lake junction the trail gains sufficient altitude to allow an occasional glimpse across the Kicking Horse Valley to the Cambrian quartzite of Vanguard Peak (2465 m) and Cathedral Mountain (3189 m). At this point the trail is rising into the upper subalpine zone, an area dominated by stunted alpine fir and whitebark pine. As the trail crosses some open avalanche slopes in the early stages of the climb watch for the occasional Douglas fir tree as well, a rather unusual species to be found at this lofty elevation.

Following a right angle turn around the flank of Paget Peak the hiker is confronted by the sheer 750 metre east face of Mount Ogden directly across the Sherbrooke Valley. Far below are the glacier-green waters of Sherbrooke Lake.

The trail ends near timberline at the Paget Lookout cabin after a rather arduous climb over the last 800 meters of trail. Paget is one of the few fire lookouts in Yoho Park that is easily accessible to the casual hiker, and, as is proper for a

Paget Lookout and the Kicking Horse Valley

lookout, it presents a superb panorama of the surrounding area: far to the northeast lie the Bow Valley and Slate Range with its highest peak, Mount Richardson (3086 m); to the southeast, directly across the valley, are the valley of Cataract Brook and the glacier-mantled peaks of the Lake O'Hara region; and to the southwest lie the Kicking Horse Valley and the Van Horne Range framed between Mounts Stephen and Burgess.

Around the lookout, a wide variety of wildflowers offset the jumbled heaps of eroding Cambrian sedimentary rock, and the early season hiker will find the immediate environs covered with the yellow blooms of glacier lilies—the first flower to appear after the melting of the snow. One might also be fortunate enough to sight the mountain goat which often roam these slopes during the summer months.

179

Sherbrooke Lake

Wapta Picnic Area to Sherbrooke Lake—3.1 kilometres (1.9 miles)

Half-day trip
Allow 1 hour to lake
Elevation gain: 185 metres (600 feet)
Maximum elevation: 1804 metres (5,918 feet)
Topo maps: Lake Louise, 82 N/8 West

Point of Departure: Drive to the Wapta Lake Picnic Area, 5.2 kilometres (3.2 miles) west of the Great Divide. The picnic area is on the north side of the highway just 300 metres west of Wapta Lake Lodge.

0.0—Trail sign located upslope from picnic shelter.

0.2—Junction. Keep left.

—Steady uphill.

1.4—Junction. Paget Lookout to the right. Straight ahead for Sherbrooke Lake.

1.9—Trail levels out.

3.1—Sherbrooke Lake (1804 m).

Hidden only a short distance from the Trans-Canada Highway and a few kilometres west of the Great Divide, Sherbrooke Lake is a popular trip for families and individuals who desire a half-day outing to a peaceful subalpine valley. A climber's access trail beyond the lake offers full day options for more energetic souls who would like to visit more open country at the head of the Niles Creek valley.

The trail climbs at a moderate grade from the Wapta Lake Picnic Area through a forest of lodgepole pine, spruce and alpine fir. After 800 metres or so, views open back to the south, offering glimpses of massive Cathedral Mountain (3189 m).

From the Paget Lookout junction to where the trail levels out near the two kilometre mark, the forest is often open and carpeted with buttercups, arnica, bunchberry, clintonia and single's delight. Once the trail has finished its climb, Sherbrooke Lake is just slightly over a kilometre away. The water of the lake bears the hue of all glacier-fed mountain tarns—a pale blue colour. The Niles and Daly glaciers, which lie to the north, grind up enormous amounts of rock material and the meltwater carries the finely pulverized sediment to the waters of Sherbrooke Lake.

Though rough and muddy in sections, the trail continues along the east shore of the lake and reaches the north end in 1.4 kilometres. Looking back toward the lake's outlet, Cathedral Mountain is once again visible. Beyond the west shore is Mount Ogden. The solitary peak rising near the head of the valley is Mount Niles (2972 m).

Continuing beyond the lake inlet, the trail eventually terminates on the upper plateaus near the valley head, some three kilometres distant. Open meadows and thundering cascades make the journey well worthwhile.

Ross Lake

1-A Highway to Ross Lake—1.3 kilometres (0.8 miles)

Nature hike
Allow ½ hour one way
Elevation gain: 90 metres (300 feet)
Maximum elevation: 1735 metres (5,700 feet)
Topo maps: Lake Louise, 82 N/8 West

Point of Departure: Drive to the trail sign on the south side of the 1-A Highway, 1.9 kilometres (1.2 miles) east of the highway's junction with the Trans-Canada and one kilometre (0.6 mile) west of the Alberta-B.C. boundary.

The short hike to Ross Lake is unexpectedly rewarding for the small amount of time and effort expended in getting there. Set within a beautiful amphitheatre carved from the rugged quartzite and limestone walls of the Great Divide, it seems strange that the lake is so seldom visited by the hordes frequenting the trails of nearby Lake Louise.

The first half of the trail travels over old fire road, through a mature subalpine forest of spruce, lodgepole pine and alpine fir. The last 600 metres is on well-kept foot trail.

The lake lies in a prime example of a glacially carved cirque. Mount Niblock contains the lake on the east, while the long north ridge of Narao Peak forms its western shore. Vertical cliffs and a steep talus slope serve as its backdrop.

Stephen Fossil Beds

Field to Fossil Beds—2.7 kilometres (1.7 miles)

Nature hike
Allow 1½ hours one way
Elevation gain: 520 metres (1,700 feet)
Maximum elevation: 1800 metres (5,900 feet)
Topo maps: Lake Louise, N/0 West

Point of Departure: Drive the Trans-Canada Highway to the town of Field, crossing the Kicking Horse River and railroad tracks to the village proper. Find 1st Street East and follow it uphill to the edge of town. A trail sign near a major stream indicates the beginning of the Fossil Beds trail.

This short but very steep trail rises from the town of Field to the slopes of Mount Stephen, where one of the outstanding fossil beds containing Cambrian age trilobites exists.

The trail is a straightforward slog up through a forest of white spruce, Douglas fir, lodgepole pine and a few birch. In addition to the interesting browsing available in the Fossil Beds, this open slope offers many fine views back to the Kicking Horse Valley and Mount Burgess beyond.

Allow the better part of a day for this trip as the trail is one of the steepest and most arduous in Yoho Park. And remember, it is illegal to remove or displace geological specimens in a national park; please leave the fossils for others to enjoy.

Lake O'Hara

In 1890 J. J. McArthur, a surveyor charting the lands within the Railway Belt, discovered an area of exceptional beauty some 13 kilometres south of Hector, British Columbia. Lieutenant-Colonel Robert O'Hara, an Irishman who heard about the region from McArthur, visited the location shortly thereafter and was so impressed that he returned repeatedly to explore its lakes, creeks and mountains. It is to O'Hara's wanderings the region owes its name.

In 1909 the Alpine Club of Canada held the first of the thirteen summer mountaineering camps it has hosted at Lake O'Hara, and by 1911 the region had gained enough popularity among alpinists to warrant construction of a mountain hut, the 'Wiwaxy Lodge'—a small cabin still standing in the Alpine Meadows.

Today the area hosts a lodge (reservations only), an ACC hut, a summer warden's cabin, a 30-site campground (just off the fire road a short distance north of Lake O'Hara), and one of the most extensive and well-maintained trail systems found anywhere in the mountain parks. These trails, built over a period of some forty summers by the efforts of Dr. George Link, Carson Simpson and Lawrence Grassi, radiate from Lake O'Hara as the spokes from a wheel hub, making the area a good location for anyone interested in a hiking vacation: a person can hike a different trail every day and return to a comfortable central camp each evening. And the nature of the hiking itself is greatly varied, ranging from a simple stroll around Lake O'Hara to a reasonably challenging expedition around the Wiwaxy Gap-Lake Oesa alpinist's circuit.

The scenery of the area is dominated by the same two peaks that form the impressive backdrop for Lake Louise, the continental summits of Mounts Lefroy (3423 m) and Victoria (3464 m). The two mountains also provide the immediate setting for one of the five distinct hiking areas found in the O'Hara environs, the Lake Oesa cirque. A second such area is the Opabin Plateau, located between Yukness Mountain (2847 m) and Mount Schaffer (2693 m), while the McArthur Pass-McArthur Lake region to the west of Mount Schaffer makes a third. The Odaray Plateau, high on the eastern flank of Odaray Mountain, constitutes a fourth, and the Duchesnay Basin, cradling the Cathedral, Odaray, Linda and Morning Glory Lakes, offers a fifth. Each of these compact hiking 'pockets' represents several hour's worth of exploration.

The Lake O'Hara region is a fascinating area: within a three mile radius of the Alpine Meadows are over twenty-five named lakes, some of the highest and most rugged mountains in the Canadian Rockies, and many kilometres of excellent hiking trails. There are also, as might be expected, an abundance of hikers and climbers. It is imperative that everyone visiting Lake O'Hara take note of the fragile nature of the environment and make a concerted effort to harmonize their activites with the land around them.

Access: The trail begins at the traffic control gate of the Lake O'Hara Fire Road. The road is reached by turning south off the Trans-Canada Highway onto the 1-A Highway, 3.2 kilometres (2 miles) west of the continental divide or 1.6 kilometres (1 mile) east of Wapta Lake Lodge. Cross the CPR tracks on the 1-A and turn right onto the gravel Lake O'Hara Fire Road (marked). Approximately 800 metres down the road is a parking area and an obvious traffic gate restricting entrance to the road spur leading to O'Hara. From this

Lake Oesa

point one has the option of either hiking the 13 kilometres into O'Hara via the fire road itself or taking the Cataract Brook trail which starts at the west end of the parking area. The Cataract Brook trail is less direct but definitely more interesting as a hike.

Bus transportation is also available to all Lake O'Hara overnight visitors and a limited number of day hikers. Any person with an O'Hara camping permit or who is registered to spend a night at the ACC hut can catch a ride to the lake on one of the lodge buses. The buses leave the lower parking area at 8:00, 11:00 and 4:00 p.m. during the months of July and August (the 8:00 run is omitted in June). In order to ensure a spot on the bus it is advisable to phone the lodge and reserve a space. The buses will also carry day hikers to the lake if there is room after lodge guests and overnight visitors are seated.

Topo maps: Lake Louise, 82 N/8 West.

Lake Oesa

3.2 kilometres (2.0 miles)

Set within a high barren cirque beneath the towering spine of the Great Divide, Oesa is one of the more exquisite of the many turquoise lakes located near Lake O'Hara.

From the Lake O'Hara Warden Cabin, the trail follows the west shore to the outlet, crosses the bridge and continues around the north shore. After walking for 1.3 kilometres, the hiker comes to the well-marked Lake Oesa trail spur. The trail cuts uphill from the lakeshore and climbs into the open subalpine forest that covers a series of rock terraces leading up to Lake Oesa. Three small lakes are passed along the way—Yukness Lake, Lake Victoria and Lefroy Lake.

Lake Oesa is exactly 3.2 kilometres distant from and 224 vertical metres above the Lake O'Hara Warden Cabin. Its name is reputed to be the Stony Indian word meaning 'ice,' so-called

because it is frozen over nearly year-round. Out from the western shore a few stunted alpine fir and Engelmann spruce grow, undoubtedly surviving at this altitude by the grace of shelter afforded by the surrounding steep-walled amphitheatre. Guarding the lake on either side are Yukness Mountain (2847 m) to the south and Mount Huber (3368 m) to the north, while hidden in the towering walls at the far end of the lake is Abbot's Pass (2922 m)—a major alpinist route between Lake O'Hara and Lake Louise.

Opabin Plateau Circuit

5.1 kilometres (3.2 miles)

Starting from the O'Hara lakeside trail, a short distance south of the Lake O'Hara Lodge, the Opabin Lakes trail (east arm) rises steeply for a little less than a kilometre to the lip of the Opabin Plateau. Once on the plateau the trail levels off to run along the foot of Yukness Mountain (2847 m) past a series of small lakes to end at Opabin Lake, high behind the terminal moraine of Opabin Glacier.

At the lake the hiker has an excellent view of Hungabee Mountain (3492 m), Mount Biddle (3319 m), and the Opabin Glacier and Opabin Peak. Mount Hungabee derives its name from the Stony word meaning 'the chieftan,' while Opabin means 'rocky.'

From the lake one can return to O'Hara via the west arm route, traversing the western edge of the plateau at the foot of Mount Schaffer to descend a steep and rocky path offering a spectacular view of Lake O'Hara, Schaffer Lake, Mary Lake and the O'Hara environs. The trail emerges at the southwest corner of the O'Hara lakeside trail somewhat closer to the lodge than the starting point.

Atlhough the main route described is just over five kilometres long, the plateau actually is covered with a network of secondary trails which are

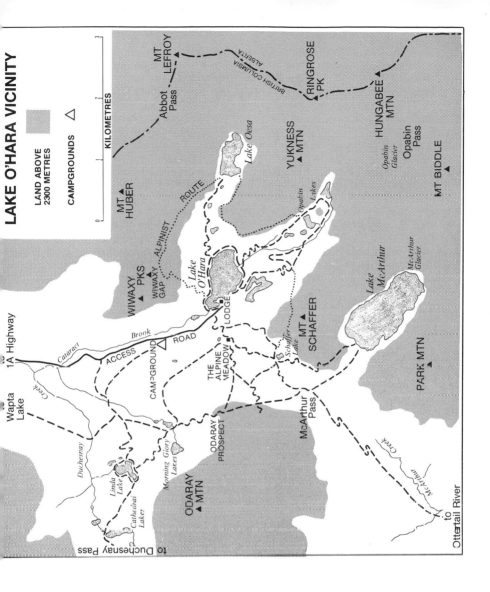

LAKE O'HARA VICINITY

LAND ABOVE 2300 METRES

△ **CAMPGROUNDS**

KILOMETRES

0   1   2   3

MT HUBER

WIWAXY PKS

WIWAXY GAP

ALPINIST ROUTE

Lake O'Hara

LODGE

Cataract Brook

Creek

1A Highway

Wapta Lake

ACCESS ROAD

△ CAMPGROUND

Duchesnay

Linda Lake

Cathedral Lakes

Morning Glory Lakes

to Duchesnay Pass

ODARAY MTN

ODARAY PROSPECT

THE ALPINE MEADOW

Schaffer Lake

MT SCHAFFER

McArthur Pass

PARK MTN

Lake McArthur

McArthur Glacier

McArthur Creek

to Ottertail River

Abbot Pass

MT LEFROY

BRITISH COLUMBIA
ALBERTA

RINGROSE PK

HUNGABEE MTN

Lake Oesa

YUKNESS MTN

Opabin Lakes

Opabin Glacier

Opabin Pass

MT BIDDLE

worthy of a full day's exploration, and it is recommended that anyone visiting the plateau find time to do some wandering on these numerous subsidiary paths.

Odaray Prospect

2.7 kilometres (1.7 miles)

Starting from the trail directly across the fire road from the Lake O'Hara Warden Cabin, hike the short distance to the ACC Elizabeth Parker Hut. The Odaray Prospect route begins in the meadows near the hut at a junction with one of the Lake McArthur trails. From the meadows the trail climbs steeply for two-thirds of its total 2.4 kilometre length, but the exceptional survey of the O'Hara region from the prospect makes the short climb more than worthwhile.

From the prospect one is able to watch the Odaray and Morning Glory Falls cascade down the northeast face of Odaray Mountain (3159 m) to the lakes of the Duchesnay Basin far below. Mount Stephen (3199 m) and Cathedral Mountain (3189 m) are clearly visible directly north across the basin. To the southeast the hiker has an excellent view of Lake O'Hara, the Lake Oesa cirque, the Opabin Plateau and the attending mountain peaks.

The vegetation of the plateau is typically subalpine with alpine larch the predominant tree. Wildflowers abound in mid-July, although the number of flowers at times seem to be equalled by the number of 'whistling' marmots that make the plateau their home.

Odaray Plateau Circuit. A recommended return trip is to complete the Odaray Plateau Circuit which continues west from the Odaray Prospect junction (the Prospect is on a short spur to the north of the main trail) and then cuts south, contouring along the flank of Odaray Mountain to McArthur Pass, a little over 1.5 kilometres distant.

At the point the trail swings south

another option, in the form of a spur trail climbing to the west, presents itself. This is an alpine route leading to the Grand View Prospect. Most hikers, however, turn south with the main trail, content with the superb views of the O'Hara environs to the east and the Goodsirs beyond McArthur Pass to the south. From McArthur Pass the trail runs back toward O'Hara past Schaffer Lake and the Big Larch Meadows, making the entire circuit route a journey of approximately six kilometres.

Lake McArthur

3.5 kilometres (2.2 miles)

Lake McArthur, named for the first white man to see the O'Hara region, lies at 2246 metres in a high and rather desolate alpine meadow enclosed on three sides by the rock of Mount Schaffer (2693 m), Mount Biddle (3319 m) and Park Mountain (2975 m). An impressive juxtaposition of water, rock, ice and sparse alpine vegetation make the lake a worthy hiking objective.

Although the number of trails in the Lake O'Hara region form a variety of possible routes to the lake, one of the more direct starts at the trail sign opposite the warden's cabin and climbs gradually through the Alpine Meadows and Big Larch Meadows to Schaffer Lake. At Schaffer Lake the hiker has the option of turning right (west) toward McArthur Pass and then back toward Lake McArthur from the pass or proceeding straight on past Schaffer Lake, thus bypassing McArthur Pass in a direct route to Lake McArthur. Beyond Schaffer Lake the latter route climbs the rocky western flank of Mount Schaffer to reach a maximum elevation (2329 m) just a short distance from Lake McArthur.

The trail summit offers a good view of the lake and the McArthur Glacier as it tumbles down across the western face of Mount Biddle. South of the lake is Park Mountain and, further to the southwest,

one can see where McArthur Creek runs by Mount Owen on its way to the Ottertail River.

Linda Lake

4.0 kilometres (2.5 miles)

Linda Lake forms the longest spoke of the trails radiating from Lake O'Hara. The most pleasing of two routes into the area passes beneath the Odaray Prospect, near the Morning Glory Lakes and on into the Duchesnay Basin, wherein lies a series of beautiful lakes surrounded by open subalpine terrain laced with alpine larch and fir. Linda Lake is the largest of the tarns and from it the hiker has many options for exploration.

From the north end of the Alpine Meadows the trail twists and rolls through a pleasant forest of fir and spruce. At the 2.9 kilometre mark it passes the Upper Morning Glory Lake and the Odaray Prospect trail junction. Odaray Mountain towers above. The route rises steeply beyond Morning Glory, then descends to the south shore of Linda Lake.

Turning west along the shore of Linda Lake, the upper Duchesnay Basin is reached in just over a kilometre. Though the trail is vague and boggy in spots the terrain is well-suited for exploration. Clustered within the open meadowland are the Cathedral and Odaray Lakes small depressions or 'kettles' formed by the melting of detached pieces of glacial ice in the detritus. To the north Cathedral Mountain (3189 m) dominates the skyline, its blocky castellate summit a popular subject for painters and photographers down through the years.

Strong hikers with a full day to spend on the trail may want to return to Morning Glory Lakes and take the spur to the Odaray Prospect—a steep climb gaining nearly 300 metres. The option makes an extremely arduous but spectacular day trip.

The Linda Lake area is also accessible via a somewhat shorter but less scenic trail which runs direct from the Lake O'Hara Campground.

Yoho Valley

The Yoho Valley was first explored in 1897 when Jean Habel, an adventuresome alpinist from Berlin, spent seventeen days on an excursion that carried him from Yoho Pass above Emerald Lake to the head of the Yoho Valley and some distance up the Yoho Glacier onto the Wapta Icefield. Habel noted that the area, featuring an impressive array of glaciated peaks, extensive icefields and the stunning 380 metre Takakkaw Falls, was one of exceptional beauty. That reputation has not been diminished over time.

Today the Yoho Valley, with its companion hanging valley, the Little Yoho, constitutes one of Yoho National Park's two major backcountry recreation areas, and while not as compact a region as Lake O'Hara, the Yoho is as popular with hikers and climbers as the O'Hara environs.

Both the Canadian Pacific Railway and the Alpine Club of Canada took an early interest in the area and built an extensive system of trails in the valley; today casual hikers and backpackers can find many hours worth of well-developed trails running from one end of the valley to the other. Many of the trails interconnect, creating hiking variations that can be tailored to the strength and available time of almost any hiking party. Thus, starting from the walk-in campground near Takakkaw Falls, one person may decide to take a short stroll to Duchesnay Lake while another may push on to Twin Falls. A stronger hiker yet may opt to return from Twin Falls via the Highline, while a backpacker will head for the Little Yoho and the Skyline via Twin Falls and the Whaleback. The options are numerous.

Beside the walk-in campground at Takakkaw Falls, there are several small campsites scattered throughout the valley. A small log chalet (reservations only) stands at the foot of Twin Falls, and a larger Alpine Club hut (members only) is found near the head of the Little

Yoho. As might be expected, the solitude Jean Habel experienced less than a hundred years ago is harder to come by these days, especially during the peak summer season, but the beauty of the area has changed little.

Access: Follow the Trans-Canada Highway to the Yoho Valley Road turnoff, 12.6 kilometres (7.8 miles) west of the Great Divide and 3.9 kilometres (2.4 miles) east of Field. Follow the valley road for 13 kilometres (8 miles). Park vehicles at the Takakkaw Falls parking area. The Yoho Valley trail commences at the north edge of the parking area.

Topo maps: Hector Lake, 82 N/9 West; Lake Louise, 82 N/8 West; and Blaeberry River, 82 N/10 East.

Yoho Valley Trail

8.5 kilometres (5.3 miles)

The 8.5 kilometre trail from Takakkaw Falls to Twin Falls Chalet is probably the most frequently hiked trail in the Yoho Valley. Not only is Twin Falls a worthy hiking objective, but the route to it serves as the starting point for several other interesting hiking options.

From the trail head at the Takakkaw Falls parking area, the trail skirts the campground and then crosses an outwash (or 'alluvial') fan, a jumbled tangle of rock rubble deposited by a stream of meltwater from the Emerald Glacier far above to the left. From the outwash the trail continues, road-width, through a pine and spruce forest to Kilometre 2.6, where it intersects with the trails to Point Lace Falls and the Angel's Staircase. Here the route jogs to the left before resuming its northerly course, now a single-file path.

The first cutoff to Duchesnay Lake is reached at Kilometre 4.0, and a short 200 metre side trip offers the best view of the

Yoho Peak from the Whaleback

small, delicately coloured lake. Beyond the Duchesnay Lake spur is another option, a short trail branching right to the edge of the Yoho River, where the hiker can observe the explosive action of this glacial torrent as it cuts its channel. Across the river, the peaks of the Waputik Mountains lie under their wreath of ice. Trolltinder Mountain (2917 m) is the predominant peak seen from the lookout.

The main trail opens out onto the valley bottom shortly beyond a second cutoff to Duchesnay Lake. At Kilometre 4.6 it runs close by the short but vociferous Laughing Falls. From the falls one can see Mount Trolltinder to the east and Mount Gordon (3203 m) to the north.

Just beyond the falls, a branch forks to the left toward the Highline and Skyline trails, a cutoff which represents the most direct—and steepest—route to the Little Yoho Valley. The Highline and Skyline can also be reached by following the main Yoho Valley trail to Twin Falls, a more scenic, if somewhat longer, route.

Beyond the Highline cutoff, the valley trail crosses Twin Falls Creek and continues its northerly course through heavy forest cover, with occasional breaks in the canopy beyond Kilometre 6.5 that allow quick glimpses of Twin Falls. At Kilometre 6.9 the trail veers to the left at the Yoho Glacier junction and starts a steady ascent toward Twin Falls, 1.6 kilometres distant.

The Yoho Valley trail ends at the small Twin Falls Chalet (limited accommodation by reservation), where one can view the falls as they drop over eighty metres off a massive cliff of Cathedral limestone. The falls are formed by a stream of meltwater from the Glacier des Poilus which splits into two branches just before plunging over the precipice.

189

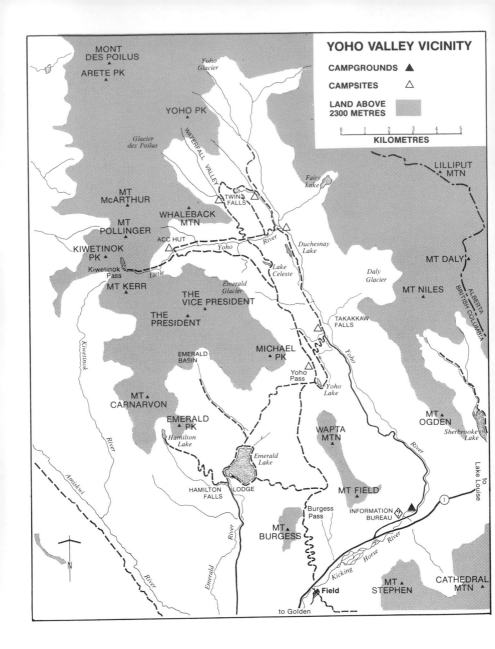

YOHO VALLEY VICINITY

CAMPGROUNDS ▲

CAMPSITES △

LAND ABOVE
2300 METRES

KILOMETRES
0 1 2 3 4 5

MONT
DES POILUS
ARETE PK
Yoho
Glacier
YOHO PK
LILLIPUT
MTN
Glacier
des Poilus
WATERFALL VALLEY
Fairy
Lake
MT
McARTHUR
TWINS
FALLS
WHALEBACK
MTN
MT
POLLINGER
ACC HUT
Yoho   River
Duchesnay
Lake
MT DALY
KIWETINOK
PK
Kiwetinok
Pass
Little
Lake
Celeste
Daly
Glacier
MT KERR
Emerald
Glacier
MT NILES
THE
VICE PRESIDENT
ALBERTA
BRITISH COLUMBIA
THE
PRESIDENT
TAKAKKAW
FALLS
Kiwetinok
EMERALD
BASIN
MICHAEL
PK
Yoho
MT
CARNARVON
Yoho
Pass
Yoho
Lake
River
MT
OGDEN
Sherbrooke
Lake
EMERALD
PK
Amiskwi
Hamilton
Lake
WAPTA
MTN
Emerald
Lake
River
HAMILTON
FALLS
LODGE
MT FIELD
to
Lake Louise
N
Burgess
Pass
INFORMATION
BUREAU
1
River
MT
BURGESS
River
River
Emerald
Kicking   Horse
Field
MT
STEPHEN
CATHEDRAL
MTN
to Golden

190

The Yoho Highline

10.9 kilometres (6.8 miles)

The Yoho Valley Highline trail, running from the Twin Falls Chalet to Yoho Lake, constitutes an exceptional 10.9 kilometre alpine hike. Lying close to treeline for much of its distance, the trail works its way through subalpine forests and meadows, past small lakes and waterfalls, and across streams and morainal deposits. Frequent viewpoints provide good opportunities to study the glaciated peaks of the Yoho Valley environs. Wildflowers abound in midsummer, and a variety of small animals make the area their home.

The Highline journey actually entails more than just the measured 10.9 kilometres—one must hike the 8.5 kilometres to reach the trail head at Twin Falls, and then another 4.8 kilometres from Yoho Lake back to the trail head at Takakkaw Falls. The total distance is 24.2 kilometres, a long day hike or a relaxed two day backpack.

From the Twin Falls Chalet the trail starts across the Twin Falls Creek gorge and along the foot of Whaleback Mountain. The view from the gorge, back across the valley to the Waputik Range, gives the hiker a good idea of what lies ahead.

With the exception of the diminutive Marpole Lake at Kilometre 0.5, the trail wanders through the forest uninterrupted until it is joined by the Laughing Falls cutoff. Here the trail turns the flank of Whaleback and starts west up the Little Yoho Valley where it is intersected by the southern end of the Whaleback trail. Another 200 metres and another junction is encountered, this time with the Skyline trail which works on up the Little Yoho. The Highline trail, however, veers left at this point and crosses the fast-flowing Little Yoho River.

Beyond the Little Yoho bridge, the trail runs through some small subalpine meadows and past Lake Celeste (Kilometre 4.5), a turquoise lake set against the impressive backdrop of The Vice President (3066 m). At Kilometre 5.6 the Skyline trail rejoins the Highline, and just beyond this junction, from the low rock ridge to the left, the hiker is afforded the finest viewpoint of the trail. An incredible array of rock, snow, water and ice is visible from the lookout—a good place to take a lengthy break and make use of a map and compass.

Beyond the viewpoint the trail stays close to the eastern face of The Vice President, descending through mixed terrain for 2.4 kilometres. Here it begins a long, open traverse of gravel outwash from the Emerald Glacier. Several swift streams of meltwater cut down across the rubble, and during early spring the runoff can create real problems for the person trying to get across. At the beginning of the traverse a trail sign indicates a cutoff to the Yoho Valley Road. The traverse is not without beauty, and it is from the wild tangle of rock that one obtains perhaps the best view of Takakkaw Falls to be found in the valley.

The trail, re-entering the high subalpine forest, soon reaches the cool green waters of Yoho Lake, presided over by the imposing north face of Wapta Mountain (2779 m). At Yoho Lake the trail is joined by the path from Emerald Lake.

From Yoho Lake the trail descends steeply through heavy timber to the Yoho Valley Road, 4.2 kilometres distant. The Takakkaw Falls parking area lies just a short distance up the road to the north.

The Yoho Skyline

10.6 kilometres (6.6 miles)

This optional hike begins at Kilometre 3.0 on the Highline trail and tours the Little Yoho Valley, running along the southern flank of Whaleback Mountain to the Little Yoho campground, then crossing the Little Yoho River and working back down the northern shoulder of The Vice President to rejoin the Highline trail at Kilometre 5.6. The entire Little Yoho horseshoe is 10.6 kilometres long.

While the ascent up the north side of the valley is forest-enclosed for much of the way, there are occasional views to the snow and glacier-covered pyramids of The Vice President and The President to the south. The Alpine Club of Canada's Stanley Mitchell Hut (members only) and the Little Yoho Warden Cabin are passed at the 5.1 kilometre mark, and the trail continues through a flat, open meadow for another five minutes or so to the Little Yoho campground.

The campground marks the apex of the Little Yoho loop, as the trail cuts across the river at this point, doubles back along the opposite side of the Stanley Mitchell meadow, and begins its ascent across the shoulder of The Vice President. Once the high point of the trail has been attained beneath the cliffs of The Vice President, the route traverses along the terminal moraines of the Emerald Glacier and descends into an expansive meadowland providing views of much of the Yoho Valley. The Yoho Skyline ends by dropping back into the forest and connecting back into the Highline trail.

From the Little Yoho campground near the head of the valley, there is a short but steep sidetrip option up to the 2450 metre summit of Kiwetinok Pass— a rocky and windswept col which boasts its own tiny lake and an outstanding perspective of both the Little Yoho Valley to the east and the Kiwetinok Valley to the west. The spur is only around three kilometres in length, branching from the Yoho Skyline immediately across the Little Yoho from the campground, but the last half of the trip is very steep and sometimes poorly defined (watch for cairns).

The Little Yoho Valley is a beautiful spot and is worthy of a day's exploration for anyone camping in the Yoho Valley environs. It is an excellent option for more energetic hikers traversing the Highline trail as it offers much more scenery than the Highline does between the 3.0 and 5.6 kilometre junctions.

The Whaleback

6.6 kilometres (4.1 miles)

The Whaleback trail, running above Twin Falls and across the southeastern flank of Whaleback Mountain, offers a spectacular option for either strong day hikers or backpackers in the Yoho Valley. A long, 22 kilometre day hike can be made from Takakkaw Falls to Twin Falls and then over the Whaleback, returning to Takakkaw via the Highline cutoff, while a primitive campsite just above Twin Falls offers backpackers a more leisurely trip and a chance at some extended hiking along the Skyline and Highline trails.

The Whaleback trail begins just north of the Twin Falls Chalet and switchbacks up the rock bands that provide the 80 metre precipice for Twin Falls. Gaining the top of the rock bands the trail descends to Twin Falls Creek and passes the Whaleback campsite at Kilometre 2.7. Beyond the campsite the hiker crosses a narrow suspension bridge spanning the turbulent waters of Twin Falls Creek and begins a gradual climb across the flank of Whaleback Mountain. The trail runs close to treeline and offers excellent views back to the north, both to the Yoho Glacier and the upper Waterfall Valley, culminating in the broad expanse of Glacier des Poilus.

The high point of the hike, both in altitude and scenery, comes at the 4.5 kilometre mark, where the trail turns the corner of the Whaleback ridge. Marked by a stone cairn and brass plaque commemorating an avalanche fatality in the area, the viewpoint offers perhaps the most commanding outlook of the Yoho and Little Yoho Valleys of any found on the trails in the region.

From the viewpoint the trail descends rapidly (300 vertical metres in 2.1 kilometres) to join the Highline trail. This is the southern end of the 6.6 kilometre Whaleback traverse, and here the backpacker who wishes to follow the Highline or Skyline will turn west, while the day hiker will probably choose to cut east toward the Yoho Valley proper.

Twin Falls

Yoho Glacier

2.5 kilometres (1.6 miles)

The Yoho Glacier hike can be made either as a trip in and of itself, or, as is frequently done, as an extension of the Twin Falls trek. From its junction with the main Yoho Valley trail at Kilometre 6.9, the Yoho Glacier trail works through dense forest cover and across relatively level terrain for 2.5 kilometres to the edge of a cutbank high above the Yoho River and the snout of the Yoho Glacier. For most hikers this vantage point will be the end of the trip, but for those wishing to observe more closely the phenomenon of a recently glaciated landscape the trail continues, dropping steeply into the valley below. It ends in the glacial debris a short distance from the glacier's ice.

Yoho Pass—Burgess Pass

Yoho Pass-Burgess Pass Loop from Emerald Lake—19.2 kilometres (11.9 miles)
Emerald Lake to Takakkaw Falls via Yoho Pass—11.1 kilometres (6.9 miles)
Field to Emerald Lake via Burgess Pass—13.7 kilometres (8.5 miles)

Day trip
Allow 6 hours for loop trip
Elevation gain: 880 metres (2,888 feet)
Maximum elevation: 2182 metres (7,160 feet)
Topo maps: Lake Louise, 82 N/8 West
           Golden, 82 N/7 East
           (last 7 kms not shown)

Point of Departure: Drive the Trans-Canada Highway to the Emerald Lake Road, 2.6 kilometres (1.6 miles) west of Field. Follow the Emerald Lake Road 8.2 kilometres (5.1 miles) to its termination at the Emerald Lake parking area.

0.0—Trail starts just beyond bridge at the north end of the parking area.

—Trail follows lakeshore.

1.4—Junction. Horse trail crosses foot trail.

1.6—Junction. Emerald Basin trail branches left. Yoho Pass trail branches left from the lakeshore circuit 100 metres beyond.

3.4—Major stream. Trail begins to climb.

4.3—Falls viewpoint.

6.3—Yoho Pass (1838 m). Burgess Pass trail branches right. Straight ahead to Yoho Lake and Yoho Valley.

—Trail contours upwards beneath Wapta Peak. Open views.

12.4—Junction. Left branch reaches Burgess Pass summit (2182 m) in 300 metres. Trail down to Emerald Lake branches right.

13.5—Mount Burgess viewpoint.

—Trail switchbacks down through forest.

18.2—Junction. Trail connects in to Emerald Lake circuit. Keep left around lakeshore.

19.2—Emerald Lake Lodge.

Of several exceptional hikes leading out from Emerald Lake to Yoho and Burgess Passes, the Yoho Pass-Burgess Pass loop trip offers the greatest variety and scenic reward. Quite simply, the loop is a triangular circuit which climbs from Emerald Lake to the summit of Yoho Pass, traverses south along the open subalpine slopes of Wapta Peak to Burgess Pass, and then descends back to the shores of Emerald.

From the parking area at Emerald Lake the trail travels northward along the lakeshore, passing across the toe of a major avalanche slope in 300 metres. Near the north end of the lake the Yoho Pass route breaks away from the lakeshore trail and crosses onto gravel outwash flats—an alluvial fan created by the washing of eroded material down from the President Range and through the narrow mouth of the Emerald Basin. (The area is often flooded after a rain.)

Beyond the gravel outwash the trail begins a steep climb toward the summit of Yoho Pass. Views back to Emerald Lake improve with the steady gain in elevation.

There is little to indicate one's arrival on the summit of Yoho Pass beyond the levelling out of terrain and a trail junction in the midst of the forest. While this is the first "corner" on the triangular circuit and hikers should now turn right for the trail to Burgess Pass, a short descent of 600 metres on the left hand branch to Yoho Lake makes a worthwhile sidetrip. Open meadow leads up to the edge of this peaceful lake, while the Cambrian cliffs of Wapta Mountain peek through the spruce and fir along its southern shore.

Back on the loop trip, the trail from Yoho to Burgess Pass climbs another 300 vertical metres in the intervening six kilometres. But despite the steady ascent, the beauty of this section makes up for the additional effort. Open wildflower mea-

The President and Wapta Mountain from near Burgess Pass

dows are scattered along the way, and there are impressive views down to Emerald Lake and back to the President Range.

The second corner of the triangle is reached at the Burgess Pass junction. While the trail to Field branches left at this point and crests the pass 300 metres beyond, the best views are back along the summit ridge just east of the junction. From an open vantage point it is possible to look over into the Kicking Horse Valley to Mount Stephen and the village of Field.

From the Burgess Pass junction, the trail back to Emerald Lake cuts downhill to the right, offering more good viewpoints before the final plunge into the forest. The lakeshore trail is reached 5.8 kilometres from the pass and the route back to the lodge and parking area stays left along the southern shore.

Yoho Valley Option. Hikers with a means of arranging transportation can make a straight traverse of Yoho Pass and descend to the Yoho Valley Road, emerging just over a kilometre from

Takakkaw Falls. Total distance for the hike from Emerald Lake to the Yoho Valley is 11.1 kilometres.

Burgess Pass Traverse. Another arrangement option runs from Emerald Lake to the town of Field via Burgess Pass. The trail from the pass to the floor of the Kicking Horse Valley is steep and switchbacking and reaches the Trans-Canada Highway just opposite the village. Total distance for the journey is 13.7 kilometres.

Highline Option. An interesting entry to (or exit from) the upper Yoho Valley can be made via Burgess and Yoho Passes. Ascending from the town of Field, the backpacker can follow the high trail from Burgess Pass to Yoho Pass and connect in with the Yoho Highline route at Yoho Lake. From this junction, he can continue on into the upper Yoho or Little Yoho country on the Highline trail. Total distance from Field to the Yoho Lake junction via this option is 13.4 kilometres. (See *Yoho Highline.*)

Hamilton Lake

Emerald Lake to Hamilton Lake—5.5 kilometres (3.4 miles)

Day trip
Allow 3 hours to lake
Elevation gain: 855 metres (2,800 feet)
Maximum elevation: 2135 metres (7,000 feet)
Topo maps: Golden, 82 N/7 East
(trail not shown)

Point of Departure: Drive the Trans-Canada Highway to the Emerald Lake Road, 2.6 kilometres (1.6 miles) west of Field. Follow the Emerald Lake Road 8.2 kilometres (5.1 miles) to its termination at the Emerald Lake parking area.

0.0—Trail sign located near the entrance to the parking area.

—Moderate uphill, crossing the Emerald Lake horse trail at 0.2 kilometre.

0.8—Hamilton Falls.

—Steady switchbacking ascent.

3.9—Emerald Lake viewpoint.

—Grade moderates.

5.5—Hamilton Lake.

A steep trail running up densely forested slopes leads to a small tarn tucked away in a hanging valley between Mount Carnarvon and Emerald Peak. While Hamilton Lake is considered by many to be one of the park's most interesting and enjoyable day trips, most hikers in the Emerald Lake area miss it entirely—a factor which enhances its appeal.

The trail to Hamilton Lake leads west from Emerald Lake and into a mature subalpine forest where Hamilton Falls is encountered within 800 metres. Dropping over a steep limestone cliff in a series of steps, the action of the water has smoothed and dissolved the bedrock to form many pothole depressions. A short distance up the main trail, at a point where it switches back, there is an excellent view of the upper falls as well.

The route is closed-in and arduous beyond the falls, and not until the four kilometre mark does the forest open briefly to disclose an aerial view of Emerald Lake. Beyond the overlook the grade moderates somewhat and the trail emerges onto open slopes overlooking the Kicking Horse Valley.

Just as the hiker has relegated himself to another half-hour or so of steep slogging, the trail cuts upward and into the Hamilton Lake cirque. Beautiful as it is unexpected, Hamilton Lake extends to the very lip of its amphitheatre, its waters riffled by the occasional down-slope breeze. By stepping across the outlet stream, one can continue along the lake's western shore to a pleasant knoll which provides views back through the cirque's entrance to the Kicking Horse Valley and the mountains beyond. Rising in the distance are the glacier-capped summit of Mount Vaux and the twin towers of Mount Goodsir—the highest mountain in Yoho Park.

Hamilton Lake and Mount Carnarvon

Amiskwi River

Backpack
Allow 2 days to Amiskwi Pass
Elevation gain: 780 metres (2,600 feet)
Maximum elevation: 1950 metres (6,500 feet)
Topo maps: Golden, 82 N/7 East
                 Blaeberry River, 82 N/10 East
                 (trail incorrectly marked)

Point of Departure: Drive to the Emerald Lake Road, 2.6 kilometres (1.6 miles) southwest of Field on the Trans-Canada Highway. Follow the Emerald Lake Road for 1.4 kilometres (0.9 miles) and take the Natural Bridge turnoff to the left. Bypass the Natural Bridge parking area and continue on down the gravel road, crossing both Emerald Creek and the Amiskwi River. Beyond the second bridge is the Amiskwi Fire Circle. Leave vehicle here and start up the fire road, running to the northwest.

*all distances approximate

The Amiskwi River trail, running from the Amiskwi Fire Circle to Amiskwi Pass, constitutes a long and remote wilderness trek. Although the view of the heavily glaciated, 3300 metre peaks of the Mummery group from Amiskwi Pass is exceptional, even for the Rockies, few parties to date have been willing to put in the long and relatively uninspiring kilometres to enjoy it.

From the traffic control gate near the fire circle, the route starts up the Amiskwi Valley tracing the western side of the river for nearly 29 kilometres via an old logging road now used as warden access. At Kilometre 21 hikers will encounter the beginnings of an extensive burn, something that will be their companion most of the way to the pass.

Beyond the end of the road the trail continues up the west side of the river as far as Amiskwi Falls, a distance of just under two kilometres. Here hikers should ford the river and continue to the pass on the east side of the Amiskwi. Owing to the forest fire the route above the falls is difficult to follow, but the general route is obvious, and the trail can be picked up again as it enters unburned forest a little over three kilometres from the pass and the Yoho Park boundary.

There are a number of campsites along the route, located roughly at Kilometre 5, 18 and 35.

Ottertail River

Wilderness access

Allow 4 hours to McArthur Creek

Elevation gain: 305 metres (1,000 feet)

Maximum elevation: 1495 metres (4,900 feet)

Topo maps: Golden, 82 N/7 East
Lake Louise, 82 N/8 West
Mount Goodsir, 82 N/1 West

Point of Departure: The Ottertail River Fire Road begins 8.4 kilometres (5.2 miles) west of Field on the Trans-Canada Highway at the former site of the Ottertail Warden Cabin (no longer standing).

From its beginning on the Trans-Canada Highway the road runs east up the north bank of the Ottertail River to the McArthur Creek Warden Cabin. From the cabin hikers have three distinct options.

McArthur Creek Option. The McArthur Creek trail veers north at the confluence of the Ottertail River and McArthur Creek (below the warden cabin), working its way up McArthur Creek and across McArthur Pass to join the Lake O'Hara trail system. Although the trail is well-maintained, most of the distance travelled (just over 12 kilometres) is through pine and spruce forest and offers little scenic reward until McArthur Pass is reached.

Ottertail Pass Option. The Ottertail Pass trail continues east up the Ottertail River, passing Ottertail Falls and crossing into Kootenay Park to the headwaters of the Ottertail. Beyond Ottertail Pass the route ties in with a trail leading down the Ochre Creek drainage system to the Banff-Radium Highway. Although the trail is maintained on the Yoho side the route is indistinct and hard to follow as it crosses to the Ochre Creek drainage. Map, compass and a working knowledge of both may come in handy.

Goodsir Pass Option. The Goodsir Pass trail branches south off the Ottertail Pass trail within a short distance of the McArthur Creek Cabin. A good foot trail angles off above the east bank of Goodsir Creek and ties in with a horse trail (running low and closer to the creek) just below the pass. The trail can be continued in Kootenay Park to make an excellent backpacking trip (see the *Helmet Creek* description in Kootenay Park).

Wapta Falls

Wapta Falls Parking Area to Wapta Falls—2.4 kilometres (1.5 miles)

Nature hike

Allow 2½ hours round trip

Elevation loss: 30 metres (100 feet)

Maximum elevation: 1120 metres (3,700 feet)

Topo maps: McMurdo, 82 N/2 East

Point of Departure: Drive 4.8 kilometres (3 miles) east of the Yoho West Gate or 25.0 kilometres (15.5 miles) west of Field to the Wapta Falls Road. A parking area 1.6 kilometres (1 mile) up the road signals the trail head. Both the road and trail head are clearly marked.

The Wapta Falls hike makes a very good family afternoon outing—it is short, the trail is well-marked and, with the exception of a rather steep descent to the falls lower viewpoint, almost level. The objective of the hike, Wapta Falls, is certainly worth the small amount of effort that goes into the walk.

The route follows a cleared access road right-of-way for a bit over 1.1 kilometres before narrowing to a single file path. The forest here is composed of lodgepole pine, spruce and aspen poplar. A concentration of ferns and Douglas maple make a dense undergrowth.

Forty-five minutes of easy walking brings the hiker to the Wapta Falls upper viewpoint. At this point the trail veers to the right and begins a steep descent to the lower viewpoint, where it is possible to fully appreciate the flow of the 30 metre falls.

Another route to the falls is a 3.5 kilometre trail that begins at the Beaver Dam Parking Area, runs 800 metres with the Ice River Fire Road, cuts into the forest to ford the Beaverfoot River and finally reaches the falls on the east side of the Kicking Horse. This route is inaccessible in the early season when the Beaverfoot is in flood.

Mount Hunter Lookout

Trans-Canada Highway to Hunter Lookout—3.5 kilometres (2.2 miles)

Half-day trip
Allow 1½-2 hours to lookout
Elevation gain: 395 metres (1,300 feet)
Maximum elevation: 1525 metres (5,000 feet)
Topo maps: McMurdo, 82 N/2 East

Point of Departure: Drive the Trans-Canada Highway to the Wapta Falls access road, 5.0 kilometres (3.1 miles) east of Yoho Park West Gate and 24.8 kilometres (15.4 miles) west of Field townsite. Park at a small pull-off just inside the Wapta Falls road entrance and walk back across the Trans-Canada to the Hunter Lookout trail sign.

0.0—Trail sign.

0.3—Cross railroad track.

—Steady uphill through forest.

0.8—Open views next 2 kms.

2.7—Grade steepens; climb back into forest.

3.5—Mount Hunter Lookout.

Despite its relatively short length and low elevation, the trail to Mount Hunter fire lookout is surprisingly rewarding. There are open views across the Kicking Horse Valley along most of the climb, and the dry western slope cover of Douglas fir and juniper found on the open ridgeline makes a pleasant change from the usual Rocky Mountain spruce-fir forest.

After crossing the CPR tracks and climbing for a short distance through a closed forest, the trail breaks out onto the crest of a ridge which leads upwards at a steady grade to the lookout tower. Here the tree cover and vegetation alter dramatically as the predominant spruce forest of the northeast slope is replaced by a much more open environment of Douglas fir and Rocky Mountain juniper on the drier southwest exposure. The ground cover is not as verdant either, as common and creeping varieties of juniper spread across the sunny slope.

The trail stays on this open ridge for nearly two kilometres, the sharp drop on the left providing open views to the Beaverfoot Range and Valley. At Kilometre 2.7 the hiker reenters a more closed forest to make the final steep climb to the lookout tower.

Beneath the fire lookout, the Beaverfoot Valley again dominates the scene. The river serves as the boundary between Yoho Park and provincial forest lands, as evidenced by the steady procession of clearcuts running southward along the slope of the Beaverfoot Range—one of the most poorly managed timber operations in all of British Columbia. More inspiring is the view to the east—the rugged summits of Chancellor Peak (3280 m) and Mount Vaux (3320 m).

The Leanchoil Hoodoos

Hoodoo Creek Campground to Hoodoos—3.1 kilometres (1.9 miles)

Nature hike
Allow 1½ hours one way
Elevation gain: 455 metres (1,500 feet)
Maximum elevation: 1585 metres (5,200 feet)
Topo maps: McMurdo, 82 N/2 East

Point of Departure: Drive the Trans-Canada Highway to the Hoodoo Creek Campground, 7.2 kilometres (4.5 miles) east of Yoho Park West Gate and 22.5 kilometres (14.0 miles) west of Field townsite. Turn off at the campground and keep right past the campground proper. The road leads to a trail sign and parking area.

A short but steep trail climbs into a narrow mountain valley wherein stand some of the most exceptional hoodoo formations to be found in the mountain parks.

The first 1.5 kilometres of trail circle through a lodgepole pine—white spruce forest and eventually arrive at the Hoodoo Creek bridge. After this flat forest prelude, the last 1.6 kilometres of trail from the bridges are steep and rigorous.

These sentinel-like pillars of silt and gravel have been formed by erosion, which has eaten away at a bank of partly consolidated glacial debris. The cap rocks on top of the remaining pillars have helped protect the material beneath from these erosive forces.

Ice River

Beaver Dam Parking Area to Upper Ice Cabin—22.5 kilometres (14.0 miles)*

Wilderness access

Allow 2 days

Elevation gain: 305 metres (1,000 feet)

Maximum elevation: 1465 metres (4,800 feet)

Topo maps: McMurdo, 82 N/2 East
            Mount Goodsir, 82 N/1 West

Point of Departure: Take the Hoodoo Creek Campground turnoff, 22.5 kilometres (14.0 miles) west of Field or 7.2 kilometres (4.5 miles) east of the Yoho West Gate, and drive to the Beaver Dam Nature Trail parking area. The trail begins at the traffic control gate on the fire road adjacent to the parking area.

*Distances approximate.

Starting at the traffic control gate at the Beaver Dam Nature Trail parking area, the Ice River Fire Road runs south along the Beaverfoot River for approximately sixteen kilometres to the lower Ice River Warden Cabin. From the lower cabin a trail cuts north up the Ice River drainage to the upper Ice River Warden Cabin. This last 6.4 kilometre section is in rather poor repair and ends at the upper cabin. (There are traces of an old trail above the cabin but it has not been maintained for several years.)

The fire road and trail combination is uninspiring hiking and is used primarily by climbers interested in the southwest ridges of Mount Goodsir. The area also contains one of the largest intrusive igneous complexes in the Canadian Rockies and is of some interest to geologists.

Kootenay National Park

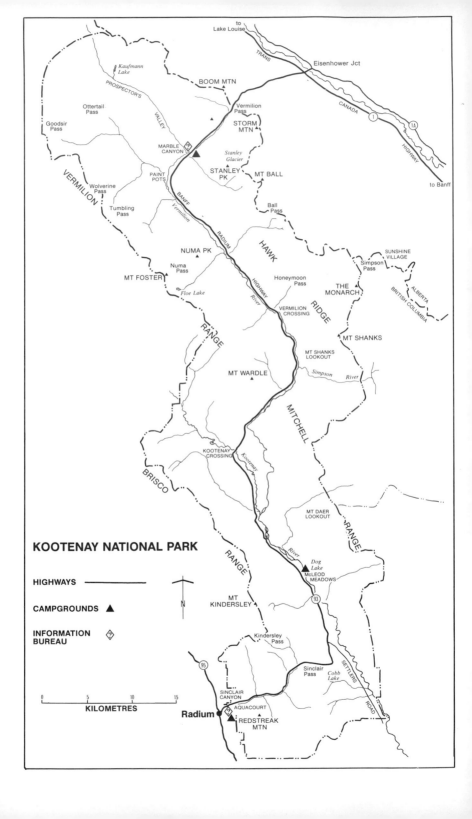

KOOTENAY NATIONAL PARK

HIGHWAYS ——————

CAMPGROUNDS ▲

INFORMATION
BUREAU

| | | | |
KILOMETRES
0   5   10   15

Radium

Kootenay National Park

Kootenay National Park, bounded partially on the north by Yoho National Park and on the east by Banff National Park and Mount Assiniboine Provincial Park, is a 1,370 square kilometre tract of rugged mountains and beautiful rivers. The park parallels the course of the Banff-Radium Highway and extends for some eight kilometres on either side of the road as it works its way from the continental divide to Radium, British Columbia, a distance of 94 kilometres. Access is gained from the north and east via the Trans-Canada Highway and from the south via B.C. Highway 95 from Cranbrook.

Kootenay is probably the least known of the four contiguous parks as a hiking park, but it would be a mistake to believe it holds little for the person interested in foot travel. Over 200 kilometres of trail offer a variety of day and half-day trips, while some of the trails in the northwest corner of the park provide challenging and scenic wilderness options for the experienced backpacker.

For the casual hiker with limited time there are several very short nature walks, some self-guided, such as the Paint Pots and Marble Canyon trails; slightly longer routes, exemplified by Dog Lake, Cobb Lake, Stanley Glacier and Kindersley Pass, provide scenic and popular half-day and day hikes. A number of excellent possibilities exist for the backpacker: a series of trails lead from the highway to the spectacular Rockwall region of the park and can be linked either together or with trails leading to Yoho Park to create extended trips. The route to Mount Assiniboine via the Simpson River, Surprise Creek and Ferro Pass is another backpacker's route that is increasing in popularity.

Backpackers are required to obtain a backcountry permit, designating the party's destination, before beginning an overnight trip. Such permits, and information concerning trail conditions and open campfire restrictions, are available year round from the Kootenay Crossing Warden Station (51.5 kilometres west of the continental divide) and, during the summer, from the Marble Canyon Information Bureau (7.1 kilometres west of the divide), and the information bureaus at the Aquacourt and Kootenay West Gate near the town of Radium.

Radium serves as a visitors' centre for the park and provides the tourist essentials: restaurants, motels, gas stations and grocery stores. There is also a very limited selection of hiking and camping supplies available. The Park Administration Building, also in Radium, is located on the road to the Redstreak Campground.

Stanley Glacier

Half-day trip
Allow 1½-2 hours to basin
Elevation gain: 365 metres (1,200 feet)
Maximum elevation: 1950 metres (6,400 feet)
Topo maps: Mount Goodsir, 82 N/1 East

Point of Departure: Drive the Banff-Radium Highway to the Stanley Glacier parking area, situated on the southeast side of the road 3.4 kilometres (2.1 miles) west of the Alberta-B.C. boundary. The trail begins at the bridge over the Vermilion River immediately below the parking area.

0.0—Vermilion River bridge.

—Switchbacks up through burn.

2.4—Trail crosses Stanley cirque outlet stream.

—Steady climb into open basin.

4.2—Trail ends atop old terminal moraine.

The trail to the Stanley Glacier basin offers an easy half-day trip which carries the hiker up the side of the Vermilion Valley and into a spectacular hanging valley, the far end of which supports the slowly retreating ice of the Stanley Glacier. It is a very pleasant hike in the spring when wildflowers blanket the trailside from beginning to end.

After crossing the Vermilion River—here only four kilometres from its source —the trail rises steadily for over two kilometres through the blackened stumps and snags of a recent burn. The result of a 1968 lightning-caused fire which consumed over 6,000 acres, the burn is an excellent laboratory for the study of the environmental processes initiated by a forest fire. Although many passing motorists believe the area is a lifeless wasteland, the hiker soon discovers that the burn has opened the forest canopy to allow an interesting variety of plants, such as fireweed, columbine, heart-leaved arnica and Labrador tea, to thrive beneath the blackened spars. Lodgepole pine, a species which needs the heat of a passing fire to open its tightly sealed cones, reforested the mountainside within two seasons of the fire, and the trees have continued a rapid growth on the open sunny slope.

Slightly over two kilometres from the river the trail crosses the small creek which finds its source in the melting waters of Stanley Glacier. At this crossing the hiker has left the major portion of the burn behind and starts into the hanging valley. Off to the right is an imposing face of Cambrian limestone which rises over 450 metres to form the southern wall of the valley. In the early spring dozens of waterfalls cascade down the length of the face, adding much to its carved beauty. Ahead one catches glimpses of the glacier through the thinning forest.

The trail runs gently up the valley for more than a kilometre, following the edge

Stanley Glacier

of the creek and a cool green remnant of spruce and alpine fir which was spared by the fire. The last few hundred metres of defined trail climbs across quite rocky terrain before ending atop an open knoll in the midst of the boulder fields of the Stanley basin.

Hikers with sturdy boots may continue on for another kilometre or so, following cairns and snippets of trail to the larch and fir-topped plateau at the head of the valley (keep to the right-hand side of the valley beneath the north wall of Stanley Peak). Though it is a stiff climb, the stream-fed meadow atop the cliff provides an outstanding viewpoint for the

toe of the Stanley Glacier.

The boulder fields of the cirque are home to both hoary marmots and pikas, and a pair of small caves dissolved from the base of the Stanley ramparts (about 100 metres beyond the major waterfall which spills over the cliff) bear evidence of these valley inhabitants. Hikers exploring the upper reaches of the basin might also take time to turn over a few rocks, for the calcareous shales found among the jumble of broken limestones and quartzites bear the fossils of trilobites—archaic arthropods which inhabited early Cambrian seas over 500 million years ago.

Kaufmann Lake

Banff-Radium Highway to Kaufmann Lake—15.0 kilometres (9.3 miles)

Backpack

Allow 5-6 hours

Elevation gain: 565 metres (1,850 feet)

Maximum elevation: 2060 metres (6,750 feet)

Topo maps: Mount Goodsir, 82 N/1 East
Lake Louise, 82 N/8 East

Point of Departure: Drive the Banff-Radium Highway to the marked Tokumm Creek turnout, situated on the northwest side of the road 6.6 kilometres (4.1 miles) west of the Alberta-B.C. boundary and 500 metres east of the Marble Canyon parking area.

0.0—Trail head (1495 m).

—Parallels above Marble Canyon trail.

1.6—Trail narrows.

3.2—Emerges onto open valley bottom beside Tokumm Creek.

—Very moderate uphill along creek.

8.5—Major tributary (bridged).

10.3—Major tributary (bridged).

10.4—Junction: Fay Hut trail cuts uphill to right. Kaufmann Lake straight ahead.

12.2—Landslide area.

13.2—Several small tributaries (bridged).

13.5—Trail begins steep climb toward lake.

14.7—Grade moderates.

15.0—Kaufmann Lake (2060 m).

Prospector's Valley is one of the more popular backpacking areas in Kootenay Park, and few trips are made up this relatively long wilderness valley that do not end at Kaufmann Lake. It is truly a 'classic' Canadian Rockies lake, a beautifully shaped and coloured body of water cradled by the towering and glacier-mantled Wenkchemna Peaks— the same 3000 metre continental divide mountains that form the backdrop to Moraine Lake and Consolation Valley in Banff Park.

Beyond the trail head the route runs northwest, parallel to the Marble Canyon nature trail in the form of an old access road. In less than two kilometres the road ends and the path proper, single file width, begins working its way through a dense coniferous forest of pine, spruce and alpine fir.

Just beyond the three kilometre mark the trail opens up onto the valley bottom and for some distance the hiker has good clear meadow walking. For the remainder of the journey up Prospector's Valley, the trail is never far away from the rushing waters of Tokumm Creek, following above its northeastern bank. The valley was named by tourist-explorer Walter Wilcox in 1899 after he discovered an old prospector's camp near its entrance; the name Tokumm apparently comes from the Stony word for 'red fox.'

Immediately after crossing the second major tributary at Kilometre 10.3, the spur trail to the Fay Hut branches up to the right. It is a stiff climb of some 2.5 kilometres to this small, well-hidden cabin which was once owned by the Alpine Club of Canada and operated as a shelter for climbers. Since then it has been turned over to the parks branch and left open to the general public (a camping permit is required). Generally speaking, it is overrun by hikers and packrats.

208

Kaufmann Lake and the Wenkchemna Peaks

The third major tributary encountered breaks into a series of small streams by the time it reaches the trail. While all of these rivulets are bridged, these crossings mark the end of the easy valley bottom hiking, for this is the outlet stream of Kaufmann Lake and there is a steep 1.5 kilometre climb ahead.

At the 15 kilometre mark, the hiker emerges onto the shore of Kaufmann Lake. Deltaform Mountain (3424 m),

Mount Tuzo (3249 m) and Mount Allen (3301 m) provide the immediate setting for the lake, and the combination of rock, ice and water make the spot one of the loveliest in Kootenay Park. Occasionally mule deer are seen along the shore, browsing among the yellow columbine, red Indian paintbrush, white Grass-of-Parnassus and purple asters which colour the meadows into late August.

Helmet Creek

Marble Canyon to Helmet Falls—17 kilometres (11 miles)*

Backpack

Allow 6 hours one way

Elevation gain: 275 metres (900 feet)

Maximum elevation: 1755 metres (5750 feet)

Topo maps: Mount Goodsir, 82 N/1 East
Mount Goodsir, 82 N/1 West

Point of Departure: Drive the Banff-Radium Highway to the Marble Canyon parking area, 7.4 kilometres (4.6 miles) southwest of the Alberta-B.C. boundary. Walk 400 metres down the highway to the trail bridge, directly opposite the Marble Canyon Warden Station.

0.0—Trail sign (1480 m).

—Follows Tumbling Glacier route for first 5.6 kms.

5.6—Junction: Helmet Creek-Ottertail Pass trail continues straight ahead. Tumbling Glacier trail branches left.

—Trail follows northeast bank of Ochre Creek at gentle grade.

8.0—Junction: Helmet Creek trail branches left and crosses Ochre Creek. Ottertail Pass route continues straight ahead.

—Trail contours into mouth of Helmet Creek and climbs at moderate grade.

17.0—Junction and Helmet Creek Warden Cabin: Trail to Goodsir Pass cuts right. Helmet Campground and Wolverine Pass straight ahead.

17.3—Helmet Falls and Helmet Creek Campground (1755 m).

*Distances approximate.

The Rockwall is a term used to describe the eastern escarpment of the Vermilion Range—an unbroken chain of mountains which forms the western boundary of Kootenay Park for over 40 kilometres. It is an apt designation for this precipitous barrier of Cambrian limestone and dolomite which, in some spots, rises sheer for 700 vertical metres and reaches elevations in excess of 3000 metres above sea level. With the hanging glaciers and larch-fringed passes which nestle against its face, the Rockwall creates one of the most natural hiking areas in the Rockies.

The Helmet Creek trail offers direct access to the northernmost end of the Rockwall and brings hikers to the base of one of the most spectacular cascades in the mountain parks—the 360 metre-plus Helmet Falls. The campsite near the falls also serves as a base for day trips to Goodsir Pass or an overnight stop for other Rockwall Highline options.

Following the same route as the Tumbling Glacier-Wolverine Pass trail from Marble Canyon, the Helmet Creek option branches from that track at the 5.6 kilometre mark. The trail continues up the Ochre Valley for another 2.5 kilometres before crossing to the southwest side of the creek and contouring into the narrow Helmet Creek drainage. The track is good and streams are bridged.

The highlight of any visit to the Helmet Creek headwaters is undoubtedly Helmet Falls and the sheer escarpment of the Rockwall which encloses the head of the valley. Limestone Peak, Helmet Mountain and Sharp Mountain are the three summits which create this massive amphitheatre, and the Sharp Glacier feeds Helmet Falls.

Wolverine Pass Option. While the Wolverine Pass area can be reached more directly from Tumbling Creek, many backpackers prefer to approach the pass from the north, particularly when following the Rockwall Highline route south to Floe Lake. Ascending the steep slopes beneath Limestone Peak, the hiker is provided with a fine aerial perspective of Helmet Falls before crossing a high saddle on the southeasterly journey. Rockwall Pass is reached eight kilometres beyond the Helmet Creek campsite, and the Wolverine Pass summit is less than a kilometre south of Rockwall Pass via the Wolverine Meadows. (See *Tumbling Glacier-Wolverine Pass*.)

Rockwall Highline Trail. With adequate time—three or more days—a traverse of the entire Rockwall may be completed by hiking to Helmet Falls and then working southward via Rockwall, Tumbling and Numa passes to Floe Lake (or vice versa). Total distance for this option, from Marble Canyon to the Floe Creek trail head, is 55 kilometres (34 miles). For people who want to add a couple of extra passes—McArthur and Goodsir—it is possible to start from (or finish at) Lake O'Hara, though the extra scenery is probably not worth the full day of hitchhiking or transportation arranging involved. (See *Tumbling Glacier* and *Floe Lake*.)

Goodsir Pass Option. The broad and extensive larch meadowlands of Goodsir Pass lie less than five kilometres north of the Helmet Creek Warden Cabin junction, but a stiff 450 metre climb away. While the pass may be visited on a day trip from the Helmet Creek campsite, most backpackers traverse it as a part of the Rockwall Highline. It is approximately 16 kilometres from Helmet Creek to the Ottertail River in Yoho Park via Goodsir Pass, and the trail is straightforward and well-maintained. (See *Ottertail River* in Yoho Park.)

Ottertail Pass Option. This seldom-used pass offers possibilities for experienced backpackers who would loop back into Kootenay Park after a northerly traverse of the Rockwall Highline. The trail is reported as good on the Yoho side of the boundary (at least as far as Ottertail Falls), but boggy and ill-defined on the Kootenay side. Total distance from the Goodsir Creek-Ottertail River junction in Yoho to the Ochre Creek-Helmet Creek confluence in Kootenay is around 19 kilometres. Expect this to be a rough and arduous journey until trail conditions are improved.

Tumbling Glacier—Wolverine Pass

Marble Canyon to Tumbling Pass—14.5 kilometres (9.0 miles)
Marble Canyon to Wolverine Pass—15.0 kilometres (9.3 miles)

Backpack

Allow 5 hours one way

Elevation gain: 745 metres (2,450 feet)

Maximum elevation: 2225 metres (7,300 feet)

Topo maps: Mount Goodsir, 82 N/1 East
Mount Goodsir, 82 N/1 West

Point of Departure: Drive the Banff-Radium Highway to the Marble Canyon parking area, 7.4 kilometres (4.6 miles) southwest of the Alberta-B.C. boundary. Walk 400 metres down the highway to the trail bridge, directly opposite the Marble Canyon Warden Station.

0.0—Trail sign (1480 m).

—Level walking.

1.9—Junction: Tumbling Glacier trail cuts right. Vermilion River trail continues straight ahead.

2.9—Ochre clay.

5.0—Major avalanche slope.

5.6—Junction: Tumbling Glacier-Wolverine Pass trail branches down to left. Helmet Creek-Ottertail Pass trail continues straight ahead.

6.0—Ochre Creek bridge.

6.1—Tumbling Creek-Ochre Creek confluence. Campsite.

—Trail rises steadily.

8.5—Tumbling Creek crossing.

11.3—Waterfall viewpoint.

12.2—Junction: Tumbling Glacier trail continues on southeast side of creek. Wolverine Pass trail branches across to right. Campsite.

12.6—Begin steep switchbacks.

14.5—Tumbling Pass (2225 m). Glacier viewpoint.

Yet another access route to the Rockwall hiking area is the Tumbling Creek trail. The trail climbs via a relatively long approach to the headwaters of the Tumbling Valley, from which point either Tumbling Pass or Wolverine Pass may be reached in less than an hour. Both passes offer larch-laced meadows and are covered with wildflowers in July and August. Tumbling Pass provides a close-up view of an alpine glacier; Wolverine Pass serves as a vantage point for the distant peaks of the Purcell Range. From both summits other lofty passes are visible north and south, beckoning hikers to further exploration along the limestone ramparts of the Vermilion Range.

Starting from the Vermilion River bridge opposite the Marble Canyon Warden Station, the trail travels downstream along the river for nearly two kilometres before branching from the river trail and up the Ochre Valley. The track is relatively level and closed-in on either side by a forest of spruce, lodgepole pine and alpine fir.

At Kilometre 2.9 the trail crosses a section of bare, rust-coloured earth and gravel. This phenomenon is created by springs which precipitate quantities of iron oxide. Dr. James Hector of the Palliser Expedition was the first white man to record the area's ochre beds after he crossed Vermilion Pass in August of 1858. There are indications that the Kootenai Indians had visited the beds long before, however, processing the clay to make body paint.

Soon the trail forks down to the left, away from the Helmet Creek-Ottertail Pass route, and crosses Ochre Creek to begin the long ascent of the Tumbling Creek drainage. Throughout the remainder of the journey the turbulent waters of Tumbling Creek are a constant companion. A beautiful waterfall is

Tumbling Glacier

passed near the 11 kilometre mark and, just a kilometre beyond, a trail junction and campsite are reached. Backpackers will find this camp an excellent base for trips to either Wolverine or Tumbling Passes.

Tumbling Pass. The final two kilometres to Tumbling Pass are up a series of steep switchbacks, traversing alongside a high terminal moraine deposited by Tumbling Glacier. As the trail grinds its way upward, views improve on all sides—the Rockwall and Tumbling Glacier to the immediate west and the open meadows of the Wolverine Pass area three kilometres to the northwest. Vegetation alters along the ascent as well, becoming distinctly subalpine with an open forest dominated by stunted alpine larch and fir. From the summit of the pass the Rockwall can be seen stretching away to the south, the high saddle of Numa Pass visible between the sheer wall of Foster Peak on the right and the rounded summit of Numa Mountain to the left.

As with other trails leading onto the Rockwall, the Tumbling route provides the hiker with a number of interesting options: a 26 kilometre loop trip via Numa Creek, emerging onto the Banff-Radium Highway at the Numa Creek Picnic Area; an even longer loop trip via the trail which branches left near the mouth of Numa Creek, hiking back up along the Vermilion River to Marble Canyon; or a trek south along the Rockwall Highline over Numa Pass to Floe Lake. (See *Floe Lake*.)

Wolverine Pass. By taking the trail spur which branches northwest from the Tumbling Creek trail at Kilometre 12.2, the hiker reaches the Wolverine Meadows and the foot of Wolverine Pass in 1.5 kilometres of steady climbing. The Wolverine environs are even more scenic than the Tumbling Pass summit, the term 'Rockwall' taking on

new meaning here. In fact, the eastern escarpment of the Vermilion Range gives such an impression of impenetrability at this point that it's not until the hiker is directly beneath the gap of Wolverine Pass that he realizes there is a cleft in the 500 metre high wall.

At the Wolverine Meadows there are actually two passes within shouting distance of one another. Wolverine is the chink in the Rockwall to the west, while the broad tundra covered saddle to the north is known locally as Rockwall Pass. A short climb brings the hiker to the summit of Wolverine Pass and extensive westward views across the Beaverfoot Range to the sharp summits of the northern Bugaboos—a range which is over 50 aerial kilometres distant.

Helmet Creek Option. By continuing northward over Rockwall Pass, backpackers can make a loop trip down into the Helmet Creek drainage or an extended journey along the Rockwall Highline into Yoho Park. (Hikers should make sure they have their passes straight, however, and not go stumbling down Dainard Creek from the summit of Wolverine by mistake, as some wayward souls have in the past.)

The Rockwall Highline makes a gradual descent from the boggy, tussock-covered heights of Rockwall Pass, skirts a terminal moraine beneath the Vermilion ramparts and makes one last stiff ascent through stands of alpine larch to the 2100 metre level before the final drop into the Helmet Creek drainage. Following close beneath the Vermilion Range ramparts, sections of this trail can be snow-covered into early August. The distance from the upper Tumbling Creek campsite to the junction at the Helmet Creek Warden Cabin is around ten kilometres, while the Tumbling Creek-Helmet Creek loop, from Marble Canyon and return, is a 40 kilometre backpack. (See *Helmet Creek*.)

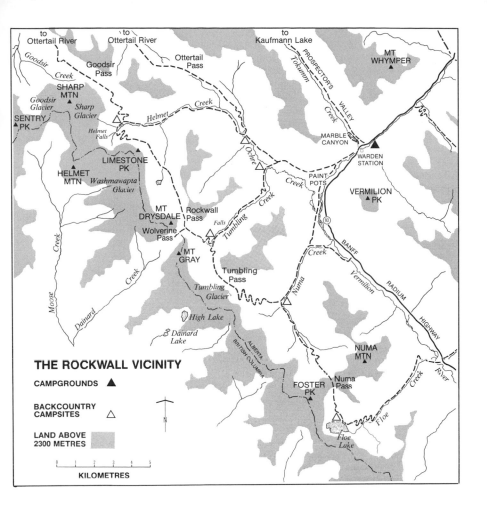

THE ROCKWALL VICINITY

CAMPGROUNDS ▲

BACKCOUNTRY
CAMPSITES △

LAND ABOVE
2300 METRES

0 1 2 3 4 5
KILOMETRES

215

Floe Lake

Day trip or backpack

Allow 4 hours one way

Elevation gain: 730 metres (2,400 feet)

Maximum elevation: 2040 metres (6,700 feet)

Topo maps: Mount Goodsir, 82 N/1 East

Point of Departure: Drive the Banff-Radium Highway to the Hawk Creek highway maintenance camp, 22.4 kilometres (13.9 miles) south of the Alberta-B.C. boundary. Watch for the Floe Lake trail sign on the west side of the road, opposite from the highway camp. Turn off and follow a dirt road 400 metres to an access gate.

0.0—Access road gate (1310 m).

—Follow road down to river.

0.4—Vermilion River and bridge.

1.7—Floe Creek and bridge.

—Moderate to steep uphill.

5.7—Steep switchbacks next 300 metres.

8.0—Steep switchbacks next 2 kilometres.

10.1—Trail levels off.

10.5—Floe Lake (2040 m).

Set beneath a sheer 1000 metre escarpment, a small glacier feeding its pale blue waters, Floe Lake is easily a match for any beauty spot in the Rockies. Above its north shore lies a subalpine forest of alpine larch and fir which grades upward into the tundra of Numa Pass—a summit which looks down upon the Floe Lake environs to provide a sublime view.

The trail to this high cirque begins near the Vermilion River. It crosses the river and, just over a kilometre l eyond, joins the Floe Creek drainage, following that narrow valley upwards for the remainder of the journey. Though travel is mainly through a forest of lodgepole pine, spruce and fir, many areas have been swept clean by avalanches along the way.

Occasionally the hiker catches a glimpse of the imposing Rockwall ahead, and at Kilometre 7.2, near the top of a short steep grade, views open back down the Floe Valley to the Ball Mountain Group on the eastern horizon. Just 300 metres beyond this viewpoint the trail enters a mature spruce forest laced with a few scattered alpine fir. Here the switchbacks begin that carry the hiker up the last two kilometres to the Floe Lake cirque. Canteens and water bottles should be filled here, for the trail is steep and there is no water until the lake.

Floe Lake is situated near the 2040 metre level, well into the upper subalpine forest zone. Trees along its northern shore are scattered and somewhat stunted, and in midsummer many varieties of wildflowers bloom in the surrounding meadows. In the autumn the golden needles of the alpine larch provide a brilliant foreground for the lake, glacier and Rockwall beyond.

The Rockwall is composed of a dark grey Cambrian limestone (Ottertail Formation) and its east-facing cliffs

form the backbone of the Vermilion Range for a stretch of nearly 40 kilometres. A small glacier clings to the foot of the wall and plunges to the southern edge of the lake; the resulting ice floes give the lake its name. It is interesting to note the lagoon which has been formed here by a terminal moraine, the ridge of which actually loops out into the lake, partitioning off a section of its waters.

Though strong hikers can reach Floe Lake and return in one day, most would undoubtedly prefer an overnight stay in this beautiful area. However, the number of campers allowed into this area hinges directly upon their ability to preserve the very delicate surrounding environment.

Numa Pass Option. For those backpacking to Floe Lake, the spur trail to Numa Pass is a must. Branching off from the lakeshore trail just before the warden cabin, the trail rises nearly 300 vertical metres in the 2.7 kilometres to the pass. The views from Numa Pass are some of the most expansive offered by any trail in Kootenay Park. Set between Foster Peak (3204 m) on the west and Numa Mountain (2725 m) to the east, it is by far the best viewpoint for Floe Lake and the Rockwall. To the north, set off by sheer walls, limestone pinnacles and hanging glaciers, the long face of the Rockwall runs toward Yoho Park. The sharp snowy mountains to the far north are the Wenkchemna Peaks, the summits comprising the Valley of the Ten Peaks in Banff National Park.

In addition to the opportunities for an extended trip along the Rockwall Highline (see *Tumbling Glacier-Wolverine Pass* and *Helmet Creek*), backpackers can complete a loop back to the Banff-Radium Highway by descending the Numa Creek trail north of the pass—an option which emerges at the Numa Creek Picnic Area eight kilometres north of the Floe Lake trail head. Total distance for the Floe Creek-Numa Creek loop is 26.9 kilometres.

Hawk Creek

Day trip

Allow 3 hours one way

Elevation gain: 885 metres (2,900 feet)

Maximum elevation: 2210 metres (7,250 feet)

Topo maps: Mount Goodsir, 82 N/1 East
Banff, 82 O/4 West

Point of Departure: The trail head is on the east side of the Banff-Radium Highway 22.4 kilometres (13.9 miles) south of the Banff-Kootenay park boundary. The trail sign is on the north side of the creek opposite the highway maintenance yard.

*Distance approximate.

While the Hawk Creek valley can be ascended to its summit at Ball Pass, the route has little to recommend it as a day trip. The trail is most often used as an entrance or exit to the Shadow Lake-Haiduk Lake area of Banff Park.

From the trail sign on the Banff-Radium Highway, the trail quickly buries itself in the forest and, within a kilometre, begins a steep steady ascent along the north side of the Hawk Creek drainage. There is no respite from this forest-enclosed climb until the seven kilometre mark when the trail branches north from Hawk Creek and ascends into the meadows and scattered larch trees of Ball Pass (2210 m).

Honeymoon Pass

Wilderness access

Allow 2 hours one way

Elevation gain: 700 metres (2,300 feet)

Maximum elevation: 1980 metres (6,500 feet)

Topo maps: Banff, 82 O/4 West
(trail not marked)

Point of Departure: The trail begins at the site of an old warden cabin at Vermilion Crossing, 41 kilometres (25.6 miles) south of Eisenhower Junction on the Banff-Radium Highway. The clearing where the cabin once stood is on the east side of the highway just north of the bridge.

A steep trail departs from the site of an old warden cabin 200 metres north of Vermilion River Crossing and climbs over Hawk Ridge via Honeymoon Pass. The route is often used as access to Verdant Creek, and experienced route finders can either follow the creek down to the Simpson River or forge up to Redearth Pass on the Great Divide.

The trail to Honeymoon Pass is a steady, forest-enclosed uphill grind, and views from the pass are limited. Continuing into Verdant Creek, a warden patrol cabin is reached seven kilometres beyond the pass. The lower Verdant Creek trail, beyond the park boundary, is not maintained and is usually in poor condition. Another undeveloped and poorly defined route crosses Verdant Creek below the falls and ascends East Verdant Creek to Natalko Lake.

218

Verendrye Creek

Vermilion Crossing to Upper Verendrye Creek—4.3 kilometres (2.7 miles)

Nature hike

Allow 1½ hours one way

Elevation gain: 210 metres (700 feet)

Maximum elevation: 1490 metres (4,900 feet)

Topo maps: Banff, 82 0/4 West
Mount Goodsir, 82 N/1 East
(trail not marked)

Point of Departure: The trail head lies at the rear of the Vermilion Crossing Picnic Area, 41 kilometres (25.6 miles) south of Eisenhower Junction on the Banff-Radium Highway.

A pleasant forest walk to near the headwaters of Verendrye Creek, the trail terminates in an open area created by avalanches, offering limited views toward the summit of Mount Verendrye (3086 m) and the sheer escarpment of the Rockwall. Unfortunately, this is one view which is better from the highway.

From the Vermilion Crossing picnic area, the trail climbs gradually through a forest of spruce and pine, then dips down at Kilometre 2.1 to cross Verendrye Creek, providing an excellent view upstream to the cliffs of the Vermilion Range. At Kilometre 3.5 the trail enters an area of avalanche paths, finally terminating 800 metres later on a large gravel outwash by the north shore of the creek. (At last report, the trail beyond the 2.1 kilometre crossing was in rough shape and several sections were washed out.)

Mount Shanks Lookout

Simpson River to Mount Shanks Lookout—4.0 kilometres (2.5 miles)*

Half-day trip

Allow 2 hours one way

Elevation gain: 425 metres (1,400 feet)

Maximum elevation: 1675 metres (5,500 feet)

Topo maps: Mount Assiniboine, 82 J/13
(trail not marked)

Point of Departure: Drive to the wooden Vermilion River bridge on the east side of the Banff-Radium Highway, 46 kilometres (28.5 miles) south of the Banff-Kootenay boundary. Cross the bridge. The trail begins at the closed traffic control gate just ahead. Parking is off the road to the right.

*Distance approximate.

From the access gate on the east side of the Vermilion River, the route follows a well-graded gravel road for the entire four kilometre journey, switchbacking up to the lookout on the southern ramparts of Hawk Ridge. (Hikers should take water on this trip.) In addition to views over the Vermilion Valley, the lookout surveys the rugged summits of Mount Wardle and Split Peak to the south.

Another trail branches up the Simpson River from the parking area, cutting to the right just before the access gate. Following the Simpson for eight kilometres to the park boundary, this is the start of the Ferro Pass route to Mount Assiniboine. (See *Assinbioine via Ferro Pass.*)

Mount Wardle Fire Road

Banff-Radium Highway to Wardle Lookout—3 kilometres (2 miles)*

Half-day trip

Allow 1½ hours one way

Elevation gain: 395 metres (1,300 feet)

Maximum elevation: 1645 metres (5,400 feet)

Topo maps: Spillimacheen, 82 K/16

Point of Departure: Drive the Banff-Radium Highway to the Hector Gorge Viewpoint, 4.0 kilometres (2.5 miles) north of the Kootenay Crossing Warden Station. A dirt road branches west from the highway opposite the viewpoint, leading to a large gravel pit. The Wardle Lookout route departs from the upper edge of this area.

*Distance approximate.

This route follows an old access road to the site of the Mount Wardle fire lookout, and though the lookout tower has been removed, the ridge still allows some panoramic views out across the Kootenay Valley and to the Brisco Range beyond.

The fire road to the old lookout site is quite straightforward but steep. The route is a dry one, so hikers should carry water on warm days.

East Kootenay Road

Banff-Radium Highway to South Park Boundary—32 kilometres (20 miles)*

Wilderness access

Maximum elevation: 1370 metres (4,500 feet)

Minimum elevation: 1095 metres (3,600 feet)

Topo maps: Tangle Peak, 82 J/12 West
　　　　　 Mount Assiniboine, 82 J/13
　　　　　 Spillimacheen, 82 K/16

Point of Departure: There are five points of access to the East Kootenay Road: (1) from its northern junction with the Banff-Radium Highway, 3.2 kilometres (2 miles) north of the Kootenay Crossing Warden Station; (2) from the Banff-Radium Highway, 1.7 kilometres (1.1 miles) north of the Dolly Varden Picnic Area; (3) from the McLeod Meadows Picnic Area, 26 kilometres (16.4 miles) north of the park west gate; (4) from the Banff-Radium Highway 500 metres north of the Nixon Creek trail head; and (5) from the Settler's Road via a bridge near the park's southern boundary.

*Distance approximate.

This is a limited access fire road which runs along the east side of the Kootenay River for some 32 kilometres from Hector Gorge on the north to the park boundary near the mouth of the Cross River on the south. The fire road is the primary means of access for anyone exploring or climbing in the Mitchell Range.

Aside from the northern junction with the Banff-Radium Highway and the bridge at the southern end connecting into the Settler's Road, the other three points of access are merely short feeder roads which bridge the river from points on the Banff-Radium Highway. Trails which branch east from the fire road up Daer Creek and Pitts Creek are poorly developed and seldom maintained. However, a branch road does switchback up to the Mount Daer fire lookout, a journey of some 13 kilometres from the bridge near Dolly Varden Picnic Area.

Kootenay River

Kootenay Crossing to Kootenay Park Boundary—10 kilometres (6 miles)*

Wilderness access

Allow 3 hours one way

Elevation gain: 30 metres (100 feet)

Maximum elevation: 1220 metres (4,100 feet)

Topo maps: Spillimacheen, 82 K/16

Point of Departure: Both the Kootenay River trail and the West Kootenay Road start near the bridge at Kootenay Crossing, 61.2 kilometres (38.0 miles) south of Eisenhower Junction on the Banff-Radium Highway. The river trail begins a hundred metres north of the bridge, the road 500 metres to the south from the Kootenay Crossing Warden Station.

*Distance approximate.

A well-developed trail follows the northeast side of the Kootenay River from the Banff-Radium Highway to the west park boundary. Beyond the boundary the route eventually runs into the logging operations extending over the divide from the Beaverfoot. The trail is valued more as a warden patrol route than for its scenery.

The West Kootenay Road makes virtually the same journey as the Kootenay River trail, though on the opposite side of the river. It is approximately two kilometres further to the park boundary via this route. A branch of this limited access fire road cuts south approximately 800 metres beyond the warden station and loops back to the Banff-Radium Highway at Crook's Meadow via Dolly Varden Creek—a journey of some ten kilometres.

Luxor Pass

Kootenay Crossing to Luxor Pass—7.2 kilometres (4.5 miles)*

Wilderness access

Allow 2½ hours one way

Elevation gain: 700 metres (2,300 feet)

Maximum elevation: 1905 metres (6,250 feet)

Topo maps: Spillimacheen, 82 K/16

Point of Departure: The Luxor Pass trail shares a trail head with the West Kootenay Road at Kootenay Crossing, 61.7 kilometres (38.3 miles) south of Eisenhower Junction on the Banff-Radium Highway. The limited access road starts from the Kootenay Crossing Warden Station.

*Distance approximate.

Following fire road for nearly half its distance and foot trail for the remainder, this route climbs to the heavily forested summit of Luxor Pass on the western boundary of Kootenay Park. It is a trail of little scenic value which can promise only solitude.

Starting from the Kootenay Crossing Warden Station, the route follows the West Kootenay Road for 800 metres then cuts left on that road's south branch. After another 2.4 kilometres of fire road walking, the hiker reaches the Dolly Varden Creek bridge and campsite. The trail to Luxor Pass cuts right from the road just across the bridge and makes a stiff 600 metre climb up the southwest side of the Kootenay Valley, reaching the pass in another four kilometres.

Dog Lake

McLeod Meadows Picnic Area to Dog Lake—2.7 kilometres (1.7 miles)

Nature hike

Allow 1 hour one way

Elevation gain: 60 metres (200 feet)

Maximum elevation: 1220 metres (4,000 feet)

Topo maps: Mount Assiniboine, 82 J/13 (trail not shown)

Point of Departure: The trail begins at the north end of the McLeod Meadows Picnic Area, 26.4 kilometres (16.4 miles) from the Kootenay West Gate on the Banff-Radium Highway.

The Dog Lake trip is an excellent half-day family hike: short, well-marked and with a good scenic objective, it is one of the more popular hikes in Kootenay Park.

From the sign in the McLeod Meadows Picnic Area the trail skirts the southeastern portion of the McLeod Campground to cross the Kootenay River via two sturdy wooden footbridges. At the far side of the river the trail swings to the north and climbs steadily above the river through a rich coniferous forest. Through the trees the hiker has many opportunities to view the expanse of the Kootenay River valley.

The lake itself is a beautiful blue body of water fed by the melting snows of the Mitchell Range. Directly west of the lake, dominating the scenery of the area, is Mount Harkin (2981 m), commemorating James B. Harkin, the first commissioner of the National Parks of Canada.

Cobb Lake

Banff-Radium Highway to Cobb Lake—2.7 kilometres (1.7 miles)

Nature hike

Allow 1 hour one way

Elevation loss: 105 metres (350 feet)

Maximum elevation: 1370 metres (4,500 feet)

Topo maps: Tangle Peak, 82 J/12 West

Point of Departure: The trail begins at the roadside pulloff on the Banff-Radium Highway, 14.7 kilometres (9.1 miles) north of the Kootenay West Gate.

A peaceful, forest-encircled lake, noted for its mirror-like reflections, Cobb Lake is the scenic goal of one of the most pleasant nature walks in Kootenay Park.

From the sign on the south side of the road the trail switchbacks down for 1.6 kilometres through dense fire succession pine, spruce and Douglas fir. Some examples of the latter species are very old and fire-scarred, their thick bark enabling them to survive the forest fires of a century ago.

After crossing Swede Creek at the 1.6 kilometre mark, the trail works slightly uphill until it reaches the lake.

Sinclair Canyon Nature Trails

Containing the Banff-Radium Highway as it rises from the village of Radium, Sinclair Canyon provides a number of interesting nature walks for casual hikers who might be camping or lingering in the Radium Hot Springs vicinity. With the exception of the Juniper Trail, all of these routes branch up side canyons from Sinclair. Only the Kindersley Pass-Sinclair Creek loop ranks as a major day hike (see separate description). The remainder comprise short trips of one to two hours duration which, while they are generally forest-enclosed and limited scenically, provide a restful diversion and an opportunity for nature study.

Topo maps: Radium Hot Springs, 82 K/9 and Tangle Peak, 82 J/12 West.

The Juniper Trail

3.2 kilometres (2.0 miles)

Of the three nature hikes branching from Sinclair Canyon, the Juniper Trail probably offers the most diversity and scenic reward. In just over three kilometres it visits a cool canyon bottom containing a lush growth of western red cedar, switchbacks up an almost arid south-facing slope where Rocky Mountain juniper and Douglas fir thrive, and climbs along the very rim of the canyon mouth to a viewpoint for the broad Columbia Valley.

Hikers usually take this trail as a loop trip, starting at the trail sign on the north side of the highway just 300 metres inside the park gates. The trail descends immediately to the banks of Sinclair Creek, then climbs up open slopes to the canyon rim at Kilometre 1.3. Another 800 metres above the rim the route reaches its summit with an overview of the Columbia River and the Purcell Mountains beyond. By continuing in an easterly direction, the hiker descends to

the Aquacourt area at Kilometre 3.2. From there it is an easy 1.4 kilometre walk back along the highway and through the canyon mouth to the trail head.

Redstreak Creek

2.7 kilometres (1.7 miles)

A very pleasant forest walk in its initial stages but somewhat disappointing near the end, this trail makes a short probe up the narrow confines of the Redstreak Creek valley.

The trail sign can be found along the south side of the Banff-Radium Highway 4.7 kilometres (2.9 miles) from the park gates. From the roadside pullout alongside Sinclair Creek, the trail climbs through a cool forest of lodgepole pine, white spruce, Douglas fir and aspen for the first 1.3 kilometres. After making a crossing of Redstreak Creek, however, the track fizzles out in open willow flats where one is greeted by somewhat limited views of the forested slopes above.

Kimpton Creek

4.8 kilometres (3.0 miles)

Similar to Redstreak Creek, the Kimpton Creek trail runs up a tight forested valley leading southward from Sinclair Canyon. The drainage is slightly longer, however, so the trail is developed a bit further from the highway. The well-shaded banks of Kimpton Creek provide a cool respite during the frequent warm spells experienced near Radium.

The trail head is reached by driving the Banff-Radium Highway 7.1 kilometres (4.1 miles) east from the park gates. The sign is located at a pullout on the south side of the road.

Kindersley Pass

Day trip

Allow 4 hours one way

Elevation gain: 1035 metres (3,400 feet)

Maximum elevation: 2375 metres (7,800 feet)

Topo maps: Tangle Peak, 82 J/12 West

Point of Departure: Drive the Banff-Radium Highway to the trail sign, situated on the west side of the highway 9.7 kilometres (6.0 miles) north of the park gates at Radium. Park on the east side of the road opposite the trail head.

0.0—Trail sign (1340 m).

2.7—Avalanche slope.

—Steady climb along edge of slide path.

6.1—Trail crests watershed divide. Grade moderates.

—Trail enters more snowslide terrain.

8.4—Kindersley Pass (2195 m). Park boundary.

—Steep ascent onto open mountainside northeast of pass.

9.8—Summit of saddle (2375 m). High trail to Nixon Creek Summit contours across the open slope to the north. The Sinclair Creek trail branches down the gully to the east.

The trail to Kindersley Pass and the high alpine ridges beyond leads hikers onto one of the most scenic day trips in the mountain parks—and one of the most strenuous.

Leading off from the trail sign in the upper Sinclair Canyon, the trail climbs steadily up a narrow, densely forested valley which is opened suddenly after Kilometre 2.7 by a number of major avalanche paths. The forest in the initial section is a mixture of Douglas fir, white spruce and lodgepole pine, but as the trail ascends above the first major slide area and crosses the small divide just west of Lookout Point a more typical subalpine cover of Engelmann spruce and alpine fir is encountered.

More avalanche paths are crossed as the trail nears Kindersley Pass, and the huge piles of snow which accumulate in the valley bottom often linger through the entire summer. Along the margins of the retreating snowbanks glacier lilies and western anemones bloom into late August.

Kindersley Pass is a bit anticlimatic after the rather stiff 8.4 kilometre climb to its summit, yet the small meadow set in a narrow gap just below timberline makes a pleasant rest stop and provides the first good views northward to the long procession of peaks which comprise the Brisco Range.

The true glory of the hike begins at Kindersley Pass. By following the trail which climbs the ridge above the pass to the north, the hiker soon ascends through the last stands of alpine larch and emerges onto the treeless alpine slopes above. At Kilometre 9.8 the highest point on the hike is reached when the trail crests a 2375 metre ridge situated between two rocky peaks. From this lofty saddle views open to the headwaters of Sinclair Creek and an

Kindersley Summit

endless sea of peaks stretching away to the northeast.

From the trail summit the hiker can continue for another two kilometres as the path contours around the head of the Sinclair Creek valley, staying just below the ridgeline and finally descending to the crest of Nixon Creek Summit. This is alpine walking at its best, and though the trail is indistinct at times, there is no problem in discerning its traces where it reappears on the open tundra ahead.

At the Nixon Creek Summit new views open along the crest of the Brisco Range and down to the forested headwaters of Nixon Creek. Experienced rock scramblers can ascend the 2530 metre peak immediately above this col to the northeast for an even better view.

Sinclair Creek Option. Dropping away from the saddle at Kilometre 9.8, the Sinclair Creek headwaters provide an excellent alternate route back to the Banff-Radium Highway. After following the Nixon Creek traverse for a short distance, watch for the Sinclair Creek trail dropping steeply down the obvious gully which leads to the head of the valley. Once the valley floor is reached near a series of small cascades, the trail follows the west side of the creek for a hundred metres, then crosses to the east where it remains the rest of the way down the drainage.

The route travels through overgrown avalanche slopes (laced with Devil's club!) in the upper valley and is rough and rocky once it enters the forest below, but it is a shorter and faster way back to the Kindersley trail head than retracing one's steps from the Kindersley Saddle. Total distance from Kindersley Saddle to the Banff-Radium Highway is only six kilometres plus an extra 1.2 kilometres back down the highway to the Kindersley Pass trail head.

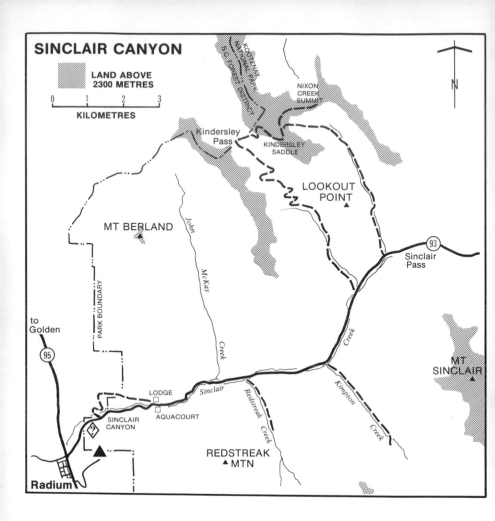

Waterton Lakes National Park

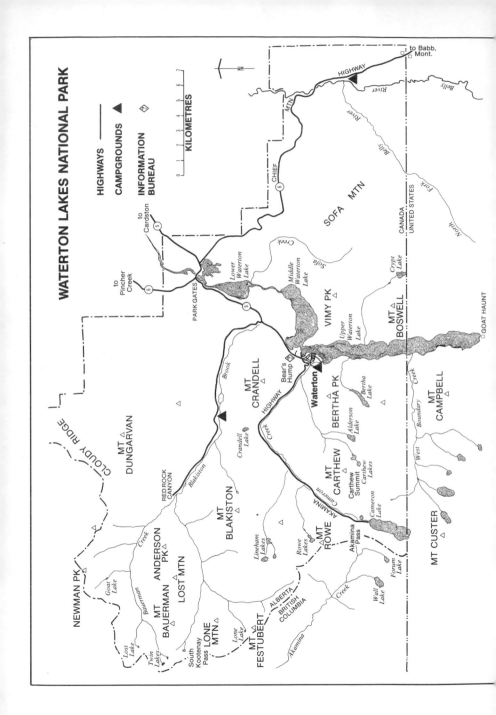

WATERTON LAKES NATIONAL PARK

HIGHWAYS ———
CAMPGROUNDS ▲
INFORMATION BUREAU ◇

KILOMETRES
0 1 2 3 4 5 6

to Babb, Mont.

HIGHWAY

Belly River

River

Belly

SOFA MTN

CHIEF MTN

to Cardston

to Pincher Creek

PARK GATES

Creek

Lower Waterton Lake

Middle Waterton Lake

Sofa Creek

Crypt Lake

CANADA
UNITED STATES

North Fork

VIMY PK △

Upper Waterton Lake

MT BOSWELL △

GOAT HAUNT

Brook

MT DUNGARVAN △

Bear's Hump

Waterton ▲

MT CRANDELL △

HIGHWAY

Crandell Lake

Blakiston Creek

RED ROCK CANYON

BERTHA PK △

Bertha Lake

Alderson Lake

West Boundary

Creek

MT CAMPBELL △

MT BLAKISTON △

Lineham Lakes

Rowe Lakes

MT ROWE △

MT CARTHEW △

Carthew Summit

Carthew Lakes

AKAMINA

Cameron Creek

Akamina Pass

Cameron Lake

MT CUSTER △

ANDERSON PK △

Goat Lake

MT BAUERMAN △

LOST MTN

Creek

Bauerman

NEWMAN PK △

Forum Lake

Wall Lake

Creek

ALBERTA
BRITISH COLUMBIA

LONE MTN △

Lone Lake

MT FESTUBERT △

South Kootenay Pass

Lost Lake

Twin Lakes

Akamina

CLOUDY RIDGE

N

Waterton Lakes National Park

Waterton Lakes National Park is a 518 square kilometres reserve located in the southwestern corner of Alberta, bounded on the west by the crest of the Great Divide, on the south of the Canada—U.S. border, and on the north and east by the rolling prairies of southern Alberta. Two provincial highways offer access to the park from the north and east, one branching south from Highway #3 at the town of Pincher Creek, the other west from Highway #2 at the town of Cardston. In addition, the Chief Mountain International Highway provides the most direct route from Glacier National Park in the United States, but is open only during the summer months.

There are over 160 kilometres of trail in Waterton Lakes Park, making its backcountry the most highly developed of the mountain parks. The trails as a whole are the best constructed in the Canadian Rockies—moderately graded, well-marked, scenically routed and, as might be suspected from such attributes, very heavily travelled.

Most trails in the park are of the shorter, day hike variety and nearly all lead to small, alpine lakes nestled in hanging valleys. Most of these short, scenic hikes can be reached from the park's main arteries—the Red Rock Canyon Road and the Akimina Highway. Several fine trips can be made directly from Waterton townsite, and one of the most popular, the Crypt Lake hike, starts from the village dock with a three kilometre boat ride.

Backpacking opportunities are fairly limited in such a small park, but a journey of more than 30 kilometres can be made along the Great Divide via the popular Tamarack Trail. In addition, a trail running south from the townsite along Upper Waterton Lake offers access to the United States and the extensive trail systems of Glacier National Park.

Waterton townsite is the only service centre for the park. Its limited facilities include a grocery store, gas stations, a laundromat, public swimming pool, and a number of hotels and motels. Some of these establishments handle items such as hiking boots, woolen clothing and socks, and a limited selection of freeze-dried foods. Waterton is a seasonal village and most businesses are closed between early October and May.

Backpackers must register for overnight trips and are encouraged to camp in designated backcountry sites. Parks Canada headquarters is located in Waterton townsite as is the main information bureau (at the town entrance) which serves as a centre for current trail conditions.

Bertha Lake

Day trip

Allow 2 hours one way

Elevation gain: 455 metres (1,500 feet)

Maximum elevation: 1770 metres (5,800 feet)

Topo maps: Waterton Lakes National Park

Point of Departure: Follow Cameron Falls Drive south for 300 metres beyond Cameron Falls. A side-road cuts uphill to a parking area on the right. The trail strikes off to the south. (This is a short walk from the townsite campground, which is located on the opposite side of Cameron Drive.)

0.0—Trail sign and parking area.

2.4—Trail junction. Stay left.

2.6—Lower Bertha Falls.

   —Trail climbs through forest and passes Upper Bertha Falls.

5.1—First view of lake.

5.8—North end of lake. Shelter.

7.4—South end of lake.

Lying just 5.8 kilometres from Waterton townsite, Bertha Lake is one of the most popular hikes in Waterton Park. With a kitchen shelter at the lake and both foot and horse trails leading to it, the area is frequented by fishermen, campers and day hikers. Although the number of people (and, unfortunately, their litter) might detract from the attractiveness of the lake, the region has a beauty and tranquility which even the most cynical mountain traveller will find hard to deny.

The trail to the lake is fairly steep but well maintained. From its origin at the extreme southwest corner of the townsite, the trail climbs gradually for the first two kilometres through a forest rich with undergrowth and wildflowers. At Kilometre 1.3, the trail breaks out of the forest briefly and onto a dry open slope which affords excellent views of the Upper Waterton Lake valley. The rather stunted and bushy looking trees which grow on this sunny exposure are five-needled limber pines—a species which thrives in just a few isolated locales throughout the park. The showy, purple-flowered horsemint also grows along this section of trail through much of the summer.

At the 2.4 kilometre mark the trail divides into horse and foot paths. Hikers should stay with the left-hand fork, and five minutes of walking will bring them to the beautiful Lower Bertha Falls. The trail crosses below the falls and begins its steep climb up to the hanging valley which contains Bertha Lake. Climbing through a typical subalpine forest of alpine fir, spruce and lodgepole pine, the trail passes the Upper Bertha Falls cascading down across the ochre-red argillite common to the region.

Just 5.2 kilometres from the trail's start the maximum elevation of the hike is reached, at which point the first

Bertha Lake

glimpse of the lake is possible. Another 700 metres to the right carries the hiker down to the water's edge and a small kitchen shelter. The trail continues down along the lake, eventually encircling the entire body of water.

The high cirque in which Bertha Lake lies was carved thousands of years ago by the motion of glacial ice as it slowly accumulated in the centre of the valley. The prevailing green hue of the rock and soil surrounding the lake comes from the green argillite of the Appekunny Formation, while the wall at the far end of the lake is composed of the grey dolomite and limestone of the Siyeh Formation and the red argillite of the Grinnell Formation. The thin, dark band stretching across the headwall is an intrusion of igneous rock which was forced between the sedimentary layers in a molten state long before the uplift of the Rockies.

The lake was named for Bertha Ekelund, once a resident of the Waterton area. Bertha achieved a certain notoriety with the locals by attempting to pass some counterfeit bills. She went to jail and was not seen in Waterton again, but her name remains behind.

Bear's Hump

Information Centre to Bear's Hump—1.2 kilometres (0.75 miles)

Nature hike

Allow 1½ hours round trip

Elevation gain: 215 metres (700 feet)

Maximum elevation: 1525 metres (5,000 feet)

Topo maps: Waterton Lakes National Park

Point of Departure: The trail head is immediately behind the parks information centre, opposite the Prince of Wales Hotel and at the entrance to Waterton townsite.

The Bear's Hump is one of the most popular nature hikes in the Waterton townsite vicinity, leading up a steep trail to a windswept ledge overlooking the entire Waterton Valley.

From the trail sign behind the park information bureau, the track switchbacks up the Bear's Hump—the southern ridge of Mount Crandell—travelling through a forest of lodgepole pine, Douglas fir and a few white birch. From the rock ledge which serves as the trail terminus there are excellent views down the Upper Waterton Lake into the United States, the distinctive U-shape of the valley disclosing its glacial origins. The trail summit also looks out over the lower Waterton Valley and onto the prairies beyond—an area which bears much evidence of past glacial activity.

Crandell Lake

Akamina Highway to Crandell Lake—0.8 kilometres (0.5 miles)
Crandell Mountain Circuit—19 kilometres (12 miles)

Nature hike or day trip

Allow 7 hours for circuit

Maximum elevation: 1585 metres (5,200 feet)

Minimum elevation: 1310 metres (4,300 feet)

Topo maps: Waterton Lakes National Park

Point of Departure: Access to Crandell Lake can be gained from either Kilometre 7.1 (Mile 4.4) on the Akamina Highway, or Kilometre 8.4 (Mile 5.2) on the Red Rock Canyon Road. The Crandell Mountain circuit is usually started and finished at Waterton townsite, and the trail can be picked up on the slope just beyond the park information bureau.

Both of these trails make for excellent family hikes, the Crandell Lake trip being a short half-hour jaunt from the Akamina Highway, while the Crandell Mountain circuit is a moderately long day trip that never strays far from the park roadways.

From the trail head on the Akamina Highway, hikers follow an old wagon road over a low ridge to Crandell Lake. Unfortunately the heavy use which the lake receives shows along its shoreline.

The loop around Crandell Mountain is not nearly as heavily travelled as that short segment to Crandell Lake. A traditional horse trip from the townsite, the broad well-graded path makes for easy hiking.

Lakeshore Trail—Mother Duck Trail

Waterton Townsite to Goat Haunt, Montana—11 kilometres (7 miles)*
Cameron Lake to Waterton Townsite—24 kilometres (15 miles)*

Day hike

Allow 4 hours to Goat Haunt

Elevation gain: 90 metres (300 feet)

Maximum elevation: 1370 metres (4,500 feet)

Topo maps: Waterton Lakes National Park

Point of Departure: Follow Cameron Drive along the west side of Waterton townsite. The parking area for the Lakeshore and Bertha Lake trails lies just above the roadway 300 metres south of Cameron Falls (watch for gravel access road cutting uphill to right).

0.0—Trail head.

1.3—Junction: Lakeshore Trail stays left. Bertha Lake trail branches right.

2.4—Bertha Bay. Campsite.

5.8—Boundary Bay. Campsite.

6.3—International Boundary.

6.8—Junction: West Boundary Creek trail enters from west.

11.0—Goat Haunt. Ranger station and boat dock.

*Distance approximate.

A seven kilometre long trail rolls along the west shore of Upper Waterton Lake from Waterton townsite to a U.S. Park Service ranger station at the lake's southern tip—an isolated piece of Montana called Goat Haunt. Day hikers and backpackers often organize an interesting loop trip, hiking the trail to the head of the lake then riding back on the tourist launch.

From the southwest corner of the townsite, the Lakeshore Trail follows the route to Bertha Lake for the first 1.3 kilometres, then branches down to the left. The trail reaches the Bertha Bay campsite near the mouth of Bertha Creek at Kilometre 2.4 and the Boundary Bay campsite at Kilometre 5.8, just before it crosses into the U.S. Less than a kilometre south of the International Boundary, the West Boundary Creek trail intersects from the right. At the end of the lake the trail swings away from the shore and across several tributary streams before circling into the ranger station—boat dock complex.

Hikers wishing to catch the International Launch back to Waterton should make arrangements at the townsite dock before setting out. Backpackers continuing south into Glacier Park, Montana should check in with the rangers at Goat Haunt.

An interesting arrangement hike can also be made by driving to Cameron Lake on the Akamina Highway and hiking back to Waterton townsite via the Mother Duck Trail. Hikers climb to Summit Lake on the Carthew trail, then descend the Mother Duck route to the West Boundary Creek trail in northern Glacier Park. The West Boundary Creek route emerges onto the Lakeshore Trail just south of the Canada-U.S. boundary, as already mentioned. Total distance for the one way trip is approximately 24 kilometres. (See *Carthew Trail*.)

Crypt Lake

Crypt Landing to Crypt Lake—8.7 kilometres (5.4 miles)

Day trip or backpack

Allow 3-4 hours one way

Elevation gain: 700 metres (2,300 feet)

Maximum elevation: 1980 metres (6,500 feet)

Topo maps: Waterton Lakes National Park

Point of Departure: The trail head is reached via a three kilometre boat ride across Waterton Lake. Check with the ticket office of the Canadian boat tours at the townsite dock and make arrangements to be dropped off at Crypt Landing. This firm has special rates for Crypt Lake hikers.

0.0—Trail sign at Crypt Landing (1279 m).

—Moderate, steady switchbacks.

2.4—Last switchback.

3.5—Twin Falls viewpoint.

5.6—Burnt Rock Falls.

—Switchbacks resume.

7.9—Campsite and shelter.

8.1—Tunnel.

8.5—Underground stream.

8.7—Crypt Lake (1950 m).

Crypt Lake is unique among all trails in the Canadian Rockies. To reach it the hiker must cross windy Waterton Lake by boat, climb a narrow valley past a series of waterfalls, crawl through a 20 metre long tunnel, and pass by a stream that suddenly materializes from beneath the ground. And if that doesn't satisfy a desire for the bizarre, one may stroll down along the lake's emerald waters and visit another country.

To reach the Crypt Lake trail head, passage must be booked on the Canadian-owned motor launch that plies the white-caps of Waterton Lake. The launch captain drops hikers off across the lake at Crypt Landing on request and arranges for pick-ups there in the evening. There is no other reasonable method of reaching the trail.

From the boat dock the trail begins to climb immediately, gaining elevation via a series of well-graded switchbacks. The way is enclosed by a forest of white spruce, Douglas fir and lodgepole pine. At Kilometre 2.4 the switchbacking ceases temporarily, as the trail heads straight up the Hell Roaring Valley, passing Twin Falls at Kilometre 3.5.

At Burnt Rock Falls, a beautiful 15 metre strand of water that tumbles off a lip of Precambrian strata, the trail takes to the open talus slopes and begins a series of steep switchbacks. After traversing high above a small green lake, it reaches the campsite and kitchen shelter at Kilometre 7.9.

The last 800 metres to Crypt Lake is not well-suited for those suffering from claustrophobia, acrophobia or obesity. A short jaunt across a talus slope brings the hiker to a halt at a sheer wall—an apparent cul de sac but for a ladder leading up into a dark hole in the rock. At the top of the ladder a 20 metre tunnel cuts through the mountain spur— a tight, cramped shaft that nearly requires the hands-and-knees approach.

Crypt Lake

Emerging from the tunnel on the opposite side, the trail is etched along an exposed precipice. A cable has been attached to the rock offering support to the faint-of-heart.

As the path enters a grove of white-bark pine and fir at the mouth of the Crypt cirque, a short spur trail branches to where the outlet stream emerges from beneath a pile of boulders. Not far away the stream plunges over a vertical wall, creating Crypt Falls.

Crypt Lake is certainly no anticlimax to its many-faceted approach. Its waters are of the deepest green and are seldom free from ice, even in the middle of the summer. The brilliant white of floating icebergs serves to accentuate the dark hue of the lake. It is the perfect example of a glacial amphitheatre, with 600 metre high cliffs rising on all but the north side of the lake.

By keeping to the east shore, one may pick a route down to the far end of the lake, which is situated precisely on the International Boundary between Canada and the United States. No customs agent or immigration officer to greet the intruder here, only the odd mountain goat above, patrolling the slopes in search of lichen. Potential smugglers will find, however, that the Wilson Range forms one of the most effective barriers to be found anywhere along the nearly 6500 kilometres of border.

Day hikers should keep an eye on their watches and allow enough time to catch the boat back to Waterton in the late afternoon, and backpackers should be aware that the Crypt Lake campsite is one of the most heavily used overnight stops in the park's backcountry.

The Carthew Trail

Cameron Lake to Waterton Townsite—20.1 kilometres (12.5 miles)

Day trip

Allow 7 hours

Elevation gain: 760 metres (2,500 feet)
  loss: 1130 metres (3,700 feet)

Maximum elevation: 2410 metres (7,900 feet)

Topo maps: Waterton Lakes National Park

Point of Departure: Drive the Akamina Highway to its terminus at Cameron Lake, 16.4 kilometres (10.2 miles) west of Waterton townsite. The trail begins at the eastern edge of the lakeshore parking area where a bridge spans Cameron Creek.

0.0—Trail sign (1660 m).

—Trail climbs gradually but steadily.

4.2—Summit Lake (1975 m) and junction. Stay left.

—Trail climbs steeply.

7.9—Carthew Summit (2410 m).

9.3—Upper Carthew Lake (2195 m).

9.8—Lower Carthew Lake (2135 m).

—Trail descends steeply.

13.1—Alderson Lake (1800 m).

19.6—Falls and power station on Cameron Creek.

20.1—Cameron Falls (1292 m). Waterton townsite.

The 20.1 kilometre hike from Cameron Lake to Waterton townsite is one of the few hikes in the mountain parks that could be considered 'complete' in having all the elements that make alpine travel the pleasurable experience it is. A beautifully constructed trail carries the hiker through a spectrum of botanical life zones ranging from dense coniferous forest to high alpine terrain where only lichens and small mosses are able to survive, past lakes and glaciers, over a high and windswept mountain pass, through delicate subalpine meadows featuring a variety of wildflowers, and at all times through some of the most colourful mountains found in any of Canada's mountain parks. The trail itself is steep in spots and the hike is a full day's effort, but these factors only add to the enjoyment of the journey for anyone truly interested in high mountain rambling.

From Cameron Lake (named after Major-General D.H. Cameron, the British Commissioner on the International Boundary Survey of 1872-76) the trail switchbacks up the southwestern flank of Mount Carthew (2620 m), climbing some 300 metres in just over three kilometres. This early section offers the hiker many fine views of Cameron Lake below and the surrounding mountains, predominantly Forum Peak (2436 m) to the west and Mount Custer (2708 m), mantled with the Herbst Glacier, to the southwest. At the three kilometre mark the trail levels off to run to the southeast across a high, thinly forested plateau to Summit Lake (1950 m). Here the scenery is dominated by Chapman Peak (2867 m), lying to the south in the United States. The North Lakes and the Hudson Glacier are clearly visible on the northern flank of Chapman Peak.

At Summit Lake the trail forks: to the left lies the path to Carthew Summit and Waterton townsite; straight ahead, the U.S. and West Boundary Creek.

Cameron Lake and Mount Custer from Mount Carthew

Three-and-a-half kilometres and 450 vertical metres from the Summit Lake junction the hiker reaches Carthew Summit after a strenuous switchbacking climb up a long and barren slope which carries him from the upper reaches of the subalpine zone well into a true alpine environment. The red scree across which the trail runs is composed of argillites and quartzites of the Kintla Formation and is responsible for the region's amazing colour. From Carthew Summit it is a brief fifteen minute scramble to the summit peak of the ridge, an effort which serves to extend the expansive view from the pass.

From the pass the trail descends a steep scree slope into the amphitheatre housing the Upper Carthew Lake. Not far below lies the Lower Carthew Lake, where the hiker again begins to encounter the subalpine forest. There is a campsite at the lower lake, but no fires are permitted; backpackers will have to carry a small stove if they plan to spend the night at the lake.

Beyond the Lower Carthew Lake the trail descends rapidly (330 metres in just over three kilometres) across two rock formations to Alderson Lake, a diminutive green body of water nestled at the foot of the impressive 780 metre north face of Mount Alderson. Camping is permitted at the lake, but all potential overnight visitors should keep in mind it is a high use area and make a special effort to protect the lake's natural beauty.

From Alderson Lake the trail runs 6.5 kilometres down the Carthew Creek valley between Buchanan Ridge to the north and Bertha Peak to the immediate south, winding its way through a heavy forest of pine, spruce and Douglas fir. A half-kilometre before reaching Waterton the trail joins Cameron Creek and bypasses the Waterton hydro-electric station to reach the townsite some 200 metres south of Cameron Falls.

Rowe Lakes

Akamina Highway to Lower Rowe Lake—4.1 kilometres (2.5 miles)
Akamina Highway to Upper Rowe Lakes—6.4 kilometres (4.0 miles)

Day hike

Allow 2-3 hours to Upper Rowe

Elevation gain: 580 metres (1,900 feet)

Maximum elevation: 2195 metres (7,200 feet)

Topo maps: Waterton Lakes National Park

Point of Departure: Drive the Akamina Highway west from Waterton townsite to the trail sign and roadside parking area, situated on the northwest side of the road 10.0 kilometres (6.2 miles) from the townsite junction.

0.0—Trail sign (1615 m).

0.3—Cascades.

   —Gradual but steady uphill.

2.3—Broad open avalanche slope.

3.9—Junction: Spur trail to Lower Rowe Lake (200 metres) branches left. Main trail to Upper Rowe Lakes continues straight ahead.

5.2—Junction and campsite: Trail to Upper Rowe Lakes branches left just across bridge. Tamarack Trail branches right.

   —Steep grade and switchbacks.

6.4—Upper Rowe Lakes (2195 m).

For casual day hikers the trail to the Rowe Lakes is one of the more pleasant outings in Waterton Park, but for strong hikers who are willing to put in a rather strenuous 15 to 20 kilometre day the area offers as much variety and exhilarating scenery as any in the Rockies.

The trail has a very pretty beginning. The first 300 metres follows along the north side of Rowe Creek which, at this point, is a long series of cascades sliding over one of the most colourful stream beds imaginable—a long chute of brilliant red argillite. Some of the most inviting streams in the Rockies flow in Waterton Park, and while the hiker may not have worked up a thirst at an early hour of the day, he had better bottle some of Rowe Creek's sparkling waters for the dry three kilometres ahead.

The first part of the climb up from the Akamina Highway is across a semi-open slope scattered with lodgepole pine, but as one ascends the Rowe Creek drainage the fire succession pine grades into a mature forest of spruce and alpine fir. Beneath the forest canopy a lush ground cover typical of the Waterton region thrives. The trail continues its steady ascent.

The Lower Rowe Lake junction is attained at the 3.9 kilometre mark, and a short spur cuts left from the main trail to reach the shore of the tiny lake in just 200 metres. Despite the lake's diminutive size, the steep walls of the surrounding amphitheatre enhance the setting, and a scattered subalpine forest along the shore helps to create a very pleasant early rest stop.

Beyond the junction the trail to the upper lakes continues its climb, finally emerging in an open basin near the head of the Rowe Creek valley. A bridge at the far edge of the meadow spans a tributary stream and brings the hiker to yet another junction. Here the Tamarack

Lower Rowe Lake

Trail branches right and begins its 500 metre vertical ascent to Lineham Ridge while the trail to the Upper Rowe Lakes cuts left and contours across a steep slope, climbing into a stand of alpine larch trees. The uppermost and largest of the two Upper Rowe Lakes is just a kilometre beyond.

The larger of the Upper Rowe Lakes is a sparkling body of water backed against the cliffs of the Great Divide and surrounded by a sparse and stunted forest of alpine fir and larch. By hiking down to the smaller of the upper lakes, one can peek over the lip of this hanging valley—a 150 metre cliff—to the waters of Lower Rowe Lake directly below. The slopes above the Upper Rowe Lake are often frequented by flocks of bighorn sheep.

For hikers who get back down to the 5.2 kilometre junction with energy and time to spare, a hike up to the 2500 metre

summit of Lineham Ridge would be a highlight of the day. Simply follow the Tamarack Trail option from the creekside junction, a trail which attains the crest of the ridge in another 3.4 kilometres of steady climbing. The views from the top are magnificent, encompassing a sea of peaks in all directions and extending as far as the Logan Pass region of Glacier National Park, Montana, to the south. On the opposite side of the ridge the beautiful Lineham Lakes lie in their verdant basin. (For more details on this option, see *Tamarack Trail*.)

One note of warning, however: Lineham Ridge should be avoided during bad weather, since high winds and poor visibility make this a very hazardous area. Hikers should also avoid the ridge early in the season when the trail is obliterated by steep snow-fields.

239

The Tamarack Trail

Akamina Highway to Red Rock Canyon—36.2 kilometres (22.4 miles)

Backpack

Allow 2-3 days

Elevation gain: 1435 metres (4,700 feet)
loss: 1525 metres (5,000 feet)

Maximum elevation: 2500 metres (8,200 feet)

Topo maps: Waterton Lakes National Park

Point of Departure: Drive to the marked trail head 10.0 kilometres (6.2 miles) up the Akamina Highway. The first portion of the trail coincides with the Rowe Lakes trail.

0.0—Trail sign (1615 m).

5.2—Upper Rowe Lake junction and campsite. Stay right.

8.5—Lineham Ridge (2500 m).

13.8—Trail fork. Stay left.

15.7—Trail crosses Festubert Mountain saddle (2225 m).

17.7—Lone Lake (2010 m). Campsite.

21.5—South Kootenay Pass trail junction. Keep straight ahead.

21.6—Blakiston Brook trail junction. Stay left.

22.2—Small lake in Peck's Basin.

24.1—Trail passes above the Lower Twin Lake.

24.8—Upper Twin Lake (1965 m). Campsite.

24.9—Sage Pass junction. Stay right.

28.0—Snowshoe Warden Cabin.

36.2—Red Rock Canyon (1495 m).

Waterton Park's Tamarack Trail is actually a combination of the Rowe Lakes trail on the south linked with the Twin Lakes-South Kootenay Pass routes on the north. Tracing a major portion of the park's west boundary along the continental divide, the Tamarack constitutes a rugged and spectacular hike of 36.2 kilometres. Because of the length and vertical profile of the trail (there are close to 3000 metres combined ascent and descent), it should be considered only by backpackers who are in fairly good shape.

The trail exhibits its steep nature right from the trail head as it climbs toward the Rowe Lakes from the Akamina Highway, rising 390 metres in 5.2 kilometres (see the *Rowe Lakes* description). At the 5.2 mark the hiker encounters the Upper Rowe Lakes-Tamarack Trail intersection and should stay to the right, continuing the long hard climb toward the ridge above the Lineham Lakes, some 500 vertical metres and three kilometres distant. The trail switchbacks high above timberline, and the hiker, approaching the ridge summit, should be careful to stay on route. Small red markers close to the top will help in this regard. The ridge is crossed at an altitude of close to 2500 metres, an elevation exceeded by only two or three other trails in Canada's mountain parks. The view is exceptional.

From the ridge the trail works west, making a long and switchbacking descent into the valley below (do not attempt to drop into the Lineham Lakes basin slightly northeast of the ridge). Toward the valley floor the trail swings south, working to the head of the valley and along its contour as it arcs back toward the north.

A trail fork at Kilometre 13.8 indicates a turn to the left and the start of the second tough climb of the trip, a 360 metre rise to the east saddle of Festubert

Upper Rowe Lakes and Mount Rowe from the Tamarack trail

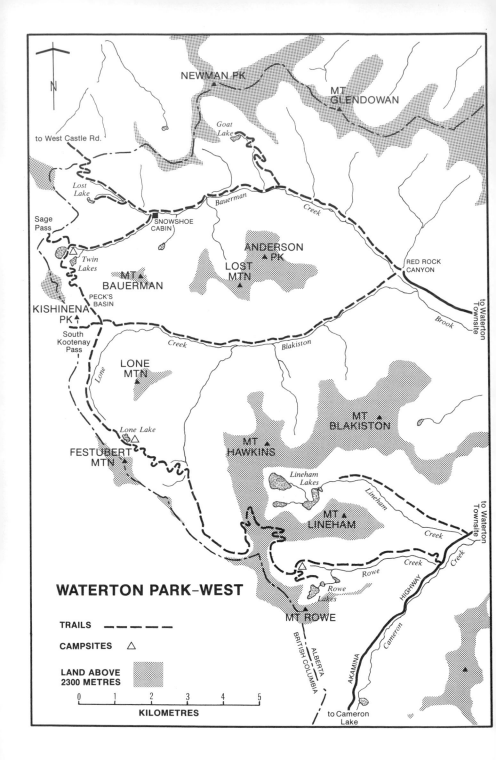

WATERTON PARK—WEST

TRAILS

CAMPSITES △

LAND ABOVE
2300 METRES

0 1 2 3 4 5
KILOMETRES

Mountain. It is a tough climb on a hot day, but scenically well-worth the effort, particularly if one scrambles up the eastern sub-summit of the mountain. From the saddle the trail drops rapidly to Lone Lake at Kilometre 17.7, marking the midpoint of the journey.

From Lone Lake the trail proceeds north at a relatively level grade, alternately working through beautiful forest and across subalpine meadows. A constant companion on this portion of trail is a spectacular rock wall to the west which marks the continental divide and the Alberta-B.C. border.

At Kilometre 21.5 the South Kootenay Pass trail intersects the Tamarack Trail, presenting an alternate route to Red Rock Canyon (see the *Twin Lakes Loop* description). For those intent on seeing the Twin Lakes, however, the route lies straight ahead to the north.

The next portion of trail runs through Peck's Basin, bypassing a sparkling lake before starting the third and final climb of the hike, a 200 metre ascent to the western ridge of Mount Bauerman. The ridge, like the ones preceeding it, is a beautiful spot for a break with map and compass. From the ridge the trail descends quickly toward the small and delicately-coloured Twin Lakes. (The last twelve kilometres of the hike coincide with the first twelve of the *Twin Lakes* trail.)

The trail is named for the many "tamarack" which grow near timberline along the way. Actually, tamarack is a general term used for the larches, and these trees are alpine larch. Also known as Lyall's larch (*Larix lyallii*), the species was named for Dr. David Lyall, a British botanist who visited this remote section of today's Waterton Park in July, 1861. The larch is a deciduous conifer which sheds its needles every fall.

Lineham Lakes

Akamina Highway to Lineham Falls—4.2 kilometres (2.6 miles)
Akamina Highway to Lineham Lakes—5.6 kilometres (3.5 miles)

Day trip

Allow 2½ hours to Lineham Lakes

Elevation gain: 550 metres (1,800 feet)

Maximum elevation: 2135 metres (7,000 feet)

Topo maps: Waterton Lakes National Park

Point of Departure: The trail head lies on the northwest side of the Akamina Highway at Kilometre 9.5 (Mile 5.9), slightly east of Lineham Creek.

The Lineham Lakes region is one of the beauty spots of Waterton Park, but the wonders of this basin are well-guarded. A 100 metre-high cliff brings the hiker to an abrupt halt just over a kilometre from the lakes, and only experienced climbers with a park climbing permit are allowed to traverse the precipice to the hanging valley above.

The first 4.2 kilometres of trail are quite straightforward, ascending the north side of the Lineham Creek drainage at a steep to moderate grade. The route up the cliff is quite exposed, however, and one corner in particular requires steady nerves and some skill.

There are five lakes situated in the Lineham basin, two ranking as the largest lakes above 2000 metres in the park. The setting is distinctively subalpine.

Twin Lakes

Red Rock Canyon to Upper Twin Lake—11.4 kilometres (7.1 miles)
Twin Lakes-South Kootenay Pass Trail Loop—24.7 kilometres (15.3 miles)

Day trip or backpack

Allow 4 hours to Twin Lakes

Elevation gain: 470 metres (1,550 feet)

Maximum elevation: 1965 metres (6,450 feet)

Topo maps: Waterton Lakes National Park

Point of Departure: Drive the Red Rock Canyon Road to its terminus at the Red Rock Canyon, 14.8 kilometres (9.2 miles) west of the junction with the Waterton Townsite Road. The hike starts at the Snowshoe Fire Road access gate, beside the warden station.

0.0—Access gate (1495 m).

—Route follows fire road.

4.3—Junction: Trail to Goat Lake branches right from road. Twin Lakes route stays with fire road.

8.2—Snowshoe Cabin. Fire road ends. Twin Lakes trail cuts south.

11.3—Junction: Sage Pass trail branches right. Twin Lakes route stays left.

11.4—Upper Twin Lake (1965 m).

12.0—Lower Twin Lake (1935 m).

13.9—Peck's Basin and pond.

14.5—Junction: Route to Red Rock Canyon branches left, following the South Kootenay Pass Trail. Route to South Kootenay Pass Summit branches right less than 100 metres farther on.

—Moderate to steep descent.

16.0—Grade moderates.

24.7—Red Rock Canyon.

When the Snowshoe Fire Road was open to the public the Twin Lakes trip was a very popular half-day outing. With the closure of the road to motorized vehicles, the heavy use of the past has moderated, so that today the area is more often visited by backpackers than day hikers. The fire road approach is admittedly mundane, but the objective, a verdant subalpine region of meadows and lakes at the foot of the Great Divide, is well worth the two or three hours of tedium.

The route from Red Rock Canyon is straightforward, following the fire road west from the access gate beside the warden residence. Over its 8.2 kilometre length the road makes a gradual but steady ascent of the Bauerman Valley, traversing to the north of Anderson Peak.

At the end of the road the foot trail takes over, the path to Twin Lakes continuing to the southwest through heavy timber and across avalanche slopes at the foot of Mount Bauerman. Just over two kilometres beyond the end of the fire road the hiker reaches Upper Twin Lake, a small, beautifully coloured body of water backed up against the Great Divide. Along with the nearby Lower Twin the lake serves as the headwaters for Bauerman Creek and has been stocked with eastern brook and rainbow trout. There is a campsite near its eastern shore.

Since it is only two kilometres further than the round trip via Bauerman Creek, most hikers will prefer to continue south through Peck's Basin to make a loop back to Red Rock Canyon along Blakiston Brook. After passing above the Lower Twin Lake the trail climbs over a saddle between Mount Bauerman and the Great Divide and descends into Peck's Basin. Less than a kilometre beyond the small pond in the centre of

Blakiston Valley from South Kootenay Pass

the basin, the lower South Kootenay Pass trail branches to the left and runs back to Red Rock Canyon via Lone Creek and Blakiston Brook. Hikers who are completing the loop can make a straightforward descent of the valley in three hours or so, while others may wish to continue south on the popular Tamarack route (see *Tamarack Trail*).

Lost Lake Option. Backpackers who are spending one or more nights in the Twin Lakes area can make a number of short and scenic excursions from their base camp. The trail to Lost Lake branches northwest from the end of the Snowshoe Fire Road and reaches this tiny but very pretty tarn in just 1.9 kilometres. A spur from the Lost Lake route climbs to the forested Castle River Divide 3.1 kilometres beyond the Snowshoe Cabin and descends to the headwaters of the Castle River on provincial forest lands.

Sage Pass Option. This 2165 metre summit is reached by means of a short one kilometre trail which branches from the Twin Lakes route just 100 metres before Upper Twin Lake. The climb is steep, but the pass offers views into British Columbia as well as back down to the upper Bauerman Valley.

South Kootenay Pass Option. Less than 100 metres south of the junction between the Peck's Basin and Lower South Kootenay Pass trails, the uppermost section of the South Kootenay Pass trail branches west from the Tamarack route. The trail is short—only a kilometre in length—and steep, actually climbing to the 2195 metre level on the ridge of Kishinena Peak where it looks down upon the summit of the pass further to the south. In addition to a fine view down the length of the Blakiston Valley, there is an excellent panorama of the peaks and valleys which comprise the provincial forest lands of British Columbia to the west.

South Kootenay Pass is one of the more historic gaps in the Great Divide, having been used by the Indians in their travels through the mountains long before the coming of the white man. In 1858 Lieutenant Thomas Blakiston made the first recorded crossing of the pass while exploring for routes through the Rockies with the Palliser Expedition.

245

Goat Lake

Red Rock Canyon to Goat Lake—6.7 kilometres (4.2 miles)

Day hike

Allow 3 hours one way

Elevation gain: 515 metres (1,700 feet)

Maximum elevation: 2010 metres (6,600 feet)

Topo maps: Waterton Lakes National Park

Point of Departure: Drive the Red Rock Canyon Road to its terminus at the Red Rock Canyon, 14.8 kilometres (9.2 miles) west of the junction with the Waterton Townsite Road. The hike starts at the Snowshoe Fire Road access gate, beside the warden station.

0.0—Access gate (1495 m).

—Route follows fire road.

4.3—Junction: Trail to Goat Lake branches uphill and right from road.

—Steep climb for remainder of trip.

5.4—First switchback.

6.2—Grade moderates. Mouth of Goat Lake valley.

6.4—Falls. First water available above Bauerman Creek.

6.7—Goat Lake (2010 m).

Goat Lake lies within a textbook example of a hanging valley, a small glacially carved cirque perched high above the Bauerman Valley. It is a shallow emerald-coloured tarn surrounded by subalpine forest and meadows, and it is enclosed by ridges of crimson argillite—the mountains which form the park's northern boundary. It is an excellent objective for day hikers, even though 4.3 kilometres of flat fire road followed by 2.4 kilometres of steep southerly-exposed mountain slope may wilt spirits a bit before journey's end.

The first hour or so of hiking follows the same route as the Twin Lakes trail—the Snowshoe Fire Road. The track itself offers little inspiration, but the way is flat and there are some fine views of the 700 metre north wall of Anderson Peak—a mountain which displays a narrow dark band of diorite (intruded igneous rock) across its face.

If hikers are feeling a little dry by the time they reach Kilometre 4.3 and the branch trail to Goat Lake, they had better fill their canteens from Bauerman Creek; the way is steep and dry ahead. Climbing from the roadside sign and a dense forest of pine, spruce and Douglas fir, the trail gains elevation rapidly and emerges onto open slopes above the Bauerman Valley in less than 500 metres. Views continue to improve for the remainder of the hike.

Beargrass is also a trail-side companion on the ascent. This member of the lily family, topped with small white flowers, often reaches a height in excess of 60 centimetres.

As the trail moderates, entering the hanging valley containing Goat Lake, watch the limestone outcroppings along the trail carefully. These rocks contain the fossilized remains of algae colonies, visible as a series of rough concentric circles in the rock—a record of one of the oldest known forms of life on earth.

Goat Lake

These colonies were part of a reef which survived in a shallow Precambrian sea over one billion years ago!

Goat Lake is a quiet body of water reflecting the forest greens that encircle it. The trail continues around its shore to an area of open meadowland to the north, where, in midsummer, yellow glacier lilies follow the melting snows. A steep scree slope descends to the water's edge on the west shore, etched by the trails of the local mountain goats. Above the slope stands the long crest of Avion Ridge, capped by the brilliant red argillite that is common throughout Waterton. Named for a town in France where Canadians fought in 1917, Avion forms part of the northwest boundary of the park. The summit beyond Avion is Newman Peak (2515 m).

Strong hikers who start early in the day can complete an ascent of Avion Ridge by following an ill-defined path to the head of the valley and then to the crest of the ridge. This arduous route climbs 425 vertical metres in 4.4 kilometres.

Vimy Peak

Y Camp to Vimy Peak—10 kilometres (6 miles)*
Y Camp to Crypt Landing—10.9 kilometres (6.8 miles)

Day hike

Allow 3-5 hours to Vimy Peak

Elevation gain: 1035 metres (3,400 feet)

Maximum elevation: 2385 metres (7,825 feet)

Topo maps: Waterton Lakes National Park

Point of Departure: The Vimy Peak trail begins at the old YWCA campsite near the eastern shore of Lower Waterton Lake. A three kilometre long access road runs to the camp from the Chief Mountain Highway, branching from that highway 500 metres south of its junction with Highway #5. (If the dirt access road has been closed to motor vehicles, it will have to be hiked, and three kilometres should be added to the distances above.)

*Distance approximate.

The trail to Vimy Peak and its lakeshore spur—the Bosporus Trail—provide the main routes of access to the region just east of the Waterton Lakes' shorelines.

From the Y Camp the Vimy Peak trail runs across relatively flat terrain for nearly four kilometres before branching east from the Bosporus route and beginning its ascent of the lower slopes of the mountain. The trail turns up a draw and continues to near the 2100 metre level, where rock scramblers can pick the line of least resistance to the summit ridge above.

The Bosporus Trail continues to the shore of Middle Waterton Lake, works its way across a point of land to Upper Waterton Lake and follows the eastern shoreline to the campsite at Crypt Landing.

The Belly River Wagon Road

Campground to International Boundary—2.4 kilometres (1.5 miles)

Wilderness access

Allow ½ hour one way

Elevation gain: nil

Maximum elevation: 1370 metres (4,500 feet)

Topo maps: Waterton Lakes National Park

Point of Departure: The old wagon road runs south from an access gate at the rear of the Belly River Campground.

The Belly River, originating in Glacier Park, Montana and running northward into Canada, has long been recognized for its excellent fishing. Eastern brook and rainbow trout, Dolly Varden and Rocky Mountain whitefish inhabit the river's pools and eddies. This old wagon road which runs south to the International Boundary provides access to this prime trout stream on Canadian territory.

Hikers may continue on into the United States, following the Belly River trail system to a number of fine lakes near the river's headwaters. Backpackers from the Canadian side of the border should check in with the ranger at the Belly River station, however.

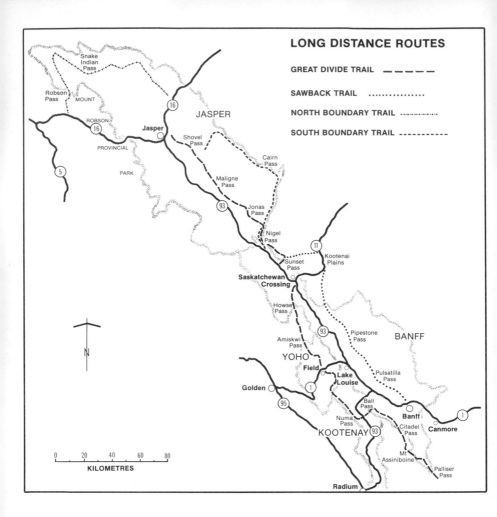

LONG DISTANCE ROUTES

GREAT DIVIDE TRAIL — — — —

SAWBACK TRAIL ⋯⋯⋯⋯⋯

NORTH BOUNDARY TRAIL ⋯⋯⋯⋯

SOUTH BOUNDARY TRAIL — — — — —

Snake
Indian
Pass

Robson
Pass   MOUNT

ROBSON
16

16   Jasper

PROVINCIAL

5

PARK

JASPER

Shovel
Pass

Cairn
Pass

Maligne
Pass

93   Jonas
Pass

Nigel
Pass

Sunset
Pass   11   Kootenai
Plains

Saskatchewan
Crossing

Howse
Pass

Amiskwi
Pass   93   Pipestone
Pass   BANFF

YOHO   Pulsatilla
Pass

Field

Lake
Louise

Golden   1

95   Ball
Pass   Banff   1

Numa   Citadel   Canmore
Pass   Pass

KOOTENAY 93

Mt
Assiniboine   Palliser
Pass

N

0   20   40   60   80
KILOMETRES

Radium

Extended Trips

When this book was first published, long distance treks were not popular in the Canadian Rockies. Even backpacks of two or three days were limited to a small minority of trail users. But with the increase in wilderness recreation during the 1970's, the interest in extended trips has mushroomed.

The mountain parks of the Rockies provide numerous opportunities for the long distance backpacker. In fact, anyone who has browsed through the preceding chapters has, no doubt, already begun linking together various hikes and trail segments to create extended journeys of one, two or more weeks. The trails are all there, most in good condition. All that's needed is a little planning and imagination.

Loop and partial loop trips are a very popular type of long distance backpack since transportation arrangements are usually not complex. Two of the longest and best known partial loops are the North Boundary Trail and South Boundary Trail in Jasper Park. Both run in excess of 170 kilometres and usually take 10 days to two weeks to traverse. The North Boundary is a 'super-highway' by normal backcountry standards, while the South Boundary is not so well developed and demands some route finding ability.

Jasper Park also possesses one of the fine complete loops in the mountain parks, the Brazeau Lake–Poboktan Pass–Jonas Pass circuit—a trip which starts and ends at Nigel Creek in Banff Park and takes five or more days to complete. And for true marathon trekkers, a super-loop of more than 260 kilometres can be made by linking the Maligne Pass–Jonas Pass trails together with the South Boundary Trail.

Banff Park boasts a number of fine, extended loop hikes, particularly in that section of the park lying to the east of the Trans-Canada Highway and the Icefields Parkway. An interesting if somewhat rough trip can be made by connecting the Dolomite Pass–Isabella Lake trail together with the Fish Lakes–North Molar Pass trail, using Pipestone Pass as the vital link. Another loop which would take five or more days to hike starts at Johnston's Canyon and traverses Mystic, Sawback and Badger Passes before returning to its starting point via Luellen Lake and Johnston's Creek. More extensive partial loops can be made into the Front Ranges of Banff Park by way of the Red Deer River, Flint's Park and Cascade Fire Road trails.

While being more linear in nature, a number of long trips can be completed through Mount Assiniboine Provincial Park using the longer approach routes running from Banff and Kootenay Parks, such as the Brewster Creek and Ferro Pass trails. Again, the possibilities are endless and it's all a matter of imagination.

For trips lasting longer than a week or two, however, backpackers find themselves forced into taking a more direct line of travel, usually following the mountain park trail systems in a general north-south direction. Two such routes—the Great Divide Trail and the 'Sawback Trail'—are outlined in this chapter.

When most backpackers think about extended trips in the Rockies, they first think of the Great Divide Trail. The Great Divide Trail concept emerged in the 1960's, spawned both by the emergence of long distance hiking trails in the major mountain ranges of the United States and Europe as well as the desire to encourage a wider variety of backcountry options in the Canadian Rockies. Picking up on the concept, Jim Thorsell—a recreational planner who conducted several trail surveys in the mountain parks during the late 1960's—drew up a provisional route for the trail running from Palliser Pass at the southern tip of Banff Park north to Mount Robson Provincial Park. With the help of the National and Provincial Parks Association of Canada, a pamphlet was published outlining the proposed route. A condensed version of this route description appeared as an appendix to the first edition of *The Canadian Rockies Trail Guide*, and while the trail still has not been formally established, continued interest in the route has prompted the authors to provide an updated version of this piece as revised by Jim Thorsell.

In addition to the Great Divide Trail, another route has surfaced which is attracting more and more use each year. Dubbed the 'Sawback Trail' by the authors, it is a long distance hike which parallels the Great Divide route for approximately 150 kilometres and can be interconnected with that trail at several points, but which runs almost entirely within Banff Park and the Front Ranges of the Rockies. An outline description of this route follows.

One final cautionary note: each season hundreds of hikers attack the major long distance trips mentioned here, recognizing the unique opportunity which the Canadian Rockies offer for 'getting away from it all.' Yet enthusiasm is no substitute for experience. Even on some of the easiest and most straightforward of these trips, such as Jasper's North Boundary Trail, the number of 'walking wounded' at trail's end is amazing. People set off on 170 kilometre treks with three days worth of food in a small rucksack, without warm clothing or foul weather gear, or with leaky tents and poor quality sleeping bags. Often hikers are simply not prepared physically or mentally to tackle extensive hiking with full packs or for the extended periods of isolation. People who come from very different parts of the continent or the world discover that they are not prepared for an alien environment. And finally, there are those who may be capable of hacking and hewing their way through the bush, but who have no concept of the 'zero impact' style of travel which is demanded in a national park. Take heed: if you haven't backpacked a number of times in the mountains of the North American west, the more isolated journeys mentioned here are not for you.

The Sawback Trail

The 'Sawback Trail' is an unofficial and undesignated route running north from Banff townsite along the western edge of the Front Ranges to the David Thompson Highway on the Kootenay Plains. By linking existing trail segments which lie to the east of the Trans-Canada Highway and the Icefields Parkway, an extended trek of some 150 kilometres (93 miles) may be completed, and the trail may be connected in with the Great Divide Trail route and the Jasper Park trail system to the north to allow more extensive travels.

The 'Sawback Trail' runs almost entirely within Banff Park and has been pieced together from the suggestions of Parks Canada personnel, detailed reports provided by long distance backpackers, and the authors' own wanderings and field studies. The name 'Sawback Trail' is a random designation used by the authors strictly for identification purposes, chosen because so much of the route passes beneath mountains composed of steeply tilted slabs of limestone which have been eroded into sharply serrated peaks.

In addition to the distinctive mountains of the Front Ranges, the trail follows very near to the strike of the Castle Mountain Thrust Fault for much of its length. This major fracture in the strata of the Rockies separates the older Main Ranges to the west from the younger Front Ranges to the east. Four alpine passes are crossed on the trail, and with the optional routes and side trips available, three others may be added to the itinerary with little additional effort. Wildflowers carpet both the passes and the many meadowed valleys during July and August, and wildlife commonly seen along the route include mountain sheep, moose, elk, wolverine and grizzly bear.

But for the terminal access points at Mount Norquay and Kootenay Plains, no part of the route intersects with a highway. However, at several points the trail dips to within a half-day's travel of main park roadways and few sections are further than one long day from civilization.

Following is an outline of the route. Most distances and elevations are estimated but, with the exception of the Siffleur Valley, all trail segments are described in greater detail elsewhere in this book. It should be noted that the northern half of the 'Sawback Trail' has not been developed for hikers. In addition to numerous fords, trails are usually more rocky and rooty, some sections are very boggy and ill-defined, and many of the more remote segments, particularly outside the national parks, are not maintained on a yearly basis. Backpackers continuing north from the Red Deer Lakes should possess a notch more experience and stamina than what is needed for most outings in the mountain parks.

SAWBACK SOUTH
Mount Norquay to Red Deer Lakes—66.7 kilometres

Starting from the Mount Norquay ski area near Banff townsite, the first half of the 'Sawback Trail' runs through the Sawback Range proper to the Boulder Pass–Skoki Valley region east of Lake Louise. With the exception of a short segment on Baker Creek, the route follows popular hiking trails through most of its distance. There are no unbridged stream crossings of any consequence, and easy access or egress is provided along the way by short spur trails which run up Johnston's Creek and Baker Creek from the 1–A Highway.

The first 30 kilometres of the journey follow the Mystic Pass trail, running up the Forty Mile Valley from Mount Norquay and crossing Mystic Pass to Johnston's Creek. Connecting into the popular Luellen Lake–Pulsatilla Pass hike, the 'Sawback

Trail' ascends Johnston's Creek, crosses Pulsatilla Pass, and descends the Wildflower Valley to Baker Creek. The Baker Creek trail makes a short but steep ascent to Baker Lake, and from there hikers have an open, easy walk northward to the Red Deer Lakes campsite and the half-way point on the route.

An interesting option is available on the first leg of the Sawback South route, bypassing Mystic Pass but adding two other fine summits to the itinerary. After reaching the Mystic Pass junction on Forty Mile Creek, hikers may continue straight ahead to the headwaters of the valley, crossing Sawback Pass to Flint's Park then turning west and traversing Badger Pass to the Johnston's Creek valley. This alternate route brings the hiker out on the Pulsatilla Pass trail just south of that summit and adds only eight kilometres or so to the overall journey.

The complete trek to the Red Deer Lakes campsite should take no longer than five to seven days, and after some exploring in the Skoki Valley area, hikers may either exit to Lake Louise via Boulder Pass or continue on to the northern half of the 'Sawback Trail.'

Distances and Elevations

	kms
Mount Norquay (1705 m) to Mystic Jct. (1830 m)	15.9
Mystic Jct. to Mystic Pass (2285 m)	6.3
Mystic Pass to Johnston's Creek Jct. (1675 m)	7.4
Johnston's Creek Jct. to Pulsatilla Pass (2345 m)	18.2
Pulsatilla Pass to Baker Creek Jct. (1815 m)	6.4
Baker Creek Jct. to Baker Lake (2210 m)	6.0
Baker Lake to Red Deer Lakes (2090 m)	6.5

Topo maps: Banff, 82 O/4 East; Mount Eisenhower, 82 O/5 East and West; Lake Louise, 82 N/8 East; and Hector Lake, 82 N/9 East.

SAWBACK NORTH

Red Deer Lakes to Kootenay Plains—82 kilometres

The northern half of the 'Sawback Trail' is definitely rougher travelling than the southern. There are several difficult stream crossings and parts of the trail receive little or no maintenance. Yet the scenery, particularly on the Pipestone River, is worth the extra effort, and there are interesting side trips to areas such as Fish Lakes and Clearwater Pass which rival any alpine beauty spots in the mountain parks.

The trail descends from the Red Deer Lakes to the Pipestone River and, after crossing the Pipestone (a healthy thigh-deep ford), ascends the valley over straightforward trail (with another stream crossing) to Pipestone Pass. Descending the Siffleur River on the north side of Pipestone Pass, Dolomite Creek must be waded just above its mouth—another troublesome thigh-deep crossing.

Once out of Banff Park and into the Siffleur Wilderness, the route should be obvious despite many branch trails and seismic lines. There is one treacherous ford across the cascades of Porcupine Creek and much deadfall over the five kilometres of trail which pass through the 1974 Siffleur burn. After reaching the logging road on the lower Siffleur, stay with it and keep right until the main logging road is encountered. Go right to the footbridge which crosses the North Saskatchewan River. From there it is a short walk across the meadows of the Kootenay Plains to the David Thompson Highway where the hiker emerges 16 kilometres west of the David Thompson Resort and 30 kilometres east of Saskatchewan River Crossing.

Two access trails run to the northern section of the 'Sawback Trail' from the Icefields

Parkway—the North Molar Pass and Dolomite Pass routes. For hikers who do not plan on extending their trip beyond the David Thompson Highway, the Dolomite Pass trail makes a preferable exit. In addition to ending the Sawback journey with some fine alpine hiking through the Dolomite meadows, this option eliminates some pretty tedious travel on the lower Siffleur.

Distances and Elevations

	kms
Red Deer Lakes to Pipestone River (1815 m)	10
Pipestone River to Fish Lakes Jct. (1935 m)	10
Fish Lakes Jct. to Pipestone Pass (2450 m)	11
Pipestone Pass to Clearwater Pass Jct. (2255 m)	3
Clearwater Pass Jct. to Dolomite Creek (1815 m)	16
Dolomite Creek to David Thompson Hwy. (1340 m)	32

Topo maps: Hector Lake, 82 N/9 East and West; Siffleur River, 82 N/16 West; and Whiterabbit Creek, 83 C/1 West.

Sawback Extensions

For hikers who are interested in continuing north into the Jasper Park area, it is possible to extend the Sawback trip beyond the David Thompson Highway, using the Cline River horse trail as a link to the Great Divide Trail route at Pinto Lake. After emerging on the David Thompson Highway from the northern section of the 'Sawback Trail', follow the road eastward some 14 kilometres to the Cline River bridge. The horse trail starts from a gravel pit 200 metres west of the bridge and follows the south bank of the Cline for some 29 kilometres to Pinto Lake.

Northward from Pinto Lake, backpackers may travel on to Jasper townsite following the Great Divide Trail, but those who have become enamored of the massive limestone mountains of the Front Ranges may wish to branch from that route at the Jonas Cutoff, continuing on to Medicine Lake via the South Boundary Trail (described in the Jasper Park chapter).

The Great Divide Trail

by Jim Thorsell

There are several feasible long distance routes through the Rockies from south to north which primarily follow existing trails. The best known of these is the Great Divide Trail route first proposed in 1967. The Great Divide Trail has been the focus of many studies since its feasibility was established, and though official policy approval of the trail was announced by Parks Canada in 1971, formal route designation or construction of the missing segments has yet to be undertaken.

Since 1971, two main developments have occurred that should be noted: Parks Canada, fearing that the Great Divide Trail passes through ecologically sensitive areas and through areas where backcountry visitation is already high, has suggested re-routing the trail away from the high ridges close to the Divide to lower, valley-bottom locations. Secondly, a southern extension of the Great Divide Trail from Banff to Waterton in lands outside the national parks has been proposed and, in part, built.*

As this revised edition of *The Canadian Rockies Trail Guide* goes to press, the situation regarding the actual development of the Great Divide Trail is unresolved. The differing views on its possible routes and, indeed, on its very legitimacy make it difficult to offer the prospective traveller a guide on exactly where best to go. All that can be definitely stated is that the route given in the first edition of this book is still essentially valid and passable. Call it what you will, the remainder of this chapter will present an updated account of the park section of the Great Divide Trail route as it originally was publicised in 1969. Remember that only the concept has received government approval and no work has been done on the rougher and missing sections. Remember too that there are other possibilities and that this is merely the one that provides the highest quality route as judged by this author.

Cautions

Remember, the Great Divide Trail has yet to be developed. There are no signs which refer to any segment of the route as 'The Great Divide Trail' and, indeed, directional signs of any kind are scarce. Trail conditions in some sections are poor. Rivers will present special problems for hikers where there are no footbridges. Although there are many primitive campsites along the route, only one shelter is now open for public use. It is important to have good lightweight equipment and be prepared for all weather conditions.

National Park regulations listed elsewhere in this book apply to all travel along this route, i.e. permits are required for any backcountry camping. Permits as well as current trail conditions may be obtained at the trail desks in park information bureaus.

Finally, most elevations in the following route description are approximate as are distances not recorded in tenths-of-kilometres. Further information on most trail segments may be obtained by reading individual descriptions elsewhere in this book (cross reference place names through the index).

---

* For information on the segment outside the parks see *The Great Divide Trail: Banff to Waterton* prepared by the Great Divide Trail Association, Box 5322, Postal Station A, Calgary, 1977.

'MEADOW' SECTION

Palliser Pass to Banff-Radium Highway—86 kilometres

Palliser Pass is at the very southerly tip of Banff Park. It is here that the national park section of the Great Divide Trail begins. Closely following the Divide for 86 kilometres, the Great Divide Trail utilises trails of the upper Spray River through the Mount Assiniboine area to the Sunshine–Egypt Lake complex and out to the Banff–Radium Highway in Kootenay Park.

The nickname 'Meadow' is given to this section because of the above-timberline location of much of the route. The entire section has good existing trails that are marked and well maintained except for a long-abandoned ten kilometre stretch along Currie Creek to Marvel Pass. As recent avalanche debris has made bush-whacking here difficult, the traveller is advised to enter the Assiniboine area via the Bryant Creek trail.

Mount Assiniboine itself is the dominant peak of the section and can be seen from Currie Pass all the way to Healy Pass. Prepare to be distracted by many side trips in Mount Assiniboine Park and around Egypt Lake, both prime hiking areas where there is usually good trout fishing. Profuse alpine flowers in early July and golden larch trees in mid-September make these the most colorful periods for travel.

Access to the southern end of the 'Meadow' Section can be gained from several directions. Palliser Pass can be reached via the North Kananaskis Pass trail running from the Kananaskis Provincial Park at Upper Kananaskis Lake. The upper Spray Valley can also be reached from the Burstall Pass trail which leaves from the Smith-Dorion Creek Road or from the west Spray Reservoir Road at the Bryant Creek trail head.

Similarly, the central part of the section in the Assiniboine–Sunshine segment can be reached by feeder trails from the east and west via Fatigue Creek, Brewster Creek, Mitchell River or Simpson River. The north end of the section emerges on the Banff–Radium Highway at Hawk Creek, although egress can also be made via Redearth Creek or Gibbon Pass to Storm Mountain Lodge.

Distances and Elevations

	kms
Palliser Pass (2090 m) to Currie Creek Jct.	8
Currie Creek Jct. to Currie Pass (2395 m)	8
Currie Pass to Marvel Pass (2150 m)	3
Marvel Pass to Wonder Pass (2375 m)	3
Wonder Pass to Lake Magog (2165 m)	2.9
Lake Magog to Citadel Pass (2360 m)	19.8
Citadel Pass to Sunshine Village (2195 m)	9.3
Sunshine Village to Simpson Pass (2120 m)	5.3
Simpson Pass to Healy Pass (2330 m)	4.0
Healy Pass to Egypt Lake Campsite (1995 m)	3.2
Egypt Lake Camp to Whistling Valley (2300 m)	3.5
Whistling Valley to Ball Pass Jct. (1920 m)	5.2
Ball Pass Jct. to Ball Pass (2210 m)	3
Ball Pass to Banff–Radium Highway (1325 m)	8

Topo maps: Kananaskis Lakes, 82 J/11; Spray Lakes Reservoir, 82 J/14; Mount Assiniboine, 82 J/13; Banff, 82 O/4 East and West; and Mount Goodsir, 82 N/1 East.

'LARCH' SECTION
Floe Creek to Field—88 kilometres

The 72 kilometres of trail from Floe Creek to Lake O'Hara via the Numa, Tumbling, Wolverine, Goodsir and McArthur Passes is one of the finest backcountry trips in the Rockies. With great differences in elevation it is also one of the most rigorous. Highlights of the trip include Floe Lake, the Tumbling Glacier, the Rockwall, the 365 metre Helmet Falls, the Goodsir Towers, and the extensive views from the Goodsir and Numa Passes. Common wildlife include goat, elk and wolverine. Larches reach their northern limit and their most impressive fall colour along this section of the Great Divide Trail. Few other places have wildflowers to match those in the Wolverine Pass meadows.

The trip should present no problem for those in reasonable physical condition. It is well marked and maintained with footbridges throughout. However, for most of the stretch between Lake O'Hara and Field there is no recognized trail; only experienced hikers should attempt the Duchesnay–Dennis Pass route as both sides of the pass are very steep and rocky, and there is heavy bushwhacking to reach the fossil bed trail on Mount Stephen.

The 'Larch' Section extends between the Banff–Radium Highway and the Trans-Canada Highway. Five days are usually required to hike the route from Floe Creek to Lake O'Hara. It is possible to exit via the Ottertail River Fire Road in Yoho, and Parks Canada has designated this as an alternative route for backpackers who would avoid the more heavily travelled Lake O'Hara region. Most hikers will choose to skip the Duchesnay Pass segment and conclude (or begin) the 'Larch' Section at Lake O'Hara.

Distances and Elevations

	kms
Banff–Radium Hwy. to Floe Lake (2040 m)	10.1
Floe Lake to Numa Pass (2353 m)	2.7
Numa Pass to Tumbling Pass (2225 m)	12.1
Tumbling Pass to Wolverine Pass (2207 m)	6
Wolverine Pass to Helmet Warden Cabin (1770 m)	13
Helmet Warden Cabin to Goodsir Pass (2210 m)	5
Goodsir Pass to Ottertail Jct. (1480 m)	11
Ottertail Jct. to McArthur Pass (2210 m)	10
McArthur Pass to Lake O'Hara (2097 m)	2.1
Lake O'Hara to Duchesnay Pass (2666 m)	8
Duchesnay Pass to Dennis Pass (2261 m)	3
Dennis Pass via Fossil Beds to Field (1242 m)	5

Topo maps: Mount Goodsir, 82 N/1 East and West; and Lake Louise, 82 N/8 West.

'GLACIER' SECTION
Field to Saskatchewan River Crossing—92 kilometres

This section extends north from Field, B.C. to Saskatchewan River Crossing, Alberta, a distance of some 92 kilometres. Despite a fifteen kilometre section missing in the middle and a lack of footbridges, the trail presents some exciting travel with a profusion of waterfalls, glaciers and wild rivers. No trail exists from Kiwetinok Pass to the Amiskwi River Fire Road, though by contouring over the northwest ridge of Kiwetinok Valley it is possible to eventually reach the abandoned logging roads leading down to Amiskwi. Likewise, from Amiskwi Pass to the Blaeberry River a thick bushwhack to the Collie Creek logging road can be shortened by keeping above timberline until the last possible moment. The upper Blaeberry trail has been improved in recent years and is now in fair condition (over Howse Pass the trail is faint until the Banff Park boundary marker is reached).

Until the centre portion of the 'Glacier' Section is built, most trail use will be concentrated at either end of this section. The Kiwetinok–Amiskwi portion may be avoided entirely by driving up the Blaeberry forestry road to the trail head 13 kilometres below Howse Pass. For the section in Yoho Park, you may gain access from the Emerald Lake or Yoho Valley Roads. Parks Canada has also designated the Amiskwi Fire Road as an alternate route to the high use Yoho Valley region.

Distances and Elevations

	kms
Field to Burgess Pass (2185 m)	6.6
Burgess Pass to Yoho Pass (1840 m)	6.1
Yoho Pass via Highline to Kiwetinok Pass (2450 m)	13
Kiwetinok Pass to Amiskwi Pass (1995 m)	13
Amiskwi Pass to Howse Pass (1530 m)	27
Howse Pass to Forbes Creek Jct. (1525 m)	2.9
Forbes Creek Jct. to Saskatchewan Crossing (1435 m)	23.0

Topo maps: Lake Louise, 82 N/8 West; Blaeberry River, 82 N/10 East; and Mistaya Lake, 82 N/15 East and West.

'CARIBOU' SECTION

Norman Creek to Maligne Lake Road—164 kilometres

From the Icefields Parkway at Norman Creek to Maligne Lake runs the longest unbroken stretch of the Great Divide Trail—120 kilometres. A minimum of ten days is required to hike this entire section. Wildlife is relatively plentiful here including caribou which are often seen in the alplands near Amber Mountain and in Jonas Pass. The six passes in this section are all high with extensive alpine meadow and encompassing views. The trails, except for a few kilometres through Cataract Pass, are in good condition and easy to follow.

The 'Caribou' Section of the Great Divide Trail is reached by car at both ends of the trail and also from the Maligne Lake Road at Maligne Lake. Feeder trails from the Icefields Parkway lead in along Nigel and Poboktan Creeks and conveniently divide this section into four roughly equal portions.

From Nigel Pass south to Sunset Pass are found some of the steepest grades on the entire Great Divide Trail. There is no trail over Cataract Pass summit to Nigel Pass, but the country is open and the route should present no problems for hikers. Horses are not allowed on the section of the route that lies within the provincial White Goat Wilderness—a bypass alternate via Coral Creek and Job Pass is suggested for those travelling on horseback.

Distances and Elevations

	kms
Icefields Parkway (1525 m) to Sunset Pass (2055 m)	8.2
Sunset Pass to Cataract Creek Jct. (1705 m)	8
Cataract Creek Jct. to Cataract Pass (2515 m)	16
Cataract Pass to Nigel Pass Jct. (2202 m)	6
Nigel Pass Jct. to Jonas Cutoff (1890 m)	6.8
Jonas Cutoff to Jonas Pass (2235 m)	9.8
Jonas Pass to Poboktan Creek Jct. (2105 m)	10.0
Poboktan Creek Jct. to Maligne Pass Jct. (1740 m)	14.1
Maligne Pass Jct. to Maligne Pass (2237 m)	7.3
Maligne Pass to Maligne Lake (1450 m)	34.2
Maligne Lake to Shovel Pass (2285 m)	17.5
Shovel Pass to Signal Mtn. Fire Road (1950 m)	18.1
Signal Mtn. Fire Road to Maligne Lake Rd. (1160 m)	8.5

Topo maps: Cline River, 83 C/2 West; Columbia Icefield, 83 C/3; Sunwapta, 83 C/6; Southesk, 83 C/11; Athabasca Falls, 83 C/12; and Medicine Lake, 83 C/13 West.

'MOUNT ROBSON' SECTION

Yellowhead Pass to Mount Robson—87 kilometres

Once the hiker completes the 'Caribou' Section and finds himself in Jasper townsite with energy to spare and a desire to see Mount Robson, what should he do? If he is intrepid (perhaps masochistic?) he may consider the route recommended in the first edition of the trail guide which follows the upper Miette and Moose Rivers. Foot travel here is not easy and is not encouraged by the Warden Service. Nor is the alternate Elysium–Thornton Pass route. Robson, a fitting northern terminus to the Great Divide Trail, can be reached, however, via the Berg Lake or North Boundary trails as described elsewhere in this book. For those still wishing to consider the preferred route, the distances are given with a warning that this section is for explorers only.

Distances and Elevations

	kms
Yellowhead Pass (1131 m) to Centre Pass (1965 m)	26
Centre Pass to Grant Pass (1937 m)	8
Grant Pass to Colonel Pass (1870 m)	5
Colonel Pass to Moose Pass (2003 m)	29
Moose Pass to Robson Pass (1651 m)	18
Robson Pass to Berg Lake (1638 m)	1

Appendix

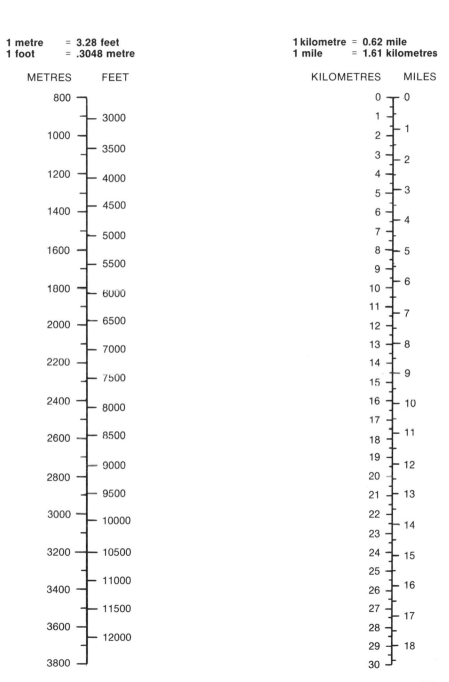

1 metre = **3.28 feet**
1 foot = **.3048 metre**

1 kilometre = **0.62 mile**
1 mile = **1.61 kilometres**

METRES	FEET
800	
	3000
1000	
	3500
1200	4000
	4500
1400	
	5000
1600	
	5500
1800	6000
	6500
2000	
	7000
2200	
	7500
2400	8000
2600	8500
	9000
2800	
	9500
3000	10000
3200	10500
	11000
3400	
	11500
3600	12000
3800	

KILOMETRES	MILES
0	0
1	
2	1
3	2
4	
5	3
6	4
7	
8	5
9	
10	6
11	7
12	
13	8
14	
15	9
16	10
17	
18	11
19	12
20	
21	13
22	14
23	
24	15
25	
26	16
27	17
28	
29	18
30	

Index

Names and pages in bold type refer to the main trail headings as used in this book.

Cover photos by Jim Thorsell
Front cover: Numa Pass, Kootenay Park
Back cover: Amiskwi Pass, Yoho Park